DISCONTENTED AMERICA

The American Moment

Stanley I. Kutler, Series Editor

DISCONTENTED AMERICA
THE UNITED STATES IN THE 1920s

David J. Goldberg

The Johns Hopkins University Press

Baltimore and London

© 1999 The Johns Hopkins University Press
All rights reserved. Published 1999
Printed in the United States of America on acid-free paper
9 8 7 6 5 4 3

The Johns Hopkins University Press
2715 North Charles Street
Baltimore, Maryland 21218-4363
www.press.jhu.edu

Library of Congress Cataloging-in-Publication Data will be found
at the end of this book.

A catalog record for this book is available from the British Library.

ISBN 0-8018-6004-0
ISBN 0-8018-6005-9 (pbk.)

For Raymond Fishler

Holocaust survivor and
an inspiration to family and friends

CONTENTS

SERIES EDITOR'S FOREWORD

POPULAR IMAGES OF THE 1920s—bathtub gin, flappers, the Charleston, the Great Gatsby, Babe Ruth, and Charlie Chaplin—are at odds with the stark realities of the time. Historical accounts tend to treat the "Roaring Twenties" and "Normalcy," as the time variously has been described, as an anomalous part of twentieth-century history. The decade falls between the stools of the politically important and momentous years of the Progressive Era and the New Deal. Against such vibrant national tribunes as Theodore Roosevelt and Woodrow Wilson, or the activist, visible leadership of Franklin D. Roosevelt, the passive figures of Warren Harding and Calvin Coolidge stand in marked contrast. The Ku Klux Klan and defenders of orthodoxy in religion and culture were on the march and it was they who put their imprint on the moment, not the reformers or organized labor or politically sophisticated dissidents, who so dominated the periods surrounding the 1920s.

The notion of an isolated decade to be measured and evaluated only by time lines is, of course, a journalistic myth. History simply does not play that way. The 1920s involved a time of confronting (or sometimes, ignoring) profound social problems, fears, and anxieties that had nagged the national consciousness for decades. David Goldberg very properly calls it a time of discontent, and in this work he thoroughly probes much of the underside of life that pitted Americans of differing classes, ethnicity, and religion against one another.

Consider, for example, the momentous National Origins Act of 1924, which imposed strict limitations on immigration. Beginning in the late nineteenth century, the nation began to question unlimited, unrestricted immigration, which had been one of the tenets of the nation since its colonial beginnings. As new immigrants poured in from southern and eastern Europe, many of them Catholic or Jewish and totally alien to the dominant culture and language, native groups feared "race suicide" and advocated restrictive measures. Their numbers involved a diverse, strange coalition, including Brahmin advocates of Anglo-Saxon superiority; Southerners deeply conscious of racial distinctions; Californians fearful of the "Yellow Peril" as they confronted a hundred thousand Japanese immigrants; and leading intellectuals, such as John R. Commons and E. A. Ross, worried that "backward races" were undermining native labor and character.

The unquenchable demands for cheap labor fueled the flow of immigrants in increasing numbers until the First World War. The war and the triumph of Communism in Russia, however, triggered a rising fear of radicalism, which incorrectly was seen as foreign in origin. A postwar recession, along with other factors, reversed the longstanding demand for more labor, and the earlier coalition for restriction was augmented with new allies from the business and political worlds. Their support for restriction culminated in legislation in the 1920s that sharply curtailed immigration from non–western European sources.

The decade was a time of profound change and happenings. Longstanding controversial problems such as immigration were "solved." The debate over the Treaty of Versailles signaled a retreat to isolation and yet another attempt to determine America's place and involvement in the world. Prohibition of alcoholic beverages was launched as the decade began, but the resultant problems of enforcement, compliance, and the growth of criminal elements are well known. Prohibition, once considered an important plank in reformist platforms, symbolized the conservatism of the era. Labor union membership sharply declined in the face of corporate America's "American Plan," a euphemism for the open shop and the barring of labor unions. The growing power of the Ku Klux Klan was, in part, rooted in a desperate affirmation of traditional beliefs. The forces of reaction everywhere seemed triumphant, nowhere more apparent than in the election of 1924, where it was difficult to discern any differences between the two major candidates, while the Progressive Party candidate, Robert M. La Follette, was overwhelmingly defeated. But by the end of the decade, the superficial prosperity with its accompanying glitter came tumbling down with the stock market crash and the ensuing depression.

As Goldberg notes, the Great Depression exposed underlying fallacies and weaknesses in the economy and provided the occasion for the great political and social transformation of the twentieth century. The achievements of the 1920s are long behind us, but the lessons of unbridled capitalism, intolerance, and the clashes between traditionalism and modernism very much remain.

Stanley I. Kutler
Madison, Wisconsin

PREFACE

THIS BOOK DESCRIBES THE various ways in which the political, social, and economic changes generated by World War I continued to affect American society throughout the 1920s. I have sought to combine the emphasis on politics and foreign policy found in older historical research with the more recent focus on social developments. In keeping with the notion that historians need to be conscious of the "pastness of the past," I have concentrated on events that appeared most important to people at the time rather than on aspects that only in retrospect served as a prelude to later decades.

Ethnic and racial conflicts roiled much of American society throughout the decade. André Siegfried, a French visitor to the United States, declared in the opening line of his 1927 account, *America Comes of Age*: "The essential characteristic of the post-war period in the United States is the nervous reaction of the original American stock against an insidious subjection by foreign blood." The debate over the Treaty of Versailles, Warren Harding's 1920 campaign, the rise of the Ku Klux Klan, the anti-immigrant movement, the attack on labor, and even the controversy over Prohibition were all influenced by the heightened postwar emphasis on Americanism. By 1925, some of the postwar tensions had eased, but, as the great outburst of anti-Catholicism during the 1928 presidential campaign indicated, many Americans remained uncomfortable with diversity.

The 1920s saw a collapse of progressivism, a movement that had influenced many aspects of American life in the immediate prewar years. In an introductory chapter I highlight the aspects of progressivism and the wartime events that are most relevant to subsequent chapters. I have also addressed the momentous 1919 conflicts in various chapters, because that year set the tone for many events in the postwar decade. I have not sought to write a complete history of the 1920s, but I hope that the emphasis on areas of American life most affected by the war will offer a new perspective on that decade.

I have benefited greatly from assistance provided by librarians at the Indiana State Library and the American Jewish Committee. I am also grateful to the students in my graduate seminar on American social movements at Cleveland State University, who have provided me with extremely useful suggestions and ideas. I received valuable assistance in preparing the manuscript from Darlene Sanders and Jim Anghilante. I am especially grateful to Glenda Rink, who in a most pleasant way aided me during the final stages of this book. Finally, I thank both Stanley Kutler and Henry Tom for their encouragement and support.

1

PROGRESSIVISM AND THE WAR

ETWEEN 1900 AND 1916, progressivism had an enormous impact on American life. Not merely a political movement, it influenced a wide range of institutions, from settlement houses to public schools and universities. By 1916, however, the conflict that had engulfed the continent of Europe began to divert the attention of Americans to foreign affairs. When the United States entered the war in April 1917, Woodrow Wilson tried to apply progressive concepts to foreign policy and convert what had been a crass struggle for power into a crusade for a new world order.

The Progressive Concerns: To Uplift and to Battle against Privilege

Progressivism was a reform movement that emerged in response to the rapid pace of industrialization in the late nineteenth century. Progressives concerned themselves with a broad range of problems, including the exploitation of female and child wage earners, unsanitary working conditions, the growth of urban slums, corrupt politics, and the abuse of power by giant corporations known as trusts. Confident in the ability of government to correct what progressives saw as social evils, they favored expanding state power to protect those who needed assistance and to check the power wielded by special interests.

Historians have had a difficult time defining the progressive movement because it included a wide variety of reformers who did not necessarily agree. Nevertheless, certain generalizations can safely be made about the progressives. Almost all came from middle-class, Protestant backgrounds; they tended to have an intensely moralistic and self-righteous approach to social problems. They sought to correct the worst abuses of capitalism rather than to attack the system as a whole. They believed in the inevitability of progress—a belief that would be shattered by the war and its aftermath. And, to an extent that would appear incredibly naive to the far more cynical postwar generation, they believed that "the people" would make the right decisions if given the power to do so. For this reason, they favored the Seventeenth Amendment to the Constitution, adopted in 1913, which mandated direct election of United States senators. They also advocated the initiative, the referendum, and the recall, measures known collectively as direct democracy and designed to increase the power of ordinary citizens.

Books published by the progressives indicate both their approach and the range of their concerns. Influential exposés of political corruption and the exploitation of children included *The Shame of the Cities* (1905) by Lincoln Steffens, *The Bitter Cry of the Children* (1906) by John Spargo, *The Treason of the Senate* (1906) by David Graham Phillips, and *The Beast* (1911) by Ben B. Lindsey and Harvey J. O'Higgins. *The Jungle* (1906), which Upton Sinclair wrote to convert people to socialism, had the most direct impact because it helped lead to passage of the federal Meat Inspection Act. Almost all of these books appeared first as serials in popular muckraking magazines, such as *McClure's* and *Cosmopolitan*, which enjoyed wide circulation among members of the Protestant middle class.

Many progressives focused their attention on urban problems. Some chose to live in cities rather than in the recently developed streetcar suburbs. Many women, in particular, became residents of settlement houses located in some of the poorest and most densely packed urban areas. Denied the vote and thus unable to participate directly in politics, female college graduates found many professions closed to them as well. The settlement house movement gave them an opportunity to use their talents and provided an outlet for women who did not want to live conventional, middle-class lives.

The settlements offered a wide range of programs aimed at immigrants and their children. Among these were day nurseries, clubs, arts and crafts, music, drama, and home economics. Like many of the progressives, the settlement house workers sought to "uplift" the poor. But the settlements also provided their middle-class residents with direct exposure to the harshness of urban and industrial life. Their personal experiences led some of them to become advocates of reform. Because of their background, these reformers served as effective spokespersons for causes ranging from the need for public-health measures to tenement house reform and the abolition of child labor.

In keeping with their middle-class reform perspective, the settlement house workers hoped to counter the saloon and the so-called evils connected to it—prostitution and gambling. In place of the saloon, they favored building bathhouses, playgrounds, and other institutions that might lure young people away from the temptations of the city streets. Although they were respectful of immigrant traditions, the settlement house workers nevertheless sought to discourage the children of immigrants from perpetuating customs and habits they considered unsuitable for life in America.

Progressives, in general, held big-city political machines responsible for many of the evils plaguing urban areas. From the perspective of the progressives, the political machines had formed an unholy alliance with saloon owners and business interests, an alliance that had led to widespread corruption and the inefficient delivery of city services. But unlike elitist late-nineteenth-century reformers, the most advanced progressives favored wide-ranging reforms to break the stranglehold of the city machines.

Samuel "Golden Rule" Jones of Toledo, Hazen Pingree of Detroit, and Tom Johnson of Cleveland proved the most successful of the progressive mayors. In all three cities, the reform administrations sought to end the influence of privilege and special interests over city government, to reform the system of taxation, and to establish municipal ownership of utilities. In 1911, Tom Johnson gave his life in a battle for a publicly owned streetcar line. The inscription on a monument in his honor in Cleveland's Public Square captured the idealism of these prewar reformers:

Beyond his party and beyond his class
The man forsook the few to serve the mass
He found us groping leaderless and blind
He found us striving each his selfish part
He left a civilization with a civic heart.

In the states, progressive governors fought for meliorative reforms such as workers' compensation, factory inspection laws, and measures establishing maximum work hours for female wage earners. On the national level, progressivism received a boost when Theodore Roosevelt became president upon William McKinley's assassination in 1901. A Republican, Roosevelt disdained reformers, whom he viewed as overly moralistic, and yet he signed measures furthering the federal regulation of the railroads and the meat-packing and drug industries, and he developed a reputation as an environmentalist. His rhetoric could be more radical than his actions, but by virtue of his national platform, Roosevelt gave a boost to calls for change and helped establish the notion that the era of unfettered capitalism had ended.

By 1912, talk of reform dominated national politics. Roosevelt became dissatisfied with the conservatism of Old Guard Republicans and upset that his successor, William Howard Taft, had not followed his lead. As a result, Roosevelt bolted from the Republican Party and ran for president as the candidate of the newly formed Progressive Party, whose platform endorsed a number of social-reform measures. The Democrats nominated Woodrow Wilson, an unusual choice in that Wilson had been a college professor and president of Princeton University rather than a career politician. He had served as governor of New Jersey, however, and had established a reputation as a reformer and as a man who would stand up to the political bosses.

Much of the 1912 campaign focused on the trusts, huge corporations formed in the 1880s. Fear over their influence led to the adoption of the Sherman Antitrust Act in 1890, but the law proved ineffective because of various court decisions. Between 1898 and 1902 a merger wave swept through American business, and by 1910 the economy was dominated by such giants as Standard Oil, U. S. Steel, International Harvester, Pillsbury, General Electric, Westinghouse, Swift, and Armour. To those who had been raised in the America of small shops and small towns, the trusts were threatening, not only because of their sheer economic power but also because they exercised considerable political influence.

Wilson and Roosevelt proposed different solutions for dealing with the trusts. Roosevelt, known as an advocate of a program called the New Nationalism, believed they should be regulated rather than destroyed. Wilson, a supporter of a reform program known as the New Freedom, believed the trusts should be broken up to return free competition to the American economy. The 1912 race turned into a contest between Wilson and Roosevelt, with Wilson becoming the first Democrat elected to the presidency since 1892. Taft finished third. Eugene V. Debs, the American Socialist Party candidate, won almost 6 percent of the vote, the highest percentage ever won by the Socialists.

Ironically, once in office Wilson carried out a reform program that resembled Roosevelt's New Nationalism more than the New Freedom. Both the Fair Trade Commission and the Federal Reserve Board, established during Wilson's first term, furthered the regulation of business, and the Clayton Act, the one antitrust measure that passed, had almost no effect. Once the United States entered the European conflict, Wilson worked closely with corporate executives, whom he no longer dared to attack. The war did much to rehabilitate the reputation of big business, although antimonopoly sentiment lived on, especially among a group of progressive Republicans based in the Midwest, including such fierce foes of Wall Street as Robert La Follette of Wisconsin and George Norris of Nebraska.

By the eve of World War I, progressivism had influenced many aspects of American life. Painters associated with the ashcan school shocked the art world by portraying and often celebrating urban life. Charles Beard and other progressive historians challenged those who idealized American history. Academics connected to the new discipline of sociology called attention to the inequalities in American society. Progressives and socialists, whites and blacks joined to form the National Association for the Advancement of Colored People (NAACP), an organization that fought for racial justice and equality. Women stepped up their efforts to win the right to vote. The federal Commission on Industrial Relations, which issued its final report in 1915, sympathized with workers who had been the victims of ruthless antiunion employers. For good reason, progressives believed they had accomplished much and that their efforts had proved the value of slow, steady, and moderate reform.

The Outbreak of the Great War

No one should have been surprised when war broke out in August 1914. In the late nineteenth century, Great Britain and France had brought much of Asia and Africa under their control. Germany, which was established as a unified nation in 1870 and had undergone rapid industrialization, chafed at being shut out of the race for colonies. By 1900, Great Britain and Germany had both expanded their military capacities in preparation for war. In the years right before 1914, the European nations had almost come to blows over disputes in North Africa and the Balkans. By 1914, imperial Germany under Kaiser Wilhelm II had formed an alliance with the Austro-Hungarian and Ottoman Empires, and Great Britain and France were allied with Russia.

It took only a small spark to set off a conflagration. In June 1914, a young Serb terrorist (or freedom fighter, depending on one's point of view), angered by Austro-Hungarian rule over land populated by Serbs, assassinated Archduke Franz Ferdinand (the heir to the Austro-Hungarian throne) and his wife during their state visit to Sarajevo. In response, the Austro-Hungarian government made a series of impossible demands on Serbia. Russia, which viewed itself as the defender of the Slavs, came to the aid of the Serbs. Germany, following a military strategy known as the Schlieffen Plan, then launched a lightning strike against France. The Germans argued that they had to follow this strategy in order to avoid a war on two fronts, because they believed Russia planned to attack them from the east. The French put up a surprisingly strong resistance. The British, following through on their commitments, entered the war on the side of the Allies. (When the war began, England, France, and Russia constituted the Allies. The German, Austro-Hungarian, and Ottoman Empires made up the Central Powers.)

French and German troops, parading before cheering throngs, marched off to battle, expecting to be home by Christmas. Instead, by the autumn of 1914, a terrifying type of combat known as trench warfare emerged on the battlefields of France. Over the next four years, millions of French, British, and German troops, living amid mud, lice, and rats, would be mowed down by machine guns, which proved to be the perfect defensive weapon before tanks had become fully operational. On the shifting eastern front, Russian troops battled the Austro-Hungarian and German armies in a war that eventually cost the czar his throne.

When the bloodletting ceased, the victors, who met at Versailles, near Paris, held Germany responsible for beginning the war. In a strict sense this was true, because Germany's attack on France had turned a Balkan conflict into a European and eventually a worldwide war. In a larger sense, however, the war was the result of the economic rivalry between capitalist and imperialist nations that had been competing with one another for the previous forty years. The war also grew out of an almost mystic belief in nationalism—a commitment on the part of the masses to fight for their nations, whether right or wrong, and a belief that loyalty to the flag came before all other loyalties. Before 1914, French, German, and other European socialists had proclaimed a belief in internationalism and pledged to oppose a war that might involve their own nations. But when the moment of truth came, French workers marched off to battle German workers, and the German Socialist Party failed to uphold its pledge to vote against appropriating money for the war.

An entire way of life perished in 1914, a date historians consider the true beginning of the twentieth century. After a far greater conflagration, the earlier conflict became known as World War I, but people at the time called it "the World War" or "the Great War," a term that captured its magnitude and impact on popular consciousness. After four years of a conflict that cost at least ten million lives, only fools still believed in the inevitability of progress. By the 1920s, Europeans would fondly remember the halcyon prewar days of Edwardian England, the French belle époque, and the civilized air of Berlin, Vienna, Prague, and Budapest. The unimaginable horrors of Hitler and Stalin would eventually grow out of the four years of death and destruction of World War I, which would in time cause even the ostensible victors to wonder what exactly they had won.

Roots of American Involvement

When the war broke out, most Americans probably heaved a sigh of relief that the Atlantic Ocean separated them from Europe. Following the advice of George

Washington, the United States had remained free of "entangling alliances," even though by the early twentieth century, most elite policymakers believed that America's interests were bound up with those of the British. Americans prided themselves on their separation from an old world they viewed as corrupt. And despite being the world's leading industrial power, the United States had only a small military, because of the sense of security provided by the Atlantic and Pacific Oceans.

In 1914, most Americans followed events in Mexico, to which Wilson had recently sent troops, more closely than the developments in Europe. But the United States was a world trading power and it could not help being affected by the conflict. Wilson called on Americans to remain neutral. Despite his professed admiration for the English form of government and system of jurisprudence, Wilson took a strictly legalistic approach and announced that the United States intended to trade with both sides. The war stimulated so much economic activity that a 1913–14 recession turned into a boom by 1916. It soon became evident that rigorous adherence to the doctrine of neutral rights aided the British because the British blockade of the North Sea made trade with Germany almost impossible. One wonders, therefore, if Wilson would have taken the same stance if such a policy had aided the Germans rather than the British.

By 1916, a flourishing trade had grown between the United States and Great Britain, and the British war effort depended heavily on its purchases of American goods and matériel. American banks extended the credits that allowed the British to make these purchases, and during the war, New York City replaced London as the center of world finance. In 1915, Wilson's secretary of state, William Jennings Bryan, resigned in protest of a policy he believed favored the British. (Robert Lansing, a more conventional choice, replaced him.) From Bryan's perspective, it would have been better to have the United States sacrifice some trade than to become so closely tied to the British that the United States could not afford to see the Allies defeated. Bryan, a Nebraska resident and a three-time Democratic presidential candidate, spoke for many midwestern residents who, either because they came from German backgrounds or because they harbored a strong distrust for Wall Street, had become disturbed by what they viewed as Wilson's tilt toward the British.

Critics had reason to believe that Wilson had not been impartial. The president strongly protested when the Germans' new submarines sank British passenger ships, leading to the loss of American lives. On the other hand, Wilson did not protest so loudly when the British violated America's neutrality rights by unilaterally widening the definition of contraband. Nevertheless, the German government in 1916 did not want to bring the United States into the war, and it pledged not to use the submarine—the only weapon that could limit the effectiveness of the British blockade.

By 1916, the war had provoked a highly contentious debate in the United States. Advocates of preparedness, led by Republican senator Henry Cabot Lodge and Theodore Roosevelt, who had rejoined the Republican Party, believed that the United States should build up its military in order to be ready to join the war on the side of the Allies. Those who followed Bryan's lead argued that the United States should stay out of the war at all costs, and they criticized Wilson for upholding a doctrine of neutrality relevant to an era before the industrial revolution had transformed warfare. Wilson and his Democratic supporters in Congress followed a middle course, favoring a limited military buildup while hoping to broker the conflict rather than to enter it.

The president's advisors, sensing the popularity of the noninterventionist position, convinced him to use the slogan "He kept us out of the war" in the 1916 presidential election, which Wilson won by a narrow margin over the Republican candidate, Charles Evans Hughes. In the meantime, facing desperate food shortages on the home front, German naval commanders convinced the kaiser to resume unrestricted submarine warfare. They knew this would bring the United States into the conflict, but they believed it would take the Americans more than two years to mobilize for the war, and that the submarine would make it difficult for the Americans to get troops across the Atlantic. According to their calculations—and they greatly overestimated the effectiveness of this weapon—the submarine would also cause devastating British losses and possibly force Britain's surrender. By March 1917, German torpedoes had sunk a number of American ships. The American public had been further aroused by news that the German government had suggested to Mexico that it enter the war on the side of the Central Powers, in order to regain territory lost to the United States between 1846 and 1848. Americans had also been influenced by the press, which had given extensive publicity to Germany's violation of Belgian neutrality and to alleged "Hun" atrocities. In this emotional climate, Wilson went before Congress on 2 April 1917 to request a declaration of war. As one would expect from an ardent progressive, Wilson used highly idealistic language to describe his hope that American participation in the conflict would lead to a new and better world:

> It is a fearful thing to lead this great peaceful people into war, into the most terrible and disastrous of all wars, civilization itself seeming to be in the balance. But the right is more precious than peace, and we shall fight for the

things which we have always carried nearest to our hearts—for democracy, for the right of those who submit to authority to have a voice in their own governments, for the rights and liberties of small nations, for a universal dominion of right by such a concert of free peoples as shall bring peace and safety to all nations and make the world itself at last free.

Nevertheless, six senators, including Norris and La Follette, and fifty representatives, including the first woman ever to serve in the House of Representatives, Jeannette Rankin of Montana, voted against the declaration.

Wilson would have had a difficult time talking about a war "for democracy" if the United States had been allied with czarist Russia. But the path for America's entry into the war had been cleared by the March 1917 revolution, which overthrew a czarist regime unraveling under the pressures of the conflict. In its stead, a new provisional government had been installed in Russia, a government that Wilson expected would bring democracy to that land. Weary of war, the Russians yearned for peace, but Wilson insisted that the provisional government would have to remain in the war (in order to force Germany to fight on two fronts) if it were to receive badly needed credits. This "no fight, no loan" stance played a significant role in paving the way for the November 1917 Bolshevik revolution.

Wilson, in his speech requesting a declaration of war, claimed that the United States had "no selfish ends to serve." This befit a president who a few months earlier, in an address to the Senate, had talked about "peace without victory" and who now sought to extend the progressive crusade to other nations. Because the United States had war goals that differed from those of the Allies, the United States entered the conflict as an associate power rather than as one of the Allies. Wilson did not even try to negotiate terms under which American troops would join the British and French, even though they badly needed American assistance to break the bloody stalemate. This omission guaranteed that the postwar wrangling would divide not merely the victors from the defeated, but the victors themselves.

The War at Home and Abroad

Wars have often caused significant domestic changes within the United States, and World War I conformed to this pattern. As Wilson's talk of a crusade for democracy permeated American society, disaffected groups heard the message and gave it a different interpretation than Wilson intended. African Americans, who began to migrate north in large numbers in 1916, had their hopes raised that the war would lead to a significant change in race relations. Women who had conducted a long battle for suffrage asked how a nation could fight for democracy and deny the vote to half of its citizens. Workers beset by an inflation that ate away at their wage increases demonstrated a new enthusiasm for joining labor unions and conducted many walkouts, confident that labor shortages would force employers to make concessions.

Wars lead to an expansion of the federal government's power. In order to mobilize the economy for warfare, the Wilson administration established a number of new federal agencies, including the Food Administration, the Fuel Administration, and the War Industries Board. Because the privately owned railroad lines could not efficiently move the large volume of traffic, the federal government took over their operation. Corporate executives headed many of these agencies, and the war did much to improve the image of big business, which churned out the matériel a modern war requires. Wilson in his first term had compromised the New Freedom, and during his second term he abandoned it; he could not attack the trusts when he needed their assistance.

Progressives, nevertheless, had reason to hope that the war would bolster the reform cause rather than destroy it. When work stoppages threatened production, the Wilson administration established another new agency, the National War Labor Board, which granted unprecedented recognition to labor. Although the government raised most of its funds through Liberty bond drives, it also put in place a progressive income tax, a measure made possible by a constitutional amendment adopted in 1913. Many liberals, especially those connected to the journal the *New Republic*, held out the hope that after the war, the federal government would use its new powers to promote social justice.

Wilson had predicted that if the United States entered the war, a wave of intolerance would sweep the nation. The president turned out to be all too prescient. Almost as soon as the United States entered the conflict, mobs forced German institutions and organizations to close. The Committee on Public Information (CPI), a government propaganda agency, produced a vast number of films, posters, pamphlets, and books that stimulated animosity toward Germans. The CPI followed Wilson's advice and maintained a distinction between the German people and the German government, but this meant little to American superpatriots seized by a hatred of all things German.

The federal government took steps to quash dissent, and "the war to make the world safe for democracy" led to one of the most repressive periods in American history. Armed with new statutory authority, the government indicted a number of the war's most prominent opponents, and barred antiwar literature from the mails. Quasi-governmental organizations such as the National Security League participated in raids against "slackers" accused of evading conscription and against radicals involved in labor organizing. Soon after the United States entered the conflict, many people became fearful of publicly expressing their views, especially because they believed that their neighbors or fellow employees might be keeping tabs on them.

A number of factors contributed to the demand for conformity. Many Americans questioned the patriotism of German immigrants, whom they accused of holding dual loyalties. A vigorous antiwar movement had emerged in the spring and summer of 1917, one that included the American Socialist Party, which had voted to oppose the war. Wilson's crusading approach to the conflict implied that anyone who opposed it had questionable motivations.

By 1918, fears of Bolshevism contributed to the hysteria. The Communists had seized control in Russia, overthrowing the provisional government, which had been in power for only six months. Many Americans believed the Germans had had a hand in the coup because the Central Powers stood to benefit if Russia withdrew from the war. In reality, Lenin's slogan, "Peace, Land, and Bread," greatly appealed to the Russian soldiers, who had suffered terribly and who yearned for plots of land they could call their own.

Just as the Bolsheviks had pledged, Russia had withdrawn from the war, although many of the Communist leaders protested the onerous terms Germany imposed on them in the Treaty of Brest-Litovsk (a treaty whose provisions became irrelevant once Germany surrendered). In 1918, a civil war broke out in Russia between the Bolsheviks and various anti-Communist armies. By midsummer of that year, at the urging of the British, the United States landed troops in northern Russia, near Murmansk, and in Siberia. Wilson never clearly stated the reason for the intervention. It sought, in part, to prevent the Germans from seizing Russian arms, to aid former Czechoslovak prisoners of war who wished to join the Allied forces, and to check the Japanese, who had designs on Siberia. Clearly, the American troops also wanted to aid the "whites," the various anti-Bolshevik forces.

The Bolsheviks maintained that the war involved rival imperial powers and that neither side had honorable motivations. To bolster their contention, the new Russian government released secret treaties that contained provisions promising Italy and Japan concessions if they joined the war on the Allied side. The United States had not been a party to the secret treaties, and Wilson believed that the Americans had far nobler motivations than other participants in the war. In order to regain the high moral ground, he made a speech in January 1918, known as the Fourteen Points address, that laid out a series of idealistic goals the United States sought to achieve by participating in the conflict. The promises of self-determination contained in the address indeed sounded noble in comparison to the program of the German government, which sought to use the Russian withdrawal from the war to gain territory.

In the spring of 1918, the Germans launched a last-ditch offensive to break the four-year stalemate on the western front. Fresh American troops, who had begun to pour into France, helped repulse the attack. By the summer of 1918, the Allies began to push the Germans back. Faced with an invasion of German territory, the kaiser abdicated, and the new democratic regime that had just taken power in Germany surrendered. Upon hearing the news of the armistice on 11 November 1918, vast crowds gathered in Paris, London, and New York, jubilant and relieved that at last the Great War had ended.

The sudden end of the war appeared to vindicate Wilson's decision to enter the conflict. The United States had mobilized for war far more rapidly than the Germans had anticipated. American power and prestige had risen as a result of the war. But would an idealistic, almost messianic president be able to frame a just and lasting peace for people who had just lived through four years of suffering and torment and who now asked: What are we going to get out of the war? These and many other questions remained to be answered in a world filled with hatred, resentment, and the desire for revenge, where the innocent optimism that had greeted the dawn of the new century seemed like a distant memory.

2

THE UNITED STATES FACES THE POSTWAR WORLD

ONCE THE GUNS STOPPED FIRING on the western front, world leaders faced an unprecedented situation. The war had destroyed the old German, Austro-Hungarian, Russian, and Ottoman Empires, and those who met at Versailles would have to decide how to replace them. Woodrow Wilson's decision to participate personally in the deliberations signaled America's emergence as a world power. As a global force, the United States also confronted a hostile Bolshevik regime, a Japanese government determined to assert power in East Asia, and the growing resentment of Latin Americans toward the United States. In attempting to deal with these difficulties, policymakers faced a vastly more complex world situation than that which had existed in the prewar era.

Woodrow Wilson and the Treaty of Versailles

Having decided that the United States should enter the war, Woodrow Wilson also became determined that America would play a decisive role in shaping the peace. Wilson believed that the war stemmed from outmoded alliances that needed to be replaced by a commitment to collective security. In the Fourteen Points address, Wilson stated America's war goals and gave his own vision of the future: a world with free trade, freedom of the seas, open diplomacy, self-determination for the subject peoples of Europe, and above all, a league of nations that would guarantee the peace. The United States stood to benefit from the more open world that Wilson envisioned, but these were not merely the words of a cunning statesman. Wilson was an idealist who believed it was his destiny to create a new world order that would ensure that such carnage would never occur again.

Unfortunately for Wilson, high ideals could be realized only through practical politics. From the time he had become president, the Democrats had enjoyed a majority in both houses of Congress. The Democrats' success had resulted from a rift that divided the Republicans into progressive and Old Guard factions. Some of the wounds had healed by 1918, and Wilson feared that the Republican Party would regain its usual majority in the off-year elections. Hoping to forestall a Republican victory, and attempting to capitalize on his popularity as a wartime president, Wilson, in the campaign's dying days, called on the American people to elect a Democratic Congress. This tactic, the first of Wilson's many political blunders during the treaty fight, backfired when the Republicans, appealing mainly to local grievances, regained control of both the House and the Senate.

Republican control of the Senate meant that Henry Cabot Lodge would head the Senate Foreign Relations Committee, which would hold hearings on any peace treaty Wilson negotiated. An ardent imperialist and advocate of realpolitik, Lodge believed that Wilson lacked a proper understanding of American national interests. Wilson and Lodge, who had deep-seated political and ideological differences, hated one another, and the elevation of the Massachusetts senator to such an important post guaranteed that any treaty favored by Wilson would face tough sledding before the Senate.

Believing that decisions reached at Versailles would shape the future of the world, Wilson announced that he would head the American delegation to the Paris peace conference. Unable to trust subordinates with the responsibility for conducting such critical negotiations, Wilson, with the aid of intellectual and academic advisors known as "the Inquiry," concentrated his attention on the upcoming peace parley and paid almost no heed to domestic issues during the postwar reconstruction period. To accompany him on the American delegation, Wilson chose his secretary of state, Robert Lansing, whose views resembled Lodge's more than those of the president; Colonel Edward M. House, his trusted confidant and aide; General Tasker S. Bliss, who served as a military advisor; and Henry White, an obscure diplomat who was nominally a member of the Republican Party. Wilson's failure to include a leading member of their party infuriated many Republicans, who began to seize any opportunity to criticize the president. Wilson might have chosen either former secretary of state Elihu Root or former president William Howard Taft, prominent Republicans who belonged to the League to Enforce the Peace, which endorsed the concept of a world organization. Failing to understand that the changed political context required him to make some conciliatory gestures to the Republicans, Wilson selected a delegation that made him vulnerable to charges of partisanship.

His weakened position at home notwithstanding, Wilson arrived in Europe in December 1918 with vast resources at his command. Despite their triumph, France and Britain had suffered devastating losses from the war. Both countries owed the United States billions of dollars, and America had replaced Great Britain as the world's leading creditor nation. Britain had lost many of its overseas markets to the United States and Japan; Britain and France had lost more than one million men; and France had suffered extensive property damage. By the winter of 1918–19, only food delivered under the auspices of the American Relief Administration kept millions of starving Europeans alive. Enthusiastic, cheering crowds greeted Wilson as he toured London, Paris, and Rome, and the president carried the hopes of millions inspired by his pledge "to make the world safe for democracy."

Wilson faced an extremely difficult task once his whirlwind tour ended and the delegates settled down to business in January 1919 amid the elegant surroundings of the Versailles palace. The Fourteen Points had been a unilateral American statement, and the French prime minister, Georges Clemenceau, scorned it. To complicate matters, Italy and Japan had been enticed to enter the war on the Allied side by promises of territory contained in secret treaties. Such wheeling and dealing violated Wilson's cherished concept of self-determination, and he claimed to have had no knowledge of the arrangements, although the treaties had been published in newspapers and the Bolsheviks had revealed those that the czar had signed. The British, French, and Italian governments needed concrete gains from the conference to justify the four years of immense sacrifice. These divisions guaranteed that some tough bargaining would take place among the members of the Council of Four (the United States, Great Britain, France, and Italy), which made the key decisions at Versailles.

Although the German revolution of October and November 1918 had replaced the kaiser with a parliamentary regime, the assembled heads of state decided that Germany would not be a party to the proceedings. Together with the decision to continue the blockade of Germany, the exclusion of the Weimar representatives demonstrated that the Allies continued to view Germany as an outlaw nation. This contravened Wilson's stated belief that the United States had gone to war against the kaiser's government rather than against the German people, but this distinction had been lost amid the passions and hysteria of war. Unfortunately for future prospects for peace, Germany's lack of representation guaranteed that the German people would view the treaty as a victor's document imposed on them against their will.

The delegates first had to decide the fate of Germany. The final territorial provisions placed some German-populated areas under foreign control. The territories that Germany lost included Alsace-Lorraine, which was returned to France, the Sudetenland, which was given to Czechoslovakia, and the Polish Corridor, which severed East Prussia from Germany in order to give Poland access to the sea. In addition, Austria was forbidden to unite with Germany without League of Nations approval, and the Austrian South Tyrol was granted to Italy. Wilson resisted Clemenceau's demand that a buffer state be created on the left bank of the Rhine. Instead, the United States and Great Britain signed a treaty to guarantee French security, and the Rhineland was placed under a fifteen-year military occupation. German sovereignty was also protected in the industrially important areas of the Saar (although the French received rights to its rich coal deposits) and Upper Silesia, where plebiscites were to be held after fifteen years. All told, Germany lost approximately 10 percent of its prewar territory and population, and the new states of Poland and Czechoslovakia contained significant German national minorities.

The Versailles delegates decided that Germany would have to pay reparations. Wilson had given assurances that the United States sought neither territory nor financial contributions, but Clemenceau went to the conference determined to assess the Germans for damages resulting from the war. Making Germany pay fit the vengeful mood of the French people, and reparations were the only means by which the French government could avoid raising taxes on its own populace. To the French, reparations meant that the subjugation of Germany would be permanent. During the British parliamentary campaign in 1918, Prime Minister David Lloyd George had talked about making Germany pay "the uttermost farthing," although he feared the harm extensive payments might do to the new German government. On the other hand, the British, like the French, needed cash if they were to have any hope of paying the enormous debt they owed the United States. The only logical way out of this conundrum was for the United States to forgive the Allied war debt, a reasonable proposition given that only the United States appeared to have profited from the war. The United States, however, would not hear of this idea, and the unbending American stance fortified French and British determination to exact reparations from the Germans.

The French proposed that Germany pay for the entire cost of the war, a sum that some experts estimated at more than two hundred billion dollars. Contrary to his earlier statements, Wilson accepted the principle of reparations, but he believed that Germany should only have to pay a reasonable sum for specific damage caused by its armed forces. At one point, Wilson became so irritated by the extreme French demand that he threatened to set sail for America. The tactic worked and the French modified their position, although the final amount, the means of payment, and other thorny questions were left up to a special reparations commission to settle.

To justify the reparations and to provide a legal basis for collecting them, the delegates inserted a special war-guilt clause in the treaty. The idea that Germany bore sole responsibility for the conflict violated Wilson's belief that the war resulted from the European balance-of-power system, but once he accepted the principle of reparations, the president had little choice other than to agree to the war-guilt clause. To punish the defeated nation further, the delegates limited Germany's army to a hundred thousand men, stripped Germany of its overseas possessions, and required Germany to pass a probationary period before being admitted to the League of Nations.

The terms could have been much harsher, and Germany still remained the strongest power on the Continent, but the treaty was a bitter disappointment to German liberals and Social Democrats. The German government had surrendered on the basis of the Fourteen Points, and the agreement repudiated promises made at the time of the armistice. Democratic forces in Germany believed that Wilson had let them down. Already the German right wing had begun to propagate the absurd notion that a Jewish "stab in the back" had caused Germany's defeat, and extreme nationalists protested "the shameful diktat of Versailles" and called for its nonfulfillment. A spirit of revenge and revanche began to take hold, a spirit that eventually played an important role in Hitler's rise to power.

In addition to addressing Germany's boundaries, the delegates had to wrestle with numerous other territorial issues. Two of the most contentious and disruptive disputes involved Italy and Japan. The Italian government had cynically offered its services to the highest bidder, and had entered the war on the Allied side in 1915 when the secret Treaty of London promised that the Dalmatian coast on the Adriatic would be granted to Italy. Italy's performance in the war had proved disappointing; nevertheless, Prime Minister Vittorio Orlando and Foreign Minister Sidney Sonnino had gone to Paris determined to collect on past promises. When Italy extended its demands to include the Dalmatian port city of Fiume, an ill and weary Wilson finally put his foot down and flatly refused the request. In anger, the Italian delegates walked out of the conference, although they eventually returned.

Wilson backed down when faced with Japanese territorial demands. Japan had entered the war in 1914 when it seized the German leasehold in China's mineral-rich Shandong Province, and at Versailles, the Japanese delegates requested that Japan be awarded the entire Shandong Peninsula. Unlike the Italians, the Japanese had a strategy to achieve their goals, and they proposed that the covenant of the League of Nations contain a racial-equality clause. The United States, Canada, Australia, and New Zealand all feared that such a provision might threaten their severe restrictions on Asiatic immigration; in addition, Wilson, a white supremacist who had reintroduced segregation to Washington, D.C., would not approve such a proposal. Having used his influence to remove the racial-equality clause from the covenant, and drained by the Fiume dispute, Wilson had little will to resist the Japanese demand for Shandong. The final treaty did contain a face-saving pledge that Japan would return Shandong to China in the future, but the outraged Chinese delegates refused to sign the final document, and senators anxious to defeat the treaty made great use of the issue.

In contrast to the unsatisfactory resolution of the Shandong controversy, Wilson succeeded in his goal of carving new nations out of the ruins of the Austro-Hungarian Empire. A hero to various Slavic peoples because of his calls for self-determination, Wilson had gone to Versailles determined to redraw the map of East Central Europe. The more-pragmatic Clemenceau, hoping to create a series of buffer states to block Bolshevik expansion, had given his consent to this idea. Representatives of the Czechs and Slovaks had already met in Pittsburgh in 1918 to draw up an agreement for a new state, and Versailles ratified their deliberations. The conference also assented to the creation of the Kingdom of Serbs, Croats, and Slovenes (renamed Yugoslavia in 1929) and restored independence to Poland for the first time since the late eighteenth century. The Treaty of Trianon disposed of the Hungarian half of the empire and awarded generous chunks of Hungarian-populated areas to Czechoslovakia, Yugoslavia, and especially Rumania.

Wilson naively believed that the successor states would almost instantly become liberal democracies on the Western model. Tomáš Masaryk, the first president of Czechoslovakia, who spoke often of his commitment to minority rights and to peace, represented the type of leader Wilson hoped would emerge. Contrary to Wilson's dreams, Masaryk and Czechoslovakia proved exceptional among East Central European leaders and nations. Members of the Inquiry were adept at drawing maps that appeared reasonable on paper, but in the villages of eastern and southern Europe, the age-old feuds of Serbs versus Croats, Poles versus Ukrainians, Rumanians versus Hungarians, and seemingly all peoples versus the Jews, fed by hatred, tribal passions, and the thirst for revenge, made a mockery of Wilson's dreams. Rather than promoting democracy, self-determination encouraged a narrow type of nationalism. Previously oppressed minorities began to oppress other minorities in what the *New Republic* in January 1919 described as "chauvinism gone mad."

Wilson's pledge of self-determination had also convinced people who lived in the colonial world that the Versailles deliberations would lead to a change in their status. Seizing on the president's lofty rhetoric, representatives of many oppressed groups, including the Irish, Vietnamese, Arabs, Kurds, and Jews, went to Paris hoping to receive a hearing. These unofficial delegates included African-American leaders who traveled to Paris incognito after being denied passports. But those who lacked credentials failed to be heard. Ho Chi Minh's experience was typical. The young future leader of the Communist revolt against the French tried to bring the Vietnamese cause personally to Wilson's attention, but he could not even get through the front door.

Only those colonial peoples who had lived in German overseas possessions or under the Ottoman Turks saw a change in status. According to a system devised by the South African Jan Smuts, the League of Nations placed these people in three different categories of mandates, determined by their supposed level of development, for a period of tutelage. As intended, the mandate system proved a great boon to the British and French, who, executing the terms of the secret 1916 Sykes-Picot agreement, reneged on their promises to their Arab allies and created new states in the Middle East (including Iraq and Kuwait) whose boundaries served Western oil interests.

Throughout the conference, Wilson made compromises in order to ensure British and French support for the League of Nations. Whatever their doubts about the feasibility of a world organization, the British decided to back the league once Wilson assured them that he would not try to break up the British colonial empire. The French gave their consent once Wilson agreed to a security treaty that pledged American aid in case of a German attack. The president also made compromises to appease domestic critics. When Wilson returned to the United States on a brief visit, Henry Cabot Lodge obtained the signatures of thirty-nine senators on a round robin that objected to the proposed league covenant on the grounds that it infringed on American sovereignty. In an address to the Democratic National Committee, Wilson had spoken of "the blind and little provincial people" who opposed him, but, given the strength of the opposition (ratification of a treaty required that two-thirds of the Senate approve), he recognized the need to make some concessions. Upon his return to

Paris, Wilson drew up a final draft that excluded tariff and immigration questions from the league's jurisdiction and contained specific recognition of the Monroe Doctrine.

Compromise had followed compromise, but after five exhausting months, Wilson had at last achieved his central goal: the establishment of the League of Nations. The league's constitution was termed a covenant, an indication of the significance the Calvinist president attached to it. Article 10 stood at the heart of the covenant and embodied Wilson's hope that a commitment to collective security would replace the balance of power. Under the vaguely worded terms of the article, members of the executive council would meet to consider the use of sanctions or armed force against any aggressor nation. Because the league did not have a military force of its own, the British and the French did not anticipate that it would actually deter aggression (which is why the French demanded a separate security treaty). But to the president, Article 10 redeemed the horrific slaughter of the past four years and his own decision to have the United States enter the war.

The treaty's final terms fell somewhere between the harsh document favored by Clemenceau and the milder peace favored by Wilson. Given the differences between the French and American war goals, compromises had to be made, but the violation of the Fourteen Points weakened Wilson's moral standing, particularly because he stubbornly refused to admit that the treaty had any defects. A mood of gloom hung over Versailles on 28 June 1919—five years to the day after the assassinations at Sarajevo that precipitated the Great War—when the German government, under protest, signed the document. Only the most optimistic individual could have believed that "the war to end all wars" had accomplished that goal.

The Senate Rejects the Treaty

Upon his return to the United States, Wilson submitted the treaty to the Senate. Although the Republicans enjoyed a two-vote majority in the upper house, most commentators predicted that the treaty would be ratified. Instead, following a bitter, acrimonious battle that focused almost entirely on the League of Nations, the Senate rejected the document that the president had worked so hard to create. A crushing personal defeat for Wilson and one that cost him his health, the treaty's rejection signaled the hostility to foreign influence that characterized the increasingly xenophobic and nationalistic postwar period.

Wilson entered the Senate fight weakened by the defection of some of the most internationally minded Americans. Prominent liberal intellectuals, already disturbed by the president's failure to fashion a domestic program of reconstruction, by the continued violations of civil liberties, and by the armed intervention in Russia, denounced the treaty as soon as they learned some of its terms. Oswald Garrison Villard, editor of the *Nation*, launched the attack in April when he returned from Paris and editorialized against Wilson's abandonment of his principles. Of greater concern to the president, the more influential *New Republic* on its 17 May 1919 cover asked "Is It Peace?" and in the following week's issue concluded "This Is Not Peace." The magazine, edited by the progressive luminaries Walter Weyl, Herbert Croly, and Walter Lippmann, had been lavish in its praise of the Fourteen Points, and its decision to call for the treaty's defeat cost the president an important source of intellectual support.

Upset by the harsh treatment of Germany and by the punitive reparations provisions, these critics argued that the Treaty of Versailles planted the seeds for another war. In dismissing the League of Nations, they maintained that Article 10 required the United States to uphold the treaty's numerous unjust territorial settlements. John Maynard Keynes's *Economic Consequences of the Peace* (first serialized in the *New Republic*) became the intellectuals' bible. It portrayed a naive Wilson outmaneuvered by the wily Clemenceau. Writing as if world leaders did not have to take mass emotions and a mass electorate into account, and betraying their own guilt for having supported the war, the liberals failed to consider whether a rational peace could have been framed in the wake of the irrational national hatreds stimulated by the conflict.

Wilson also suffered from the defection of certain ethnic groups. Italian Americans, for example, asked why the president gave in on Shandong and stood so firm on Fiume. Angered by the president's hard-line stand, leaders of the Sons of Italy and other Italian-American organizations cheered when the proto-Fascist, nationalistic poet Gabriele d'Annunzio in September 1919 led a private army that temporarily seized Fiume.

The disaffection of Irish Americans promised to be far more damaging to the treaty's cause. Strongly Democratic in their political loyalties, Americans of Irish descent had often provided moral, financial, and even military support for their brethren across the seas. British repression of the 1916 Easter rebellion had infuriated Irish Americans, and Wilson's call for self-determination had fed their hopes. Irish bishops dominated the American Catholic church, and they, along with the Catholic press, gave vigorous support to the struggle against "perfidious Albion."

Irish-American representatives had gone to Paris determined to press the Irish cause. When they learned that the treaty made no provision for Irish independence, they were outraged. How, they asked, could the supposed champion of the rights of small nations not stand up for Ireland? Irate at Wilson's refusal to challenge British imperialism, Irish Americans vowed to oppose the treaty and turned out in great numbers when Ireland's provisional president, Eamon de Valera, toured the United States during the summer of 1919.

Despite these setbacks, the president remained a commanding figure. Polls showed support for the document, and prominent Republicans who belonged to the League to Enforce the Peace continued to favor a world organization. Unfortunately for the president, Henry Cabot Lodge served as Senate majority leader as well as chairman of the Senate Foreign Relations Committee. A Harvard Ph.D., Lodge intended to reassert senatorial power vis-à-vis the president and to position the Republicans for victory in the 1920 election. He was an early advocate of entering the war on the side of the Allies, and he believed that the United States should continue to cultivate close ties with the British and the French. A believer in power politics, he approved of the punitive aspects of the treaty but did not feel that collective security could be achieved through the League of Nations. Lodge was determined to carry on the Rooseveltian foreign-policy tradition following the former president's death in January 1919, and he set out to oppose an agreement that he thought endangered American national interests.

A savvy and often meanspirited politician, Lodge devised the strategy that led to the treaty's defeat. After consulting with other Republican Party leaders, Lodge decided that the Senate Foreign Relations Committee (packed with the treaty's opponents) would attach reservations to the document. The Republican strategists intended to present Wilson with a Hobson's choice: either accept the treaty with reservations that altered the very nature of American participation in the League of Nations or oppose the reservations and run the risk of the treaty's rejection. Eventually, the committee voted in favor of fourteen reservations (to match Wilson's Fourteen Points), including those that (1) guaranteed that the United States could withdraw from the league at any time; (2) required that regardless of Article 10, American troops could not be sent overseas without congressional approval; (3) exempted domestic questions from the league's jurisdiction; and (4) removed the Monroe Doctrine from the league's purview. The reservations had a distinctly nationalistic tone, an indication that the Republicans intended to portray themselves as the defenders of Americanism who stood firm against Wilsonian internationalism.

Most of the forty-seven Democratic senators supported ratification of the treaty without reservations. The Republicans divided into groups known as mild reservationists, strong reservationists, and irreconcilables. The irreconcilables vowed to oppose the treaty even with the reservations attached. The views of the irreconcilables varied. For example, the most radical, such as Republicans Robert La Follette and George Norris, had been ardent reformers before the war, had opposed the United States' entry into the conflict, and had been extremely critical of American intervention in Russia. Distrustful of Eastern economic interests, they viewed the treaty as an imperialist document that strengthened British power in the world. Other irreconcilables such as Senators Hiram Johnson of California and William Borah of Idaho, shared an anti-imperialist perspective with La Follette and Norris, but also made demagogic appeals to Americanism and railed against foreign influence.

Some of the irreconcilables appealed to the most provincial, narrow-minded, and bigoted attitudes of Americans. Senator Lawrence Sherman of Illinois argued that the inclusion of Catholic countries guaranteed that the pope would control the League of Nations; Democratic senator James A. Reed of Missouri warned that the inclusion of nations such as Haiti and Liberia meant that the organization would become "a colored league of nations"; Colorado senator Charles S. Thomas feared that the International Labor Organization, created by the treaty, would become a "socialistic supergovernment." A number of senators appealed to Anglophobia and predicted that Great Britain's six votes in the league (including those of its dominions) would ensure British control of the world organization. Irreconcilables and other Republicans also took advantage of the furor aroused by the Shandong settlement. Ostensibly, they criticized Wilson for his failure to back up the Chinese delegates at the Paris Peace Conference. In reality, many of the senators focused on this issue in order to appeal to the anti-Japanese prejudice that remained virulent on the West Coast.

Lodge proved a master strategist and convinced the irreconcilables on the Senate Foreign Relations Committee to vote in favor of reservations, even though they intended to vote against the final treaty whether or not the reservations were attached. Every time the mild reservationists threatened to side with the Democrats, Lodge made conciliatory gestures toward them. He did not allow his own scorn for Italian immigrants to prevent him from catering to the Italian disaffection over Fiume, and he blatantly appealed to "America First" sentiments.

As the hearings dragged on through September, nothing went right for Woodrow Wilson. Few believed his claim not to have known about the secret treaties. William Bullitt, a disillusioned former Wilson supporter, informed the

Senate Foreign Relations Committee that Robert Lansing privately opposed the treaty. When it came time for the secretary of state to give his own testimony, he infuriated the president by his weak defense of the document. Wilson had an especially difficult time explaining Article 10. As senators pressed him to explain what responsibilities the United States assumed under this article, Wilson replied that it involved a moral rather than a legal obligation. This prompted Borah to inquire how Article 10 could be "binding" if it was not a "legal obligation." Wilson lacked an adequate reply.

The president refused to compromise and rebuffed those Democrats who urged him to accept some reservations in order to save the treaty. Arguing that he had already incorporated the critics' points in the final draft, Wilson further maintained that if the senators voted in favor of the reservations, the entire treaty would have to be renegotiated. Less and less open to criticism, the embattled president often appeared more interested in delivering soliloquies than in engaging in hard bargaining with Congress.

Wilson, buffeted by criticism from all sides, faced a desperate situation. Nine months earlier, cheering crowds had hailed him as the world's savior; now it appeared that the Senate would defeat the treaty he had done so much to fashion. Although he had never fully recovered from an illness he contracted in Paris, Wilson decided on a last-ditch effort to salvage his handiwork. He would take his case directly to the people through a speaking tour of the midwestern and western states, the very heart of antitreaty sentiment.

Traveling by train, Wilson delivered forty addresses in twenty days. The speeches reflected Wilson's mood swings. At times, the president reached his past oratorical heights and spoke of his hopes for world peace. Forced to respond to inane congressional criticism, Wilson repeatedly assured his audiences that Article 10 did not negate the right of Congress to declare war. At other times, the besieged president accused his opponents of disloyalty and engaged in hyperbole, calling the treaty "the greatest humane arrangement that has ever been adopted."

As the trip progressed, Wilson learned of Bullitt's disheartening testimony about Lansing and of the Republicans' continued insistence on attaching reservations to the treaty. Searching for scapegoats, Wilson blamed immigrants for undermining the treaty's chances in the Senate. During the war, old-stock Americans had accused recent immigrants of having dual loyalties and had spoken derisively of hyphenated Americans, and Wilson began to make use of these themes. In a St. Paul, Minnesota, speech, he declared "the most un-American thing in the world is a hyphen." In Pueblo, Colorado, he stated that "any man who carries a hyphen around with him carries a dagger that he is ready to plunge into the vitals of the republic whenever he gets a chance." Except for the Irish, immigrant groups had played only a minor role in stimulating opposition to the treaty, and the attacks indicated the president's desperation.

The trip ended abruptly in Pueblo. Ever since his Paris illness, the president had suffered migraine headaches; now they became so severe that he could not continue. His personal physician ordered Wilson to return to Washington and told the press that the president suffered from "nervous exhaustion." In early October, a severe stroke paralyzed Wilson's left side and rendered him incapacitated for the duration of his presidency.

The rest of the treaty fight proved anticlimactic. With the president confined to the White House, the Senate finally scheduled votes on the treaty for November 1919. On the first vote, a bizarre coalition of Wilson's Democratic loyalists and irreconcilables voted against the treaty with reservations. Then Republicans and irreconcilables joined to defeat the treaty without reservations. The treaty did not receive even a majority from the Senate on either vote.

Although they were shaken by the result, the treaty's supporters refused to give up. On the Republican side, Elihu Root and William Howard Taft led a new effort to arrange a compromise. On the Democratic side, prominent party leaders pleaded with Wilson to make concessions. But the principals stuck to their guns. Lodge actually strengthened what he called his "American reservations," and a sickly, feeble Wilson grew even more intransigent. Upon learning that his secretary of state had called cabinet meetings in his absence, he charged Lansing with insubordination and dismissed him. Finally, in March 1920, the treaty came up for another vote. Enough Democrats deserted Wilson that a majority of the senators voted for ratification with reservations, but the treaty still fell seven votes shy of the required two-thirds majority.

The League of Nations proved vulnerable to the same forces that would feed the Red Scare, the Ku Klux Klan's revival, and nativism. Attempting to counteract a rising tide of nationalism, defenders of internationalism appeared unpatriotic in the fervid postwar atmosphere. Ironically, the president who fell victim to these forces had set them in motion through his decision to have the United States enter the worldwide conflict. Having accurately predicted that people would lose their sense amid the passions of war, the president became engulfed in a tide of emotions that in the end obscured the reasoned arguments either in favor of or in opposition to the treaty.

For all the fury of the debate, the League of Nations would have remained ineffectual even if the United States had joined. The treaty's defeat also spelled death for the French security treaty, which never made it out of committee. The defeat jolted British and French confidence in American reliability, but the United States eventually participated in efforts to revise the Treaty of Versailles and to stabilize postwar Europe. In the meantime, the United States confronted revolutionary movements in Russia and Mexico and the rising tide of Japanese power in East Asia. These issues, which had been obscured by the heat of the treaty debate, faced policymakers in the new and highly unstable postwar world.

The End of Intervention and a New Russian Policy

When Woodrow Wilson decided to land American troops in Russia, he justified their presence on military grounds. Once the armistice had been signed, the rationale for intervention disappeared. Wilson could no longer claim the need to protect Allied military stocks from the Germans or the need to aid former Czechoslovak prisoners of war trying to reach the western front. Nevertheless, fourteen thousand American troops remained stationed in northern Russia and in Siberia two months after the surrender of Germany.

The diplomats who gathered at Versailles viewed Russia as an outlaw nation that did not deserve to be represented at the conference table. Indeed, some Allied leaders, such as Britain's Winston Churchill, expected the Bolsheviks to be overthrown and pressed Wilson to step up the American commitment of troops and matériel. Wilson despised the Soviets, but he recoiled at the thought of large-scale American involvement in the Russian civil war, and he rejected the entreaties.

Wilson also faced countervailing pressures from Congress. Despite the hysterical atmosphere engendered by the Red Scare, progressives led by Hiram Johnson, Robert La Follette, and William Borah opposed American involvement in Russia. Arguing that the presence of American soldiers on Russian soil violated Wilson's own commitment to self-determination, these senators sponsored a resolution calling for the withdrawal of all American troops from Russia. It nearly passed the Senate in February 1919.

Nineteen nineteen proved to be the critical year of the Russian civil war. A reinvigorated Red Army led by Leon Trotsky took the offensive and smashed the White Russian forces, some of which were led by former czarist officers. By the spring of 1919, all American forces had been withdrawn from the Archangel-Murmansk region, but eight thousand American troops remained to guard the Trans-Siberian Railroad and to check a much larger contingent of Japanese troops. These forces were the de facto allies of the dictatorial White Russian commander Admiral Kolchak, although Wilson's military representative, William Graves, had informed the president of atrocities and depredations committed by Kolchak's forces. The Red Army captured and executed Kolchak in early 1920 and the Americans finally withdrew in the spring of that year, although the Japanese remained in Siberia until 1922.

The intervention had turned into a fiasco, but this was not the cause of the Soviet hostility to the West. Lenin scorned the Western governments, which he contemptuously referred to as "bourgeois democracies," and Allied military intervention did not come as a shock to him. The Soviet regime in subsequent years would follow a pragmatic two-pronged policy, seeking to develop political and economic ties with Western nations and simultaneously founding and directing the Comintern, which sought to overthrow the same governments.

In the years following the Bolshevik consolidation of power, the Western governments, with the exception of the United States, granted recognition to the Soviet regime. To the president, recognition implied a grant of legitimacy that should be withheld in selected cases. In Wilson's eyes, by challenging the right to private property, by using force to take power, and by withdrawing Russia from the war, the Bolsheviks had forfeited all claims to be considered a legitimate government. By the early 1920s, liberals in the United States pressed for the opening of diplomatic relations, but the policy of nonrecognition remained in place until Franklin Roosevelt took office in 1933.

Nonrecognition did not prevent the United States from saving millions of Russians from starvation during the terrible Soviet famine between 1921 and 1923. The famine was brought on by a severe drought, devastation wrought by the civil war, and the peasants' refusal to plant crops. Conditions became so severe by July 1921 that the Russian writer Maxim Gorky issued a stirring appeal, "To All Honest People," seeking humanitarian assistance.

The United States, the only country in the world with huge stocks of surplus food, responded. Since the end of the war, the American Relief Administration, under Herbert Hoover's direction, had distributed tons of food and medicine to war-ravaged areas of Europe. In 1921, Hoover was appointed secretary of commerce in the Harding administration. Having taken on a number of domestic and foreign-policy tasks, he assumed responsibility for the new American relief effort. By providing assistance, Hoover hoped both to boost declining farm prices and to moderate or even fatally weaken the Bolshevik regime. Distrustful of liberal groups that did not share these goals, Hoover sought to ensure that all relief efforts would be handled by a quasi-governmental organization. The Soviets, desperate for assistance, willingly accepted what they called "bread intervention." After a difficult set of negotiations at Riga, Latvia, the American government won the right to distribute food on its own terms. Despite the mutual suspicions, the actual provision of relief went surprisingly well. By August 1922, the Americans were feeding more than ten million people per day, and mass inoculations and the supply of medicines helped prevent the spread of disease.

When bountiful harvests returned in 1923, the emergency program came to an end. Moving quickly to quash expectations that the goodwill engendered by the relief effort would lead to diplomatic ties, the State Department strongly iterated the nonrecognition policy. Nevertheless, a number of contacts between Russians and Americans occurred during the early 1920s. The American industrialists Armand Hammer and Julius Hammer signed their first trade agreement with Lenin in 1921. A left-leaning trade union, the Amalgamated Clothing Workers of America (ACWA), aided the modernization of the Soviet clothing industry. The Russian government granted concessions to a number of Western firms. Many of these contacts continued even after Stalin consolidated his hold on power in the late 1920s, and lines of Soviet-American communication remained outside government channels.

From the perspective of the State Department, the Bolshevik threat had receded by the early 1920s. Having failed to spark revolutionary movements in the West, the Soviets became preoccupied with consolidating their hold on power. The Comintern served as a rather ineffectual tool of Soviet foreign policy. As the domestic and foreign Red Scare faded, many American policymakers expressed greater fears about Japan, a rival capitalist industrial power, than about the Soviet Union.

The Uneasy Relationship: The United States, Japan, and China

During the late nineteenth and early twentieth centuries, the United States emerged as a Pacific power. Having acquired Hawaii, Guam, and American Samoa, United States troops fought a nasty and brutish war in the Philippines between 1899 and 1902 before completing the conquest and colonization of that island nation. A number of actions signaled the determination of policymakers to assert American influence in East Asia: American troops participated in the suppression of the Boxer Rebellion in 1900; Theodore Roosevelt sent the fleet around the world in 1907; William Howard Taft actively encouraged American corporations to invest in China; and the completion of the Panama Canal in 1914 opened up new possibilities for world trade and a truly effective two-ocean navy.

Japanese civilian and military leaders resented the expansion of American influence in East Asia. Having rapidly industrialized in the late nineteenth century, Japan (a resource-poor nation) intended to assert its power in a region it considered within its sphere of influence. In short order, Japan defeated China in a war (1894–95), scored a stunning victory over Russian forces (1904–5), completed the colonization of Korea (1910), seized Shandong (1914), and issued the Twenty-One Demands (1915), which surpassed the Europeans' imbalanced treaties in attempting to infringe on Chinese sovereignty. American diplomats began to view Japan as their chief Pacific rival, and naval leaders developed War Plan Orange in anticipation of a future conflict with Japan.

Racial tensions exacerbated Japanese-American diplomatic relations. The Japanese deeply resented efforts to limit Japanese immigration and to restrict Japanese land ownership in California. Sensitive to any suggestion of inferiority, the Japanese bristled at the notion of the Yellow Peril propagated by racist writers in Western nations. In any case, fear of rising Japanese power required those who made American foreign policy to accommodate Japan. The Root-Takahira Agreement of 1908 and the Lansing-Ishi Agreement of 1917 both sought to maintain the balance of power in East Asia.

In contrast, the Chinese government continued to be treated with contempt by the Western powers. Since 1842, European nations had burdened China with a series of unequal treaties that reduced that nation to semicolonial status. As a symbol of its inferiority, China had been forced to accept the concept of extra-territoriality, which exempted foreigners from Chinese laws. The proud inheritors of a civilization thousands of years old, the Chinese had stood by helplessly as Congress in 1882 passed the Chinese Exclusion Act (barring all Chinese immigrants except for those with specified exemptions), a measure extended in later years.

Despite the anti-Chinese immigration laws, the United States government claimed to be a friend of China. Secretary of State John Hay's Open Door Notes of 1899 and 1900 had appeared to protest the carving up of China, although they only requested that all countries be guaranteed equal access to foreign spheres of influence. Nevertheless, the Chinese looked to the United States for protection. President Wilson had withdrawn government support from a consortium he considered unfair to the Chinese, and his calls for self-determination had stirred the hopes of Chinese intellectuals. Anticipating a place at the conference table, the Chinese government had declared war on Germany and had sent more than a hundred thousand laborers to the western front. Because they had such high expectations, the Shandong settlement, known in China as "the betrayal of Versailles," came as a shock to the Chinese. On 4 May 1919, student protests exploded in Beijing's Tiananmen Square and spread to other parts of the nation, marking the emergence of the modern Chinese nationalist movement, one of the signal events of the twentieth century.

While the Chinese protested, the Japanese government acted. Well aware that the Russian civil war and the exhaustion of the European nations had created a power vacuum, the Japanese sought to expand their influence in East Asia. In an effort to gain control over eastern Siberia, the Japanese government shocked Woodrow Wilson (who had agreed to their participation in the intervention) by sending seventy thousand troops, who acted as if they intended to become a permanent occupation force. In the immediate aftermath of the war, the Japanese also occupied the Russian half of Sakhalin Island, strengthened their hold over Korea, and continued to seek a special status in China.

Between 1919 and 1921, Japanese-American tensions steadily increased. The Shandong issue figured heavily in the treaty fight, both the United States and Japan expanded their naval capabilities, and the United States government expressed its displeasure at aggressive Japanese moves. Stung especially by the furor over Shandong, the Japanese had a ready reply to what they perceived as an American double standard. What about the Monroe Doctrine, they asked. What about the American military occupations of Haiti and the Dominican Republic? What about the threats against Mexico? What about America's continued refusal to grant independence to the Philippines?

Discrimination against Japanese immigrants contributed to the deterioration of relations. Jealous of the success of Japanese-American farmers, in 1919 a coalition of California groups had formed the Japanese Exclusion League. This organization played an important role in 1920 when California voters passed an alien land law more restrictive than the original measure enacted in 1913. Fearful of further alienating the Americans, the Japanese government in 1921 agreed to new restrictions on Japanese immigration, as it had done in 1907 and 1908.

By the early 1920s, it had become routine for commentators to refer to Japan as "the Prussia of the East" and to predict that America's next war would be with Japan. Between 1920 and 1922, Lothrop Stoddard's *The Rising Tide of Color against White World-Supremacy*, Sidney Osborne's *New Japanese Peril*, and Walter Pitkin's *Must We Fight Japan?* all appeared. The authors' perspectives varied, but the provocative titles suggested the possibility of war with Japan. Similarly, Japanese military leaders anticipated that their next war would be with the United States, the only country that could conceivably block Japan's goal of becoming the dominant power in East Asia.

At this time, countervailing forces existed on both sides. Japanese civilian leaders distrusted their military counterparts and believed that a disproportionate share of tax revenues was going to the military. Likewise, Warren Harding had campaigned on a platform calling for economy in government and lower taxes. Moreover, peace sentiment had begun to make itself felt. A number of prominent Republicans and women's organizations had criticized the Wilson administration's naval buildup and had called for disarmament. Disillusioned by Versailles, many Americans had begun to question whether the United States should have entered the war. Viewing the result of the recent conflagration, they feared, as the *Nation* put it, "if another war comes, civilization perishes."

Critical of the excessive expenditure for armaments, William Borah in December 1920 introduced a resolution in the Senate calling on the United States to negotiate with Great Britain and Japan to cut back their naval forces 50 percent over the next five years. Tapping into the growing antimilitarist sentiment, the resolution captured the public imagination. The Harding administration, anxious to cut government expenditures, responded. Working closely with the British, who also faced growing pressure to reduce military spending, Secretary of State Hughes expanded on Borah's suggestion. He invited France and Italy to join the naval disarmament talks and invited all countries with a stake in the western Pacific (excluding the Soviet Union and colonial countries) to participate in conversations concerning China's status. Hughes reacted positively to the peace sentiment for practical reasons. He knew that the American public would not support the use of force to check Japanese ambitions in China, and that only a general diplomatic agreement could deter Japan. In addition, he sought to terminate the Anglo-Japanese Alliance signed in 1902, which he believed encouraged Japanese aggression in East Asia.

The ensuing Washington Conference was a major diplomatic success for the United States. When the delegates assembled in Washington in November 1921, Hughes seized the initiative with a bold proposal that the major powers freeze their naval strength at existing levels. The Japanese and the British responded positively, and the conferees signed three major agreements: (1) a Four-Power Treaty, in which the nations pledged to respect one another's insular possessions and to confer in case of an armed threat from another power, thereby negating the Anglo-Japanese Alliance; (2) a Five-Power Treaty, which maintained British and American supremacy over Japan in capital ships at a 5:5:3 ratio; and (3) a vaguely worded Nine-Power Treaty that, without making tangible changes in China's status, pledged to respect "the sovereignty, the independence, the territorial and administrative integrity of China." As part of the harmonious mood, Japan promised to withdraw its remaining troops from Siberia and to phase down its involvement in Shandong.

Despite the euphoria that surrounded the conference proceedings, the treaties did little to resolve the fundamental disagreements between the United States and Japan. In 1924, tensions once again surfaced when Congress, as part of a nativist immigration law, passed a measure that in effect barred all Japanese from immigrating to the United States. Strongly opposed by the State Department, the measure passed Congress by a wide margin even though only a tiny number of Japanese immigrants would have been allowed into the United States under existing laws. The measure produced a storm of protest in Japan. Patriotic and right-wing organizations staged demonstrations, the Tokyo press proclaimed a national day of mourning, and militarists seized the opportunity to challenge civilian leaders' belief that Japan and the United States could peacefully coexist.

Although they caused loud protests, controversies over immigration had been only an irritant in United States–Japanese relations. Japanese and American military leaders continued to plan for war against each other. In Japan, right-wing nationalists still believed that only the United States could block Japanese expansion in East Asia and, in 1923, naval planners developed a new war plan that anticipated a conflict with the United States. Likewise, American naval planners in 1924 revised War Plan Orange in expectation of a war that would be fought in Japanese home waters. A different situation prevailed in the Western Hemisphere, where the United States lacked a strong challenger to its paramount position.

Developing a New Latin American Policy

Beginning with the Spanish-American-Cuban War of 1898, the United States had sent troops to Latin America on a regular basis. American military intervention had occurred most commonly in the Caribbean, a region that United States policymakers treated as an American lake. Between 1906 and 1916, the United States had sent forces to Cuba, the Dominican Republic, and Haiti, and had established protectorates over all three nations. Military intervention had bred anti-Americanism in Latin America, and during the postwar period, the State Department sought alternative means for maintaining stability in the Caribbean.

The nations of Haiti and the Dominican Republic, which shared the island of Hispaniola, provided the first opportunity for the Americans to work out new methods of control. The United States had first sent troops to the Dominican Republic in 1916. During the American occupation, some improvements had been made in road building, education, and public health, but in 1917, a rebellion broke out in the eastern sugar-growing regions. Led by localist caudillos, the Dominican uprising gained the support of peasants dispossessed by a new land law. To suppress the rebellion, the United States established a national police force, the Guardia Nacional. When the force proved unable to defeat the guerrillas, the United States in 1919 committed more than three thousand troops to the fight. These forces removed peasants from guerrilla-controlled areas and even used aerial bombardment before finally subduing the rebels in 1922.

Opposition to American military occupation also sparked a nationalist movement based in the capital city of Santo Domingo. Disturbed by the rising level of protests, the military authorities in the spring of 1920 enforced a strict censorship decree and arrested prominent Dominican intellectuals. In response, even the archbishop of Santo Domingo joined in denouncing the suppression of civil liberties and the brutalities committed by American troops. Outraged by the Wilson administration's failure to support self-determination when it threatened American interests, the middle-class Dominican nationalists in December 1920 rejected a phased withdrawal plan developed by the State Department.

During the 1920 campaign, Warren Harding criticized Wilson's frequent resort to force in the Caribbean, and Dominican nationalists had high hopes when the new president took office in March 1921. Expectations also ran high because the United States Senate had formed a special committee to investigate conditions in the Dominican Republic and Haiti. But the Senate report was a whitewash, and the Dominicans eventually had to accept a phased withdrawal plan developed by State Department advisor Sumner Welles that led to the removal of all troops by 1924. Whatever the peaceful claims of the Republican administrations, the occupation had long-lasting negative effects for Dominicans. Liberalized land laws forced peasants to become cane cutters on huge sugar plantations, the Guardia Nacional trained the future dictator Rafael Trujillo, who joined the guard in 1919, and the Dominican Republic essentially remained a protectorate of the United States.

The United States also had to step up its military involvement in Haiti before new means of control could be implemented. The American government had first sent troops to that nation in 1915 on the pretext that Haiti had failed to fulfill its financial obligations. As in the case of the Dominican Republic, the desire to block a possible German base heavily influenced the decision. The occupying troops had forced the client government to accept a treaty that reduced Haiti to a protectorate and had insisted on the adoption of a constitution that permitted foreigners to own land.

As part of a road-building program, the marines had resurrected the policy of the corvée, which required Haitian men to labor outside their home districts. Nationalist protests led to the discontinuance of the corvée in 1918. By then, however, a full-scale revolt, led by Charlemagne Peralte, had broken out in Haiti's mountainous northern region. The American-trained Gendarmerie d'Haiti tried to put down the insurrection, but in March 1919, the marines took charge of the fight. From their perspective, American forces enjoyed a splendid success in suppressing the rebellion. Marines captured and killed Peralte (a widely circulated photo showed his body tied to a flagpole) and by the end of 1919, the American military claimed to have killed 3,250 Haitians and to have suffered only 13 casualties.

Haiti had been a point of pride to African Americans ever since it won its independence in 1804, and the marines' boasts of their kill rate led black leaders to suspect that American forces had engaged in the indiscriminate murder of Haitians. News of the marine actions came soon after the bloody Chicago race riots of 1919 and fed the growing disillusionment of black intellectuals. Throughout 1919 and 1920, the *Crisis*, the journal of the NAACP, gave extensive coverage to the Haitian events. Further aroused by reports that southern white officers had brought Mississippi-style "justice" to the island, the NAACP dispatched its field secretary, James Weldon Johnson, and its publicity agent, Herbert Seligmann, to Haiti to conduct an investigation. Upon their return, the *Nation* published a series of articles by Johnson and Seligmann accusing occupation authorities of indiscriminately slaughtering Haitians, of suppressing news about the atrocities, and of opening Haiti up for a takeover by the National City Bank of New York.

Republicans, anxious to expose the hypocrisy of Wilson's claim to support the rights of small nations, responded sympathetically to the protests. During the campaign, Harding seized on the claim of Democratic vice presidential nominee Franklin Roosevelt to have written Haiti's 1918 constitution and pledged that he would be far more restrained in his use of military force in the Caribbean. Following the election, a delegation of Haitians traveled to the United States to protest the occupation, and a group of prominent American lawyers issued a highly critical report entitled "The Seizure of Haiti by the United States." Facing additional pressure from a bloc of progressive Republicans, the

United States Senate formed the Special Select Committee on Haiti and Santo Domingo. The senators who traveled to Haiti heard extensive testimony, but, much to the dismay of the critics, the final report called for an administrative reorganization rather than withdrawal from Haiti.

The Senate report set the tone for the new Republican policy. Unlike in the Dominican Republic, the troops remained in Haiti, and a military officer, Colonel John Russell, assumed the post of high commissioner. A Georgian and a supporter of segregation, Russell worked closely with the dictator Louis Bruno. Despite the expectations of investors, little economic development occurred, and thousands of impoverished Haitian peasants migrated to Cuba to work for a pittance on American-owned sugar plantations.

Cuba provided another opportunity for the United States to implement alternatives to the constant use of force. Following an occupation between 1898 and 1902, Cuba had become an American protectorate. The United States had sent troops there in 1906, 1912, and 1917. When sugar prices collapsed during the postwar depression, the Wilson administration in 1920 assigned General Enoch Crowder to straighten out Cuba's finances. Crowder essentially took over the Cuban government and initiated reforms that furthered the American domination of the Cuban economy. Thus, the United States appeared to have found a way to maintain its control without sending troops. The change, though, did not appease opponents of American influence. Beneath the surface, Cuban and other Caribbean nationalists continued to resent their treatment as "banana republics."

The case of Mexico demonstrated that diplomacy and American financial power could be used more effectively than force to protect American economic interests. Mexico had been in the throes of economic, social, and revolutionary turmoil ever since the overthrow of the dictator Porfirio Díaz in 1910. Radical leaders threatened to expropriate American property, and Wilson had twice sent troops to Mexico, first in 1914 to aid the constitutionalist forces of Venustiano Carranza, and again in 1916 to pursue the peasant leader Pancho Villa. Unlike in the Caribbean, the United States faced a potentially strong foe in Mexico, and both interventions had been limited.

During the war, the Wilson administration had wanted to avoid antagonizing the Mexican government, but once the armistice had been signed, relations between Mexico and the United States soured. The flash point this time was Article 27 of the 1917 Mexican constitution, which reserved the ownership of all subsoil natural resources to the Mexican government. Advocated by nationalists, who used the slogan "Mexico for Mexicans," the provision threatened the property of the American oil companies, which had been welcomed with open arms by the Díaz regime and whose investments had made Mexico second only to the United States in oil production.

Oil's importance increased in the postwar period. Spurred by the growing use of the internal combustion engine, oil had replaced coal as the world's most important fuel source. Getting a jump in the race for petroleum, the British had gained extremely favorable concessions in the Middle East. Oil firms and other companies with investments in Mexico, knowing that the United States government feared being shut out in the race for petroleum, had formed the National Association for the Protection of American Rights in Mexico, which lobbied for a tough American stand against any implementation of Article 27. Coupling Mexico with Russia (an association often made at the time) and appealing to Catholics unhappy with Mexico's anticlerical legislation, this organization received a sympathetic hearing from Albert Fall's Senate subcommittee on Mexico. Fall, a conservative Republican from New Mexico, was a close associate of Edward Doheny, whose Pan American Petroleum Company pioneered Mexican exploration. Witnesses before his committee called for military intervention to prevent Mexico from enforcing its constitution.

During the autumn of 1919, the Wilson administration faced intense pressure to take action against Mexico, but the president, who understood the pitfalls of military intervention, firmly opposed sending troops. Instead, Wilson insisted that Mexico sign a treaty guaranteeing that Article 27 would not be applied to property acquired before 1917. Fortuitously, the overthrow of Carranza by the military commander Alvaro Obregon Salido gave Wilson a familiar tool to enforce this demand, and he refused to recognize the new government unless it adhered to American terms.

Wilson passed the recognition issue to the incoming Harding administration, and Secretary of State Charles Evans Hughes continued to insist that Mexico sign a treaty guaranteeing American property rights. Obregon, anxious to dampen revolutionary ferment, desired improved relations with the United States but resented the bullying tactics that humiliated his country. Mexico's financial distress finally provided a solution to the crisis. In 1922, the House of Morgan banker Thomas Lamont arranged for Mexico to reorganize its external debt and to receive badly needed loans. This paved the way for the Bucarelli Accords of 1923, by which Mexico pledged to respect subsoil resources purchased before 1917. In turn, the United States recognized the Mexican government and shipped arms to Obregon to aid the suppression of a revolt of nationalists who were unhappy with the "sellout" to the Americans.

The postwar race for oil also affected United States relations with other Latin American nations. In 1921, the Senate ratified a treaty that apologized for American intervention in the 1902 Panamanian revolt and appropriated a twenty-five-million-dollar indemnity to make amends. The Senate's action paved the way for United States oil companies to exploit Colombia's rich petroleum reserves. In Venezuela, the State Department encouraged an aggressive petroleum policy that helped win American firms rich concessions.

In general, the war enhanced American economic and political influence in Latin America. Believing the time had come for the United States to rehabilitate its reputation, Charles Evans Hughes used the hundredth anniversary of the Monroe Doctrine to reassure Latin American nations that the United States intended to be a good neighbor. Despite the peaceful claims, however, the United States government remained ready to use the big stick. The Coolidge administration sent troops to Honduras in 1924, and the United States kept troops in Nicaragua for much of the decade. With no strong power to oppose it, the United States was free to set its own course in the Western Hemisphere.

The United States and Postwar Europe

Following the defeat of the Treaty of Versailles, many Americans began to question the desirability of continued involvement in Europe. Stung by the reluctance of the English and the French to pay their debts, Americans viewed their former allies as ingrates who should be left to fend for themselves. Warren Harding captured the prevailing mood when, in a May 1920 address delivered in Boston, he called for "not submergence in internationality but sustainment in triumphant nationality."

Upon taking office, the Harding administration followed an autarkical policy that appeared almost deliberately designed to block European recovery. In 1922, the Republican Congress raised tariff rates, making it difficult for other industrialized countries to sell their goods in the United States. At the same time, the United States flooded the world with its exports and insisted that England and France pay their debts, which, including interest, totaled more than twenty billion dollars. Determined that the United States solidify its position as the world's leading creditor, both Treasury and Commerce Department officials scoffed at any notion of debt forgiveness, leading Europeans to chastise "Uncle Shylock" for attempting to keep them subservient.

By any assessment, Europe remained in desperate straits more than two years after the conclusion of the war. In Germany, misery and a sense of desperation characterized much of the population. In Britain, the working class suffered hard times, and unemployment rose to more than two million by the early 1920s. In France, the population appeared so demoralized that one would have thought they had lost the war. Throughout Europe, a bitter and hateful mood prevailed, and conditions seemed to confirm the writer Norman Angell's 1910 prediction that there could be no victors in a modern war.

Germany's need to pay reparations limited the possibility of a European recovery. After a great deal of haggling, England and France had finally presented the Germans in May 1921 with a bill for 132 billion gold marks. Despite the size of the sum, a strong German government might have been able to raise sufficient taxes to pay the amount. But the weak Weimar regime, beset by rightist and nationalist opponents, could not pay up and survive. A general cancellation of debts continued to afford the only way out. In the Balfour Note of 1922, the British suggested they would forgo sums owed them if the United States would do likewise. The Harding administration, though, insisted that repudiation would wreck the international credit structure.

In 1923, the French occupation of the Ruhr, Germany's chief iron and steel region, provoked a crisis that led to a restructuring of the brittle Versailles settlement. Resentful of both the British and the Americans for failing to understand France's security needs, the French sent their forces across the border when the Germans failed to meet their reparations obligations. In response, the German government financed a campaign of passive resistance and discovered an easy way to pay off its debts: it deliberately sponsored a program of hyperinflation. Although the strategy caused extreme hardship for German citizens, by the end of 1923 the lack of support from its erstwhile allies led France to back off from its hard-line policy.

Rattled by the breakdown of the Versailles settlement, Washington reconsidered whether it could afford to remain aloof from the European difficulties. In 1924, Herbert Hoover helped establish a commission, headed by the Chicago banker Charles G. Dawes, that arranged for a scaling-down of Germany's yearly reparations payments, although the total sum remained the same. To finance the obligations, American bankers agreed to extend the Germans significant loans. Thus the United States became a principal guarantor of stability on the European continent, and after 1924, American capital financed German reparations payments that in turn allowed the French and British to pay off some of their debts to Americans. But the United States still refused to consider debt relief or lower tariffs, even though the United States enjoyed unbounded prosperity compared to any other country in the world. Totally dependent on the export of American capital, the entire structure collapsed in the months following the stock market crash of 1929.

Even before the onset of the Great Depression, it became apparent that the old European order had been destroyed forever. Benito Mussolini and his followers seized power in Italy in 1922. Exalting violence and calling for "Respect for Italy," the Fascisti fed upon dissatisfaction with the new world order created at Versailles. In their appeal to national myths, the Blackshirts previewed a romantic nationalism that would reach its apogee in Adolf Hitler's National Socialist movement. Many Americans who were taken by Mussolini's anti-Communism praised his regime for bringing law and order to Italy. Others understood that in its appeal to the irrational, the growth of the Fascist movement indicated that the prewar faith in democracy, inevitable progress, and rationality had not survived the four years of bloodletting.

3

ANYTHING BUT "NORMAL"

POSTWAR AMERICAN POLITICS AND THE DEMISE OF PROGRESSIVISM

THE POSTWAR YEARS presented an unusual political context. Caught off guard by the sudden end of the war, the Wilson administration in 1919 confronted unprecedented labor unrest and the Red Scare, which it had helped stimulate. Constitutional amendments providing for women's suffrage and Prohibition further upset the balance of American politics. Despite regaining the presidency in 1920, the Republican Party faced a resurgence of progressivism stimulated by the 1920–22 depression. Meanwhile, the Democratic Party became so torn by disputes that its 1924 convention turned into a prolonged donnybrook between factions supporting William Gibbs McAdoo and Al Smith. Only with the return of prosperity and the election of Calvin Coolidge did American politics appear to regain the "normalcy" promised by Warren Harding in 1920.

The Wilson Administration and Postwar Reconstruction

In giving their support to the war, many progressives had hoped that the overseas conflict would lead to constructive changes at home as well as abroad. The wartime repression of dissidents had caused them to bite their tongues, but progressives had been greatly encouraged by the Wilson administration's embrace of wartime collectivism. Having established new federal agencies such as the Food Administration, the Fuel Administration, the War Industries Board, and the National War Labor Board, Wilson appeared to have abandoned the backward-looking features of the New Freedom and to have embraced many of the more forward-looking aspects of Theodore Roosevelt's New Nationalism.

Liberals and progressives held numerous conferences in the months following the armistice, and a journal entitled *Reconstruction* publicized many of the most advanced proposals. The *New Republic* and the *Survey* published the British Labour Party's manifesto "Labour and the New Social Order," and liberal publications gave great publicity to the National Catholic War Council's "Bishop's

Program of Social Reconstruction." Whether emanating from Catholic bishops or progressive intellectuals, the proposals shared a belief in the need for the continuation of high taxes on the wealthy, government controls over the economy, and guarantees of labor's right to organize.

Wilson greatly disappointed his progressive followers. His December 1918 State of the Union message barely mentioned domestic affairs, and the president moved quickly to dismantle the various wartime agencies, including the National War Labor Board, which had made rulings favorable to labor. Wilson followed this course for a number of reasons. He had become preoccupied with peacemaking, he had no intention of using the wartime mobilization as a basis for domestic reform, and he faced pressures for cuts in spending from the postwar Congress. An economic spurt in 1919, stimulated by easy credit, continued overseas demand for American goods, and pent-up consumer demand further eased pressures on the president to continue government controls over the economy. Token efforts to alleviate the rapid rise in the cost of living and to move against profiteers did little to dampen the impression that the president had lost all interest in domestic reform.

The return of the railroads to private ownership signaled the progressive retreat. During the war, the railroads had been taken over by the federal government, which brought order and efficiency to what had been a chaotic industry. Faced with postwar business pressures to return the railroads to private ownership, labor unions and many intellectuals had rallied behind the Plumb Plan (named for the railroad union's general counsel, Glenn Plumb), which called for shared ownership by the public, the railroad corporations, and the unions. Critics labeled the Plumb Plan "naked socialism," and not even Senator La Follette's moderate proposal that the railroads remain under temporary government control had any chance of passage. Labor threatened to elect a "Plumb Plan Congress" in 1920, but the Esch-Cummins Transportation Act, enacted that year, returned the railroads to their former owners, though it did create the Railway Labor Board to protect labor's collective bargaining rights.

The Red Scare

Any hope that reform efforts might be carried into the postwar period also fell victim to the 1919 Red Scare, which saw a continuation of the wartime violations of civil liberties. Communists attacked what many Americans held sacred—religion, private property, and democracy. Some radicals hoped that the Russian events could be emulated, but a Bolshevik-style revolution could not have occurred in the United States. Nevertheless, a number of events in 1918 and 1919 stoked the hysteria. Russia's withdrawal from the war damaged the Allied war effort; the Bolshevik revolution inspired short-lived revolutions in Hungary and the German state of Bavaria; a strike wave affected much of American industry; bombs had been sent through the mails to a number of public figures.

Relishing the opportunity to smear labor with a red brush, business interests sponsored a nationwide ad campaign warning about "the Grasping Hand of the Bolshevik." Quasi-governmental groups such as the National Security League and the American Protective League, which raided homes and meetings of alleged German sympathizers during the war, now turned their attention to "Reds." Small-time opportunists also sensed their chance. Ole Hanson, mayor of Seattle during that city's February 1919 general strike, provides a good example. Once the labor rebellion had been broken, Hanson resigned his position and toured the country warning about the Red Peril. Hanson even developed presidential ambitions and wrote a book, *Americanism versus Bolshevism*, but by 1920 he had returned to his accustomed obscurity.

"One hundred percent Americanism," a term coined in 1915 by Theodore Roosevelt, became the rallying cry of the anti-Red crusaders. The American Legion made good use of the slogan. Founded in March 1919 by army officers stationed in Paris, the legion tolerated and often encouraged its members to raid socialist meetings, attack radical gatherings, and brutalize members of the Industrial Workers of the World (IWW). State governments joined vigilantes in attacking those accused of supporting communism. In New York, a special legislative committee known as the Lusk committee, armed with search warrants, seized the records and correspondence of numerous left-leaning unions and organizations. In January 1920, the New York State Assembly even expelled five Socialist Party members elected from New York City districts. (They were later reelected.) Numerous states passed criminal syndicalism laws banning advocacy of "subversive" doctrines. In a nation uneasy with its ethnically heterogeneous population, any hint of the desecration of the flag could bring instant punishment. Even those who claimed to support free speech appeared to have lost sight of its meaning. In December 1919, the governor of Missouri, Frederick D. Gardner, wrote labor lawyer Frank Walsh, "While we are intensely loyal out here and will not sanction anything that smacks of disloyalty to our government, yet there must be no effort on the part of any one to prevent free speech. Free speech, of course, means loyalty to the country."

In a nation still affected by the war-induced hysteria, those who protested the delirium had difficulty being heard. The most notable defender of civil liberties was the American Civil Liberties Union (ACLU), which assumed that name in

1920. Founded in 1917 as the National Civil Liberties Bureau, the organization had initially devoted itself to defending conscientious objectors and other critics of the war. In the postwar period, the ACLU attempted to monitor the countless violations of First Amendment rights, although its protests had little impact.

Progressives disheartened by the chain of events looked to the White House. Surely Woodrow Wilson, a believer in the rule of law who had tolerated abuses during the war, would finally speak out. But having spent the first part of 1919 in Paris, the president made no effort upon his return to protest the tawdry spectacle of hundred-percenters trampling the Bill of Rights underfoot.

Once Wilson suffered his stroke, the administration fell into total disarray. Wilson's personal physician did not inform the country of the seriousness of the president's condition. Totally disabled during the autumn of 1919, Wilson did not even resume cabinet meetings until the spring of 1920. He was paralyzed on the left side, and never again delivered a full-fledged speech. In effect, the country did not have a functioning president for the last year and a half of Wilson's term.

Even before Wilson's illness, the president had given cabinet members a free hand in shaping domestic policy. A. Mitchell Palmer, who had been appointed attorney general in early 1919, welcomed the unusual degree of latitude. Before the war, Palmer had been one of Wilson's most loyal supporters in the House of Representatives. A Quaker, Palmer had undergone, according to historian Stanley Coben, "a startling metamorphosis" during the war when the "former pacifist became one of the most aggressive belligerents." Appointed to serve as alien property custodian, he had been charged with seizing and administering property owned by German nationals. Nevertheless, upon Palmer's assumption of the attorney general's post, liberal publications such as the *New Republic* applauded the selection.

Progressives soon had reason to despair. Whether because his home had been the target of bombs or because he harbored presidential ambitions, Palmer joined the anti-Red crusade with extraordinary zeal. Acting on his own, he established a special Radical Division within the attorney general's office; it was renamed the General Intelligence Division in 1920. Palmer appointed the twenty-four-year-old J. Edgar Hoover to head this bureau, and Hoover promptly began sedulously to amass files on suspected radicals, a project he pursued for the next fifty years.

Palmer and Hoover primarily targeted immigrants. Under a special 1903 law, aliens (immigrants who had not yet become citizens) could be deported after administrative hearings rather than jury trials. During February 1919, thirty-six Wobblies (members of the IWW) were taken to Ellis Island, and in November

1919, the Justice Department raided the offices of the Union of Russian Workers and deported 249 suspected radicals, including the anarchists Emma Goldman and Alexander Berkman. The press applauded the deportations on the so-called Soviet Ark, which encouraged Palmer to continue his feverish antiradical campaign.

The climax came on 2 and 3 January 1920, when the Justice Department, with the aid of local police and deputized citizens, staged simultaneous raids on homes, clubrooms, and meeting places in more than thirty cities, rounding up more than three thousand suspected radicals. Ukrainians, Jews, Lithuanians, Russians, and Poles—those most suspected of supporting Bolshevism—constituted the vast majority of those taken into custody. Coordinated raids of this sort had been conducted during the war against the IWW and alleged slackers. The distinguishing feature of the Palmer Raids, as they came to be known, was the widespread use of informers who had infiltrated various groups and called many of the meetings that had been broken up.

Protests, especially by the courageous assistant secretary of labor, Louis Post, limited the number of deportations. Most of the detainees were released following days or weeks of harrowing confinement. Palmer, however, persisted in defending his actions. In a February 1920 article that appeared in the *Forum*, he warned that "alien filth" and "alien criminals" advocating "unclean doctrines" needed to be swept out of the nation. By scapegoating immigrants, Palmer illuminated the distance many Americans had traveled from the heady, buoyant New Freedom days of 1912 to the sour, fearful, and far more pessimistic mood of the Red Scare.

By the spring of 1920, the extreme fear of Bolshevism had begun to fade. Palmer appeared ridiculous when his prediction that a communist uprising would occur in May 1920 proved false. Labor unrest lessened and right-wing forces in Europe were more powerful than those on the left. Even a terrible Wall Street bombing in September 1920 that took more than thirty lives evoked surprisingly little response. But the fears lingered. Accusations of advocating communism continued to be used against liberals and progressives, despite their own battles with the American Communist Party.

The 1920 Presidential Election

Shut out of the White House for eight years, the Republican Party entered the 1920 election year confident of victory. Skyrocketing inflation had led to consumer protests over the high cost of living. President Wilson had played into the hands of Old Guard Republicans by focusing attention on the treaty rather than on domestic issues, over which Republicans remained divided. Believing that the League of Nations retained popular support, Wilson, in a January 1920 letter sent to Democratic Party leaders, had called for the election to be "a great and solemn referendum on the Treaty." Republicans salivated in anticipation of an election in which they would campaign against "Mr. Wilson's League," as they liked to refer to it.

A number of candidates sought the Republican presidential nomination. General Leonard Wood appealed mainly to eastern conservatives, and Illinois Governor Frank Lowden won the support of many midwestern moderates. Senator Hiram Johnson of California carried the progressives' hopes. Known before the war as an antimonopoly crusader, Johnson proved a poor standard-bearer for the progressive cause. Preoccupied by his opposition to the Treaty of Versailles and by his hatred of Japanese immigrants, Johnson campaigned for his version of "pure Americanism," which meant staying out of the league and restricting immigration.

When the Republicans gathered in Chicago, none of the leading contenders could gather sufficient support to gain the nomination. On the tenth ballot, the convention chose Senator Warren Harding of Ohio. Harding had been mentioned as a possible candidate but had not been given much of a chance. To party regulars, though, he appeared to be an ideal choice. A small-town newspaper editor, he had rarely taken a strong stand on any issue. Handsome and convivial, Harding was most comfortable bantering with the "boys" during late-night poker games. To much of the American public, which was tired of Wilson's crusades, Harding offered a welcome change. In his oft-quoted Boston address he called for "not heroism but healing, not nostrums but normalcy, not surgery, but serenity, not the dramatic but the dispassionate, not experiment but equipoise, not submergence in internationality but sustainment in triumphant nationality."

For vice president, party bosses had planned to nominate Irvine L. Lenroot, a moderately progressive senator from Wisconsin. But an unanticipated rebellion from the floor led to the nomination of Governor Calvin Coolidge of Massachusetts. Coolidge had been a relative unknown until the Boston Police Strike of 1919, when he gained great national publicity for having warned the president of the American Federation of Labor (AFL), Samuel Gompers: "There is no right to strike against the public safety by anybody, any time, anywhere!" Coolidge exaggerated his own role in crushing the walkout, but he became a symbol of tough resistance to labor. If Harding appealed to the middle classes' desire for a "return to normalcy," Coolidge appealed to their fear of unions, and the two made a formidable team.

Meeting in San Francisco, the Democrats knew they had little chance of holding on to the presidency. Wilson, ill and forlorn, had not resumed holding cabinet meetings until April 1920. Those close to him knew the president could not possibly run for a third term, but uncertainty about the seriousness of Wilson's condition had prevented candidates from entering the race.

By June, William Gibbs McAdoo, A. Mitchell Palmer, and James Cox had emerged as the leading contenders for the Democratic Party nomination. McAdoo, a former secretary of the treasury, possessed considerable strengths. Hailing from Tennessee, he was guaranteed southern support and had become popular with labor when he served as director-general of the Railroad Administration during the war. But McAdoo, who was married to Wilson's daughter, had proven a hesitant candidate, and his support of Prohibition had alienated urban political bosses. Palmer's star had faded as fears of revolution receded and evidence of corruption in the alien property custodian's office became public. This left Cox, a three-term governor of Ohio, who received the nomination on the forty-fourth ballot. Bland and colorless, Cox had earned a reputation as a progressive but he had never been ardent in support of any cause. Big-city Democrats liked him because he had been a critic of Prohibition. Cox was a resident of the Buckeye state and a newspaper editor; his background resembled Harding's background. Hoping to add some dash and energy to the ticket, the Democrats nominated the young, ambitious assistant secretary of the navy, Franklin Delano Roosevelt, for vice president.

Any Democrat nominated in 1920 had to run in Wilson's shadow. Cox had not voiced a strong opinion on the league, and some commentators interpreted his nomination as a slap in the face to Wilson. But shortly after the convention, Cox visited Wilson in the White House. To the delight of Republicans—who planned to emphasize Americanism in the campaign—the Democratic candidate fully endorsed the Treaty of Versailles.

Much of the American public, absorbed in Babe Ruth's assault on the major league home run record, responded to the nominations of Harding and Cox with yawns. Those on the political left reacted with disgust. Disappointed and disillusioned by Wilson's compromises at Versailles, by the Russian intervention, by the dismantling of wartime agencies, and by the assault on labor and civil liberties, committed progressives began to talk in earnest about the need for a third political party.

By 1919, two separate movements to form such a party had begun. One, inspired by the spectacular rise of the British Labour Party, focused on workers. Advocating a broad program calling for social reconstruction and "democratic control of industry," these third-party advocates believed that the time had arrived for labor to develop its own political vehicle. The other movement emanated from disenchanted progressives and intellectuals who called themselves the Committee of Forty-Eight (standing for the forty-eight states). They framed a program calling for public ownership of the railroads and other natural monopolies, restoration of civil liberties, and guarantees of collective bargaining for labor. Many third-party supporters believed that the nascent labor party and the Committee of Forty-Eight should join, uniting "hand and brain." Such a party could also count on the support of farmers, who, in states such as North Dakota and Minnesota, had backed a radical organization known as the Non-Partisan League.

Disaster struck when the disparate third-party forces met in Chicago in July 1920 to discuss the possibility of fusion. Despite the groups' agreement on many issues, disputes broke out over the extent to which the proposed new party should favor the nationalization of industry. As often occurred on the left, bickering, name-calling, and endless debate over fine points replaced reasoned discourse. Observing the shenanigans, Senator Robert La Follette, the presidential choice of most of the delegates, made it clear he would not accept a nomination. Once some of the members of the Committee of Forty-Eight bolted the floor, the newly formed Farmer-Labor Party nominated the totally obscure Parley Parker Christensen of Utah for president. To the surprise of no one, the party proved not to be a factor in what many on the left termed a "sham" election because it ignored vital issues. The left had blown a major opportunity, but third-party advocates did not give up; they pressed forward, hoping for a different result in 1924.

Republican hopes soared as the campaign commenced. Not only did Cox have to wear the Wilsonian mantle but the postwar economic boom had come to an abrupt halt during the summer of 1920. Caused in part by the Federal Reserve Board's deflationary policy, the economic plunge led to mounting factory layoffs and plummeting agricultural prices, which were sure to work to the Democrats' disadvantage.

Under the direction of Will Hays, the shrewd Republican national chairman, the Republican Party mounted an election drive modeled on William McKinley's 1896 campaign. Harding, who might have embarrassed himself on the stump, remained home in Marion, Ohio. Republicans, their campaign coffers full, hammered away at the league and at foreign influences. Striking a nationalistic chord, the Republican campaign appealed to America First and anti-European sentiments stimulated by the battle over the League of Nations. For example, an advertisement placed by the Republican National Committee in the news weekly *Literary Digest* said Harding and Coolidge "stand for these things":

> Absolute control of the United States by the United States. No foreign dictation. No foreign control expressed or implied . . .
>
> Americans can govern their country without Europe's assistance . . .
> On the Fourth of July, in future as in the past, one flag will be seen—
> One is enough.
>
> This country will remain American. Its next President will remain in our own country. American public affairs will be discussed by American public servants in the City of Washington, not in some foreign capital.

Such chauvinistic language did not allow for the "solemn referendum" that Wilson desired. Edging away from labor and from domestic reform, Cox, who became an avid campaigner, tried to present a reasoned defense of American participation in the League of Nations. But the Democrats also tolerated the circulation of rumors that Harding had Negro blood. To veterans of the 1912 and 1916 campaigns, the desultory battle between the two Ohio newspaper editors— described by Walter Lippmann in the *New Republic* as "provincial, ignorant politicians"—provided a depressing spectacle.

Harding's call for a "return to normalcy" captured many Americans' disillusionment. On election day, the Republican ticket won an impressive 60 percent of the popular vote. Republicans also gained control of both the House and the Senate by wide margins. Only 49 percent of eligible voters had bothered to cast ballots, a reflection of voter apathy and Irish disaffection with the Democrats because of the treaty's terms. To some observers the election was the death knell of progressivism, but this prediction turned out to be premature as the recession in the fall of 1920 turned into a depression.

The election did prove to be a last hurrah of sorts for the American Socialist Party. In the immediate prewar period, the Socialists had elected a couple of members of Congress and a number of mayors in medium-sized cities. Optimistic members even believed that the party could emerge as a significant political force. America's entry into the war destroyed these hopes. Meeting in emergency session in St. Louis in April 1917, the American Socialists vowed to oppose a conflict they considered imperialistic. In turn, Socialist Party members, along with members of the IWW, had been singled out for harsh repression by the Wilson administration.

Eugene V. Debs was the best known and most admired American Socialist. Hailing from Terre Haute, Indiana, he began his career as a craft unionist and Democratic representative in the Indiana state legislature. In 1894, as head of the American Railroad Union, he called on railroad employees to walk out in sympathy with striking Pullman workers. Debs was imprisoned for having violated a federal court injunction, and shortly thereafter became a socialist. Beloved by many workers, who did not necessarily share his socialist beliefs, he had traveled the country in support of labor causes.

Debs agreed with his party's antiwar position and spoke out on myriad occasions in opposition to the overseas conflict. Indicted for a speech he delivered in Canton, Ohio, he was sentenced to ten years in prison for violation of the Sedition Act. He appealed the sentence, and did not begin serving his term until March 1919, five months after the conclusion of the war. Friends and supporters pleaded for clemency but A. Mitchell Palmer considered him a dangerous radical. A bitter and vindictive Woodrow Wilson concurred, and after a short stay in a jail in Moundsville, West Virginia, Debs was transferred to the imposing Atlanta fortress.

Despite having run a campaign confined to press releases, Debs, who wore the Atlanta federal penitentiary number 9563, polled almost one million votes in 1920. But prowar Socialists had already abandoned the cause, and many of those who applauded the Bolshevik revolution had joined the Communists. An admirer of Tom Paine and Wendell Phillips, Debs, who was pardoned by Harding in 1921, could never fully embrace a movement inspired by Marx and Lenin. Ironically, Debs and Wilson became political enemies, but they had shared the optimism of the prewar days and appeared out of step in a postwar world of Bolsheviks, Babbitts, and businessmen.

The Harding Administration

As Harding prepared to take the oath of office, the *Nation* claimed that this was "the most material, the most sightless Administration ever to begin its rule in America." Some of Harding's cabinet choices confirmed the *Nation*'s observation. For attorney general, Harding tapped his longtime mentor and crony Harry Daugherty, a man totally unprepared for such an office. Harding selected

Albert Fall, a confidant of oil investors, for secretary of the interior. Harding did choose some men of ability (no women were selected) for other cabinet posts. Henry C. Wallace, well regarded by farmers, became secretary of agriculture, and the multimillionaire industrialist and banker Andrew Mellon, a favorite of businessmen, became secretary of the treasury. For secretary of state, Harding chose Charles Evans Hughes, and for secretary of commerce, Harding turned to Herbert Hoover, a choice widely applauded by progressives.

Harding had called for "triumphant nationality," and the new administration moved quickly to enact an America First program. During the campaign, Harding had straddled the issue of the League of Nations. Once in office, he made it clear that the United States would not join a "super government." In response to growing anti-immigrant sentiment, the Republican Congress in 1921 enacted the Emergency Immigration Act, which established the principle of quotas. According to the law's provisions, the United States would accept a maximum of 3 percent of any European country's nationals residing in the United States in 1910. Similarly, the Emergency Tariff Act of 1921, the protectionist Fordney McCumber Tarriff Act of 1922, and the refusal to grant debt relief reflected the prevailing nationalistic, anti-European sentiment.

Progressives still exercised some muscle in Congress. Mellon did not succeed in repealing all of the wartime taxes, nor did he gain the drastic cut in the top bracket of the income tax that he desired. Likewise, Henry Ford encountered unexpected resistance when he attempted to purchase a government-owned dam and nitrate plant at Muscle Shoals, Alabama. Progressives still carried some weight because no one was yet talking about the Roaring Twenties during Harding's first two years in the White House. Instead, public attention focused on the severe postwar depression, which deepened throughout 1921 and only lessened somewhat in 1922. The economic downturn, a delayed reaction to the end of the war, led to angry marches by the unemployed in Great Britain and unrest in much of Europe. In the United States, the economic crisis represented the most severe depression since the 1890s and led to demands for government action.

To address the mounting unemployment problem, Harding turned to Herbert Hoover. Still basking in his wartime popularity, Hoover had entered the cabinet on the condition that he be given a major voice in a number of areas, including foreign trade, agriculture, and labor. A highly successful engineer, Hoover had harshly criticized industry for its waste and inefficiency. He was a firm believer in private enterprise, and he hoped the federal government could cajole business into being more responsible.

Faced with a rising unemployment rate in the autumn of 1921, Hoover convinced Harding to convene a conference on unemployment. Harding delivered the opening address, in which he warned that he "would have little enthusiasm for any proposed relief which seeks either palliation or tonic from the public treasury," but Hoover dominated the proceedings. The final report requested business to stabilize employment and local governments to carry out public works, but it did not recommend any significant expansion of the federal government's role.

Hoover addressed the problem of unemployment by using nontraditional methods to arrive at solutions that did not threaten the status quo. Changes resulting from constitutional amendments providing for Prohibition and women's suffrage could not be so easily managed. By bringing new issues to the forefront of American politics, the Eighteenth and Nineteenth Amendments further threatened Harding's quest for "normalcy."

The Impact of Women's Suffrage

The fight for women's suffrage formally began when the historic women's rights convention held in Seneca Falls, New York, in 1848 included it as one of its demands. Throughout the nineteenth century, the struggle for women's suffrage rested primarily on the natural-rights philosophy, which emphasized that women should have the same political and legal rights as men. Disappointed in 1869 when Congress failed to include women in the terms of the Fifteenth Amendment (intended to guarantee suffrage to African-American men), the early suffragists participated in an often lonely campaign to win the ballot.

Beginning in the late nineteenth century, new arguments began to be heard in support of the cause. Accepting the notion that women belonged in the home, some advocates believed that women were more moral than men and would vote to protect the home against evils such as the saloon and prostitution. Many of those active in the progressive movement maintained that, if given the right to vote, women would be more likely than men to favor reforms such as a ban on child labor. Some of the advocates of women's suffrage even queried: How can the country deny suffrage to women when it has granted it to such "inferior" types as recent immigrants from southern and eastern Europe and African-American men?

Militant and radical women continued to emphasize the natural-rights approach. Contrasting ideological approaches led to contrasting tactics. The moderate National American Woman Suffrage Association, which was the largest suffrage organization, favored lobbying to win support for the cause. The smaller National Woman's Party favored direct action. Its members were imprisoned for engaging in civil disobedience; they received extensive national publicity when they had to be force-fed. Both groups capitalized on the war, during which many women moved into jobs previously held by men. Wilson's call for "a war for democracy" made him appear hypocritical in refusing to endorse women's suffrage. In September 1918, Wilson, embarrassed by picketing of the White House, had at last capitulated and announced his support for the cause. In May 1919, Congress approved the constitutional amendment by the required two-thirds margin; on 26 August 1920, Tennessee capped the struggle begun at Seneca Falls by becoming the thirty-sixth state to ratify the amendment.

Ratification delighted suffragists, but the low turnout in the November 1920 election—when less than half of the eligible female voters cast ballots—disappointed many of them. Despite the poor showing, activist women believed that they now had the political influence to convince Congress to enact their legislative agenda. In order to coordinate their lobbying activities, members of ten voluntary organizations formed the Women's Joint Congressional Committee, which began to pressure Congress to pass laws of special concern to women, including measures to protect women in industry, to extend federal aid to public education, and to promote disarmament.

The first notable victory came in 1921 when Congress enacted the Sheppard-Towner Act, which aimed at reducing the shockingly high infant mortality rate in the United States. According to some estimates, more than two hundred thousand babies died each year before the age of one. An additional twenty thousand mothers died yearly in childbirth. Nevertheless, the measure had faced opposition from the Roman Catholic church, which opposed any government intrusion into the family, and from the American Medical Association, which considered the measure "Bolshevistic."

Passage of the bill indicated that Congress respected the potential voting power of women and that Progressive Era concerns survived in the more conservative postwar period. According to the law's terms, states received federal aid to fund visiting nurses, to staff clinics, and to provide a range of other pre-natal and maternal services. By the mid-1920s, every state but Illinois, Connecticut, and Massachusetts had moved to implement this innovative piece of social legislation.

A second victory for newly enfranchised women came in 1922, when Congress enacted the Married Women's Independent Citizenship Act, popularly known as the Cable Act. Before the passage of this measure a woman's citizenship followed that of her husband and an American-born woman lost her citizenship if she married a noncitizen. The new law ended this galling practice, although a woman still lost her citizenship if she married an alien ineligible to become a citizen (a category that applied primarily to the Japanese).

The Cable Act turned out to be the last significant legislative victory won by women in the 1920s. After 1922, male politicians paid less attention to issues of special concern to women. Female voter turnout remained low and wives generally cast their ballots along the same lines as their husbands. To the surprise of some suffragists, a female voting bloc had not emerged. One leading magazine even asked, "Is Woman Suffrage Failing?" The lack of female candidates also hurt the cause. By the mid-1920s, only a paltry number of women had been elected to Congress or to state legislatures. Candidates had difficulty raising funds and encountered hostility when attempting to enter a male domain, but many women also evinced a reluctance to leave the predominantly female sphere of voluntary organizations for the male-dominated world of party politics.

A nasty rift between women activists further reduced female political influence. The division began when the National Woman's Party, headed by Alice Paul, framed the Equal Rights Amendment (ERA), which supporters introduced into Congress in December 1923. The amendment aimed at making all forms of discrimination against women illegal; the critical clause read, "Men and women shall have equal rights throughout the United States and every place subject to its jurisdiction."

The amendment's wording appeared to threaten state laws protecting women workers, including statutes that barred night work by women, limited the number of hours that women could work, and prevented women from working with certain machines. Such laws, known as protective labor legislation, had been favored by female activists partly because Supreme Court rulings had made it impossible to enact legislation applicable to both men and women, but many reformers also advocated these laws because the reformers believed women needed special protection.

As the debate flared, the sides traded invective. Supporters of the ERA accused its critics of accepting a dependent status for women; opponents of the ERA accused its supporters of being "ultra" feminists. The amendment itself stood no chance in Congress, and the division damaged the overall cause of women. As a sign of the weakening political influence of women, Congress in the late 1920s ceased all funding for the Sheppard-Towner Act. By way of contrast, the Prohibition amendment provoked controversy that deepened as the postwar decade progressed.

Wets versus Drys

Efforts to restrict the consumption of alcohol dated back to the 1820s, when the temperance movement first emerged. Concerned about the damaging effects that high rates of alcohol consumption had on the nation's health, Protestant, middle-class reformers had also become disturbed by the drinking habits and customs of Irish and German immigrants. Temperance advocates, not content to rely solely on moral suasion, sought legislation against John Barleycorn. In 1851, Maine became the first state to enact Prohibition, but the cause lost momentum during the Civil War.

The Ohio-based Women's Christian Temperance Union (WCTU), founded in 1874, revived the agitation. The first mass-membership organization of women in the United States, the WCTU attracted large numbers of women concerned about the damaging effect alcohol had on the home. They shared with the earlier temperance reformers a belief that the elimination of the liquor traffic would lead to a more well-ordered, sober, and industrious society. The WCTU gained its greatest support from evangelical Protestants who belonged to pietistic denominations. Often the victims of drunken and abusive husbands who wasted their precious wages on drink, these brave and dedicated women invaded saloons in order to confront the sinners.

In 1895, the Anti-Saloon League (ASL) joined the WCTU's campaign against alcohol. The ASL resembled the WCTU in that it drew its members from the Protestant churches, but the Anti-Saloon League proved far more adept at developing a sophisticated organization, and it pioneered many of the techniques used by other single-interest pressure groups. As its name indicated, the ASL focused its attention on the saloon, an urban institution that the Anti-Saloon League identified with vices such as gambling, prostitution, and political machines. Part of a nativist attack on immigrants' social customs, the war against the foreign-born saloon keeper won the support of many Protestant ministers, some of whom took leadership roles in the organization.

The Anti-Saloon League's accusations were partly true; the saloons had often provided a base for corrupt ward politicians and for criminal activities. But many of the saloons' patrons would not have recognized the ASL's portrayal of this social institution. Coal miners, packing-house employees, and steelworkers relied on saloons to quench their thirst after a hard day's work, and the saloon's free lunches (well salted, of course) provided nourishing meals. For Slavic immigrants in particular, saloons served as social centers where neighbors exchanged news, held meetings, and escaped the harshness of urban life.

The ASL's campaign gained support from efficiency-minded businessmen concerned that drinking caused industrial accidents and from white southerners who believed that alcohol corrupted African Americans. The drive against the "liquor trust" also won the support of many progressives, who viewed abstinence as a way to uplift the urban poor. Initially, the ASL sought laws restricting consumption on the local and state level, but at its 1913 convention, the Anti-Saloon League decided to campaign for a constitutional amendment that would eliminate the liquor traffic entirely. None of its members expected this to be an easy fight, and the ASL anticipated that it would take many years before it would accomplish its goal.

Instead, the victory came with amazing rapidity. The Anti-Saloon League triumphed easily, in part because brewers, who believed that beer would be exempted, refused to join distillers in a fight against the proposed amendment. The cause, above all, benefited from America's entry into the war. Accepting the Prohibitionists' argument that grains such as barley and rye should not be wasted, Congress essentially enacted wartime Prohibition during the so-called national emergency. The wave of anti-German hysteria that swept the country further aided Prohibitionists, who could now identify the numerous German owned breweries with the enemy. Many fervent drys (the term used for those who favored Prohibition) had already won election to Congress in 1916, which soon thereafter submitted the Prohibition amendment to the states. In January 1919, Nebraska became the thirty-sixth state to ratify it, ending a hundred-year battle against "demon rum."

The amendment banned the "manufacture, sale, or transportation of intoxicating liquors," but it did not define "intoxicating." Many people expected Congress to permit the continued sale of light wines and beer, but the enforcement statute, known as the Volstead Act (named for its sponsor, Representative Andrew Volstead of Minnesota), categorized any drink containing more than 0.5 percent alcohol as "intoxicating." Drafted by America's so-called dry boss, Wayne Wheeler, the president of the ASL, the statute shocked the AFL, which threatened a strike in defense of beer, the workingman's drink.

Drys expected that the amendment would be enforced and did not anticipate the myriad difficulties that authorities faced throughout the decade. It proved impossible adequately to police the Canadian and Mexican borders and the open seas. The Volstead Act contained loopholes in that it allowed special exemptions for medicinal, industrial, and religious purposes. The measure did not forbid consumption or possession of alcohol, which complicated the enforcement problems. The economy-minded Congress never appropriated adequate funds for enforcement, and the drys hesitated to request additional funds for fear of exposing how widespread violations had become. Congress placed enforcement in the Treasury Department's Bureau of Alcohol, Firearms, and Tobacco, renamed the Prohibition Bureau, which, because of a special civil-service exemption (eliminated in 1927), became rife with corruption.

Young, middle-class urban residents who patronized speakeasies took special delight in defying a law they identified with Puritanism. Many historians believe that because of the elimination of the saloon, the working class drank less during the 1920s but the middle class, including many women, imbibed more. Indeed, illicit drinking became fashionable in a decade when many people rejected Victorian notions of propriety and began to enjoy new forms of leisure and entertainment.

Throughout the 1920s, a decade that saw a declining interest in politics, Prohibition was one of the few issues that aroused strong emotions. Drys, in defending the amendment, cited the decline in arrests for public drunkenness and the decrease in alcohol-related illnesses such as cirrhosis of the liver. By the mid-1920s, many drys even claimed that great prosperity had resulted from Prohibition and that the money saved on alcohol had stimulated the strong consumer demand for other items.

The wets marshaled their own arguments. They lamented the disappearance of the workingman's social club and ridiculed the hypocrisy of a law that eliminated the saloon while jet-setters drank at "fancy hotels." Observing the rise of organized crime and the spread of a "crime wave," they argued that Prohibition encouraged disrespect for the law. Aided by the Association Against the Prohibition Amendment (AAPA), an organization modeled on the Anti-Saloon League, wets maintained that the law violated the "personal liberty" of all Americans and established a dangerous precedent for federal intervention in private matters.

Republicans generally supported the Prohibition amendment, but the Democrats were divided. Southern and western Democrats strongly favored it; most northern Democrats opposed it. Protestants tended to vote dry and Catholics to vote wet. Wets scored a major victory in 1923 when the New York legislature, with the encouragement of Al Smith, the most prominent Roman

Catholic politician in the United States, voted to repeal its state enforcement law. Smith became a hero to many Democrats, but other members of his party vowed to thwart his presidential ambitions.

Many progressives regretted that a war against the bottle threatened to replace the war against special privilege as the nation's top political issue. Encouraged by an unexpectedly strong showing in the 1922 elections and by a faltering Harding administration, they had hoped instead to refocus the public's concern on many of the unresolved postwar issues.

The Indian Summer of Progressivism

The revival of progressivism in the early 1920s was largely the result of widespread agricultural discontent. Following the dismal years of the early 1890s, farmers had done quite well between 1896 and 1916, when world prices for agricultural commodities enjoyed a steady rise. When the United States entered the war, agricultural prices boomed. Encouraged by the easy credit policies of the Federal Reserve Board, by government-guaranteed prices, and by the Food Administration, which told them "Food Will Win the War," farmers in 1917 and 1918 brought millions of previously untilled acres into cultivation.

The golden era for farmers ended abruptly in 1920–21, when deflationary Federal Reserve Board policies and lessening European demand for American agricultural produce inaugurated a decade-long agricultural depression. Signs of distress quickly became apparent throughout the agricultural states. Between 1920 and 1921, cotton prices fell from a dollar a pound to twenty cents a pound. In 1919 it took six bushels of corn to buy one ton of coal; in 1921 it took sixty bushels to buy a ton. Many wheat farmers could not sell their produce even at the cost of production. Nearly one million farmers lost their homesteads to foreclosures and bankruptcies in 1920 and 1921. Feeding their resentments, farmers found themselves portrayed as hicks in magazines and films that identified the city with modernity and the farm with backwardness.

Faced with a deepening agricultural crisis, congressional representatives from rural states grouped themselves into the Farm Bloc, also known as the Progressive Bloc. Despite this identification, the rural representatives did not necessarily have the same perspective. Those who were more business oriented affiliated themselves with the American Farm Bureau Federation, which had been formed in 1920 from preexisting state organizations. These representatives pushed the McNary-Haugen bill (named after the Senate and House sponsors), by which the government would guarantee prices by buying and storing agricultural goods until prices rose and by dumping the surplus overseas. Those who were more radical sought alliances with other discontented groups. Primarily based in a band of states that included Wisconsin, Minnesota, Iowa, the Dakotas, and Nebraska, these Farm Bloc representatives desired in particular to build ties with labor.

The 1922 elections revealed the extent of the agrarian discontent in the upper Midwest. Those elected to the Senate included Robert La Follette of Wisconsin, Farm-Labor Party member Henrik Shipstead of Minnesota, Non-Partisan League member Lynn Frazier of North Dakota, Smith Brookhart of Iowa, and R. B. Howell of Nebraska. Criticizing Federal Reserve Board policies, the Esch-Cummins Transportation Act, the use of injunctions to break strikes, the high tariff, and Wall Street influence, most of the progressive senators and representatives belonged to the insurgent wing of the Republican Party. Many of them had opposed the war, which may have helped them in states with large German populations.

Dissidents could point to other victories that made 1922 a progressive year in politics. The Democrats, demonstrating strength in urban areas, picked up an astonishing total of seventy-eight House seats. In New York, Al Smith regained the governorship; in Pennsylvania, the insurgent Gifford Pinchot defeated an Old Guard Republican in the gubernatorial primary and easily won the regular election. In Kansas, voters repudiated Governor Henry Allen, who had backed an industrial court that required compulsory arbitration of labor disputes, a measure strongly opposed by the labor unions.

Progressives' hopes for the 1924 elections rose as the AFL expressed disgust with the antilabor stance of the Harding administration and of the Supreme Court. Already angered by the Court's interpretation of the 1914 Clayton Act, the usually cautious AFL leadership exploded with anger in 1922 when, in a matter of months, President Harding sought to undermine a massive bituminous coal strike and Attorney General Daugherty gained a sweeping injunction (known as the Wilkerson injunction) to break a nationwide strike of railroad shopmen.

Labor's growing dissatisfaction with the probusiness orientation of the courts received support from female activists when, in a 1923 decision known as *Adkins v. Children's Hospital*, the Supreme Court ruled that Washington, D.C.'s minimum wage law for women was unconstitutional. Ever since the 1908 *Mueller v. Oregon* decision, the Court had accepted the idea that women could be protected by special labor legislation. But now, recent Harding appointee George Sutherland, in the five-to-three decision, ruled that such legislation invalidated the constitutionally protected right of employers and employees to make contracts on an individual basis.

The Court's reversion to late-nineteenth-century legal thinking outraged reformers, already upset by a 1922 decision that forbade Congress from outlawing child labor. (The same Court granted major league baseball owners exemption from the antitrust laws.) William Jennings Bryan compared *Adkins* to the Dred Scott decision, and progressives denounced the usurpation of congressional power. The veteran reformer Florence Kelley called for the appointment of a woman to the Court, and William Borah suggested that seven votes be required before the Supreme Court could overturn a congressional measure.

Progressives also believed that business interests exercised total control over the Harding administration. Not only had the four Harding appointees to the Supreme Court exhibited a procorporate bias, but Treasury Secretary Andrew Mellon persisted in his efforts to cut taxes on the wealthy. As a sign of the growing discontent, dissident senators balked at a ship subsidy bill that allowed for the sale of government-built ships to private investors at bargain-basement prices. In 1922, the Senate came close to expelling Michigan senator Truman Newberry, whose exorbitant campaign expenses had become a symbol of the power of money in politics.

By the summer of 1923, the Harding administration was floundering. Rumors circulated about Harding's philandering and about the flow of liquor in the White House. In May 1923, Daugherty's close friend Jess Smith, who had received kickbacks from German bankers, committed suicide in the attorney general's apartment, and the press began to speculate about possible Republican challengers to Harding.

Smith's suicide gave the public the first hint of the Harding scandals, which did not become fully public until after the president's death. Harding was betrayed by his cronies, otherwise known as the Ohio Gang. Smith, it turned out, had used his connections with the attorney general to arrange favorable deals for gamblers and bootleggers. Daugherty had become enmeshed in a web of corruption that led to his forced resignation in February 1924. Charles Forbes, the head of the Veterans' Bureau, had bilked the government out of nearly two hundred million dollars. And in the biggest scandal of all, Interior Secretary Albert Fall had sold oil leases at Elk Hills, California, and Teapot Dome, Wyoming, in return for cash payments.

During the summer of 1923, Harding became more and more aware of his friends' betrayal. Confused and despondent, the embattled president set out on a vacation trip to Alaska. Stopping in Seattle on his way home, he suffered a fatal heart attack. Harding's death proved timely from the Republican Party's perspective because the mantle of power passed to Calvin Coolidge, the poker-faced, rock-ribbed symbol of Yankee moral rectitude who bore no taint of scandal. Nevertheless, despite an improving economy, Republican regulars showed concern when, in the summer of 1923, Swedish-born "dirt farmer" Magnus Johnson, the candidate of Minnesota's Farmer-Labor Party, won that state's special senatorial election. Early in 1924, persistent investigative work by Montana senators Burton K. Wheeler and Thomas Walsh began to uncover the full scope of the Teapot Dome scandal, and progressives remained convinced that the "radical swing" would be carried into the presidential year.

The 1924 Presidential Election: The Democratic Divide and the Progressive Demise

The 1924 election took place in a boom year; the American economy appeared to have fully recovered from the postwar depression. Coolidge had practically disappeared from public view as vice president, but he acquitted himself well during his first ten months as president. After some initial hesitation, he had removed the offenders from office and replaced Daugherty with the highly respected Harlan Fiske Stone. Hiram Johnson offered only token opposition in the Republican primaries, and when the Republicans gathered in mid-June at Cleveland's glistening new convention hall, the delegates nominated Coolidge on the first ballot. The taciturn Coolidge proved an appropriate choice for a party anxious to demonstrate its faith in American business. Old Guard politicians played a smaller role at the 1924 convention than they had at the convention in 1920. Instead, Herbert Hoover and Andrew Mellon stood as the foremost representatives of the new Republican Party. As a sign of their business-mindedness, the Republicans nominated the banker Charles Dawes, the first director of the federal budget and the author of the Dawes Plan, for vice president.

The Democratic convention, which convened a week later in New York City, conveyed a different image. The Republicans had been quiet and orderly. The boisterous Democrats shouted and yelled at one another. The vast majority of Republican delegates came from Protestant backgrounds, but Catholics played a prominent role at the Democratic convention. The Republicans nominated their candidate on the first ballot; the Democrats took a record 103 ballots. Indeed, there has never been a political gathering like the 1924 Democratic convention, when the ethnic, social, and cultural tensions roiling the nation came to the surface. (Much to the Democrats' embarrassment, the proceedings were broadcast on radio.)

Williams Gibbs McAdoo and Al Smith emerged as the leading contenders for the Democratic nomination. McAdoo, the front runner, appealed mainly to Democrats from the South and the West. McAdoo was a critic of Wall Street, a Wilsonian progressive, and a dry. Fearful of alienating his supporters, he refused to condemn the Ku Klux Klan. He retained the support of many workers who fondly remembered his tenure as head of the Railroad Administration. But his reputation had been badly tarnished when, amid the Teapot Dome revelations, the public learned that he had accepted a sizable retainer from oil tycoon Edward Doheny.

Al Smith, a two-term governor of New York, appealed to urban Democrats from the big cities of the Northeast and the Midwest. He signed the bill repealing New York's Prohibition enforcement law, and also strongly supported an "antimask" measure aimed at suppressing the Ku Klux Klan. An urban progressive, he had backed social legislation protecting female employees. Despite his provincialism, many commentators believed that Smith would have been a shoo-in for the Democratic nomination except for one drawback: he was a Roman Catholic in a nation where many Protestants could not abide the notion of a Catholic president.

The religious issue figured prominently throughout the convention. When the platform committee drafted a plank that criticized bigotry but failed to condemn the fiercely anti-Catholic Ku Klux Klan by name, Smith supporters, anxious to embarrass McAdoo, forced a floor debate on the issue. With Madison Square Garden's galleries packed with Smith backers, vociferous denunciations of the Klan received thunderous applause. Put on the defensive, McAdoo supporters argued that the Klan danger had been exaggerated. Finally, when the vote was tallied, the convention voted to uphold the majority by an incredibly slender one-vote margin. (The delegates attending the Republican convention, who were almost all Protestant, had hardly considered the issue.)

The Klan debate forced into the open the issues that tore Americans apart: wet versus dry; Protestant versus Catholic; critics of immigrants versus their defenders; small towns versus big cities; the South versus the Northeast. Whether or not they wanted to, Smith and McAdoo had come to represent diametrically opposite conceptions of America. Complicating the Democrats' task of selection, a rule requiring that any nominee receive two-thirds of the ballots gave southern delegates virtual veto power over any nominee.

Once the balloting started, chaos reigned. Any mention of McAdoo's name brought chants of "Oil! Oil! Oil!" from the fiercely partisan Tammany Hall denizens who packed the galleries. The meanspirited crowds booed William

Jennings Bryan, who, in his declining years, voiced the fears of a rural America in decline. Ballot after ballot failed to break the deadlock. As the convention stretched into its second hot, steamy week, some Democrats suggested that the proceedings be moved to another city. Finally, on the record 103d ballot, the exhausted delegates chose a compromise candidate, John W. Davis of West Virginia. Davis had served as solicitor general and as ambassador to Great Britain. Since the war, he had been employed by a Wall Street firm. Hoping to balance the ticket, the Democrats chose William Jennings Bryan's undistinguished brother, Representative Charles Bryan of Nebraska, for vice president.

The Democrats' disarray doomed whatever chance they had of regaining the White House. But the nomination of a Wall Street lawyer to run against the big-business team of Coolidge and Dawes reinforced the belief of many third-party advocates that 1924 would be their year to make their mark in American politics.

Third-party supporters had developed new organizational forms in an effort to recover from the debacle of 1920. Early in 1922, the railroad unions had called a conference of progressives that led to the formation of the Conference for Progressive Political Action (CPPA). Hoping to unite labor, agrarians, socialists, liberals, and intellectuals, the CPPA began to hammer out a platform. Disappointed by the abandonment of reform by the middle class, a number of former Wilsonians now looked to labor. Many AFL leaders, in turn, angered by the federal government's and the courts' role in crushing strikes, began to cast aside labor's traditional opposition to independent politics.

CPPA activists, however, proved far more adept at holding conferences than at carrying out grass-roots organizing. Moreover, for all the talk of a third party, only the Socialists believed that such a party should be formed immediately. Conscious of its own weakness, labor, in particular, lacked the will to follow the example of the British Labour Party. The Farmer-Labor Party, the only other potential third-party vehicle, had been taken over by the Communists. As a result, when the 1924 presidential year rolled around, third-party supporters needed someone whose passion, fire, and charisma could make up for their organizational deficiencies.

Only Robert La Follette fit this description. When the diverse groups that made up the CPPA gathered in Cleveland for their July 1924 convention, practically all of the delegates agreed that "Battling Bob" would be the independent candidate. The war-horse of the progressive movement, La Follette had stuck to the causes that had motivated him since the turn of the century. A strident foe of monopolies, a critic of concentrated wealth, and an anti-imperialist, La Follette had fought against all forms of special privilege. He had been hated by superpatriots for his opposition to American entry into World War I; the Senate had seriously considered expelling him. But other Americans, disillusioned by the war's outcome, now admired his position and the courage it took to express it.

Echoing La Follette's lifelong concern with the trusts, the first sentence of the Progressive platform read: "The greatest issue before the American people today is the control of government and industry by private monopoly." Labor concerns showed up in planks that called for the repeal of the Esch-Cummins Transportation Act, a limit on injunctions, and the adoption of a constitutional amendment allowing Congress by a two-thirds vote to reenact measures declared unconstitutional by the Supreme Court. Other planks called for the public ownership of water power and the withdrawal of American troops from Haiti, the Dominican Republic, and Nicaragua. Despite addresses by representatives of the NAACP and the League of Women Voters, neither the platform nor the campaign made much effort to reach out to African-American or to female voters. But in an attempt to appeal to Democrats unhappy with the choice of a corporate attorney as their presidential candidate, the convention nominated Burton K. Wheeler, a prolabor Democrat from Montana, for vice president.

La Follette's antimonopoly rhetoric harked back to a nineteenth-century America of small towns and small shops, but many mainstream politicians and publications treated him as if he were a dangerous radical. Accusations of Communist sympathies began to be made against La Follette as soon as he received the nomination, although he had made every effort to dissociate himself from the Communist Party. Mindful of the Soviet Union's repression of dissidents and harboring no sympathy for a Marxist-Leninist organization that employed secretive and conspiratorial methods, La Follette had read the Communists out of his movement. Nevertheless, La Follette could not shake the "Red" label that Republicans attached to him throughout the campaign.

The Cleveland convention had brought together more than a thousand enthusiastic delegates still committed to a progressive vision for America. Bolstering the independents' hopes, the AFL, shaken by a severe membership decline, had taken the unprecedented step of endorsing the third-party ticket, although some union leaders backed Coolidge. Few commentators believed the Progressives could actually win, but some thought La Follette could garner enough electoral votes to throw the election into the House of Representatives.

The 1924 election turned out to be a bitter disappointment for the Progressives. Soon after endorsing La Follette, the AFL leaders began to question the wisdom of their action and only contributed a paltry twenty-five thousand dollars to his cash-starved campaign. La Follette, always more of a maverick than a team player, had difficulty gaining the support of other progressive Republican senators. Because he stubbornly refused to create a third party, his independent candidacy lacked organization on the local level.

In contrast, the Republicans entered the electoral drive with plenty of money to spend. An industrial boom enhanced their argument that the Republicans had restored prosperity. Rather than aiming their fire at the lackluster Davis-Bryan team, they focused on the dangers posed by La Follette. Portraying the contest as one between Americanism and communism, they appealed to the lingering postwar fears of radicalism. The Republicans were blessed with a candidate who epitomized old-stock America, thus assuring themselves of a large share of the nativist and dry vote.

Despite the excitement caused by the La Follette candidacy, fewer than 50 percent of the eligible voters bothered to go to the polls. Coolidge won 54 percent of the popular vote, Davis 28.8 percent, and La Follette 16.6 percent. La Follette's total provided a gauge of progressive sentiment. Winning the electoral votes only of Wisconsin, he ran second in eleven states west of the Mississippi. Despite the candidate's weakness in most large urban centers, the La Follette vote revealed pockets of working-class discontent. He carried the city of Cleveland, headquarters of the railroad brotherhoods and a progressive redoubt dating back to the mayoralty of Tom Johnson; he carried Passaic County, New Jersey, an area hit hard by the slump in textile production; he ran well in Rochester, New York, a bastion of the Amalgamated Clothing Workers of America.

La Follette's defeat can be viewed in various ways. It represented the last serious antimonopoly campaign in American history. It marked the end of progressivism as a major political movement. It exposed the political weakness of the American left and of labor. It capped a period (1919–24) when a sustained effort to form a labor-based political party ended in failure.

From a larger perspective, the 1924 election launched a new era in American politics, one in which business was ascendant. Soon after the election, Coolidge observed in a speech: "The business of America is business." In 1926 Mellon's tax proposals breezed through Congress, and Herbert Hoover, forgetting his earlier, more cautionary statements, sang paeans of praise to American capitalism. Coolidge's name became associated with prosperity, and chambers of commerce rose to a new position of prominence. Discouraged by the materialistic strivings of the American masses, labor writer J. B. S. Hardmann spoke for many disconsolate activists when he lamented in his introductory essay to the book *American Labor Dynamics in the Light of Post-War Developments*: "The world has grown not only older but old. . . . We seem to be generations away from the age of missions and large enterprise: only pilgrimage—to fleshpots—seems to be the order of the current day."

Significantly, a number of figures who had cut their political teeth in the prewar era died between 1924 and 1926. Woodrow Wilson, never fully recovered from his stroke, died in 1924. William Jennings Bryan, ridiculed by urban sophisticates, collapsed and died shortly after his defense of Tennessee's law banning the teaching of evolution at the 1925 Scopes "monkey trial." La Follette, disheartened by the outcome of his campaign, died of a heart attack in June 1925. Debs, never the same after his imprisonment, died in an Illinois sanitarium in 1926. Great orators all, Wilson, Bryan, La Follette, and Debs represented different strains of American reform and radicalism. But they had shared an optimism, idealism, and naiveté poorly suited for the more materialistic world of postwar America.

In the wake of the movement's failure, many progressives searching for explanations wrote autobiographies and memoirs. In the best known of these works, *Confessions of a Reformer* (1925), Frederic Howe asked: "What has become of this movement that promised so much twenty years ago? What has become of the prewar radicals?" The question implied that all the reformers had given up the cause, but this was hardly true. In particular, many women, such as Alice Hamilton, Grace Abbott, and Lillian Wald, who had always been more comfortable operating outside the narrow political sphere, remained adherents of reform all the way through the New Deal. Nevertheless, progressivism as a movement never recovered from the 1924 defeat. Significantly, the CPPA disbanded in 1925. Labor had invested a great deal of hope in the CPPA, and labor's decline illuminates why the postwar decade proved so disappointing to reformers and radicals.

4

CAPITAL TRIUMPHANT

THE POSTWAR DECLINE OF THE AMERICAN LABOR MOVEMENT

AMERICAN LABOR entered the postwar period full of high expectations. Having benefited from a number of National War Labor Board rulings and having launched successful wartime organizing drives, the AFL anticipated further growth. But major American corporations believed that labor had taken undue advantage of the "national emergency." Conflicting goals and expectations meant that 1919 would be a memorable year for labor-capital confrontations. Capital scored a decisive victory in the most important of these battles, the 1919 steel strike, but labor retained and even extended many of its gains until the depression began in mid-1920. At that point, American business, proclaiming its belief in the open shop, fully reasserted its power at the workplace. AFL unions conducted defensive strikes in 1922, but by the mid-1920s, a badly battered labor movement had practically disappeared as a significant factor in an America resplendent with "Coolidge Prosperity."

The 1919 Strike Wave

More than four million workers participated in strikes during 1919. Major walkouts included the Seattle General Strike; work stoppages conducted by Butte, Montana, copper miners and textile workers in Passaic, New Jersey, and Lawrence, Massachusetts; a New England telephone operators' strike; the Boston Police Strike; and nationwide walkouts in the steel and coal industries. Recent immigrants to the United States from southern and eastern Europe played a notable role in many of the work stoppages. Unable to return to their homelands during the war, they had enjoyed steady wartime work and had begun to view themselves as permanent industrial employees. Motivated by a desire to earn a living wage, many immigrants now viewed unions as a vehicle by which they could gain both a measure of security and respect on the job.

Participants in the 1919 strikes voiced grievances that they had nursed through-out the war. Whenever walkouts occurred, employees expressed irritation at the war-imposed speed-ups, corporate profiteering, runaway inflation, and coerced contributions to the so-called voluntary Red Cross and Liberty loan drives. Arguing that it was time for some democracy at home, they seized upon Wilson's idealistic language and applied it to their own lives. Calling for an end to "Kaiserism in industry," employees in far-flung mill towns announced their readiness to do battle with "Junkerish" bosses and the "Hun in America," and told employers that it was now time for them to make some "sacrifices."

Two of the most noteworthy 1919 strikes occurred in Seattle and Boston. In Seattle, sixty thousand laborers shut down the entire city in sympathy with strik-ing shipyard workers. For one week in early February, workers essentially ran the city, but the general strike collapsed because of unclear overall objectives, government threats of repression, and divisions among its supporters. In Boston, most of the police force walked out in an attempt to win a wage increase and in support of its leaders who had been fired. Considerable rioting accompanied the walkout until the National Guard restored order. In the aftermath, the po-lice officers, who belonged to an AFL union, lost their jobs.

The Seattle and Boston events scared a middle class already prone to blame labor for the high cost of living. Ole Hanson and Calvin Coolidge were not the only politicians to take an antilabor stance. Erstwhile progressive supporters of labor also began to reconsider their backing for what they now considered a selfish and class-bound movement. During his September 1919 speaking tour, President Wilson denounced the Boston Police Strike as a "crime against civi-lization." Attorney General A. Mitchell Palmer distanced himself from the AFL, and Wilson's alter ego, Secretary of War Newton Baker, embraced the antiunion campaign of the Cleveland Chamber of Commerce. Furthermore, with the dis-mantling of the National War Labor Board, the Wilson administration signaled that labor could no longer count on sympathetic government intervention dur-ing walkouts.

Emboldened by its wartime gains, labor pressed ahead despite the loss of gov-ernment support. Of all labor's planned organizing drives, the boldest involved a full-fledged effort to organize America's steel industry. Steel—the very sym-bol of America's industrial might. Steel—a bastion of antiunionism ever since the crushing of the 1892 strike in Homestead, Pennsylvania. Steel—an indus-try which used spies and blacklists to weed out labor organizers. Steel—home to America's largest industrial firm, the U. S. Steel Corporation. Steel—where almost half of all employees worked a twelve-hour day and a seven-day week.

From labor's perspective, if steel could be organized then perhaps all of America's mass production industries could be organized.

The drive to unionize steel got underway in the summer of 1918 when two experienced organizers, John Fitzpatrick and William Z. Foster, headed the National Committee for Organizing Iron and Steel Workers. Fitzpatrick and Foster had the formidable task of coordinating the efforts of the twenty-four AFL unions that claimed jurisdiction over some part of the steel industry. The campaign picked up steam in the spring of 1919 when organizers in Chicago, Gary, Cleveland, Buffalo, and other districts met an unexpectedly enthusiastic response from Slavic (Polish, Slovakian, Czech, Slovenian, Croatian, Serbian, Bulgarian, Ukrainian, and Russian), Hungarian, and Lithuanian workers. These recent immigrants, whom older Americans often scornfully called "hunkies," did the vast bulk of the unskilled and semiskilled work in the steel mills. Hailed for their contributions during the war, immigrants resented that many old-stock Americans once again referred to them as "foreigners" as soon as the war ended. They eagerly embraced the twelve demands made by the steel organizing committee, especially those calling for an end to the twelve-hour day and the seven-day week, and demanding collective bargaining.

For the steel drive to succeed, organizers had to crack the Pittsburgh district, the center of America's steel industry. In this region, mill towns such as Ambridge, Aliquippa, New Kensington, Homestead, Braddock, Duquesne, and McKeesport lined the Monongahela, Allegheny, and Ohio Rivers. From a distance, lighting up the sky with a red glow in the night, the mills awed visitors. Seen up close, the mill towns, with their belching smokestacks, decrepit housing, and barren hillsides, served as a reminder of the ugliness that accompanied industrialization.

First Amendment rights did not exist in these small municipalities where mayors often held supervisory positions in the mills. Aliquippa, for example, could not be penetrated by the unions' flying squadrons. Even the less tightly controlled towns required permits for meetings, banned foreign-language speakers, and discouraged hall owners from letting workers use their facilities.

Despite these barriers, the enthusiasm of the immigrant workers forced the National Organizing Committee to establish 22 September 1919 as the strike date. On that day, more than 250,000 steelworkers walked picket lines rather than reporting to work. Never before had there been a steel strike of such magnitude. Deeply affected by their wartime experiences, worker after worker voiced the same opinion: only a union could guarantee that employees would be treated with decency and respect.

Steel executives scoffed at the notion of collective bargaining. Determined to run their businesses as they had before the war, without any outside interference, steel executives, led by U. S. Steel head Elbert Gary, made plans for a long strike. Counting on the support of local, state, and federal officials, management expressed confidence that the organizing drive could be defeated.

The gap separating the two sides in the steel dispute became evident at an industrial conference that the Wilson administration convened in early October. Meeting against the backdrop of the intensifying steel walkout, union representatives and members of the public called for recognition of collective bargaining, but management representatives adamantly refused to sign any statement that acknowledged the legitimacy of labor unions. The failure of the conference made it clear that the strike would force an all-out struggle between capital and labor.

The steel strike was an unequal battle. In the Pittsburgh district, local police and the state constabulary—called "Cossacks" by workers—broke up meetings, smashed heads, and even invaded workers' homes. In Gary, Indiana, federal troops headed by General Wood acted in a similar manner. Many of the native-born skilled workers refused to strike alongside the "hunkies." In the Pittsburgh region, the mill owners brought in trainloads of African-American strikebreakers from the South. Seizing on William Z. Foster's previous involvement in radical causes and the association of eastern Europeans with the Russian Revolution, steel magnates also used the press to portray the strikers as Reds. Steel executives knew the battle was about unionism and had nothing to do with revolution (except to the extent that collective bargaining represented a revolution to them), and Slavic workers, devoted to the church, expressed little sympathy for the Russian Revolution, but charges of Communist influence carried weight in the highly charged Red Scare atmosphere.

Labor's position looked hopeless by comparison. The AFL's insistence on retaining a craft-union structure made no sense in an industry where the majority of workers did not do skilled jobs. Samuel Gompers and other AFL leaders never gave their full support to the walkout. In November and December 1919, workers began to drift back to the mills, returning, as Thomas Bell described in his novel *Out of This Furnace*, with a "beaten sag" to their "shoulders."

The mill owners had scored a decisive victory. Having used much of their savings during the strike, many workers vowed never again to join a union and voiced suspicion that organizers had made off with strike funds. As late as 1927, workers told a reporter for the *Survey* magazine about their resentments over having been "left alone, without relief, without leadership." Above all, fear continued to dominate the lives of steelworkers: fears of spies, blacklists, discriminatory bosses, and layoffs. The twelve-hour day remained in force as a new decade began, and it seemed as if all the wartime hopes of the steelworkers for "industrial democracy" had been thwarted.

Coal miners, participants in the other major strike in the autumn of 1919, appeared to have fared better. Working in a highly dangerous industry, coal miners often formed strong bonds of solidarity that transcended nationality and racial divisions. More than five hundred thousand miners belonged to the United Mine Workers (UMW), the largest union in the AFL; it gained many new members during the war when industry's insatiable demand for coal led to the opening of countless new pits. Headed by John L. Lewis, a shrewd, calculating, tough-minded son of Welsh immigrants, the UMW had organized the entire anthracite (hard coal) region of northeastern Pennsylvania and most of the bituminous (soft coal) mines in western Pennsylvania, northern West Virginia, Ohio, Indiana, and Illinois. Most remarkably, in 1917 and 1918 the union had begun to make inroads in the fiercely antiunion southern Appalachian region of southern West Virginia, Kentucky, and Alabama.

With the conclusion of hostilities, coal miners rushed to cast off the wartime restraints, and the UMW's September 1919 convention resolved to seek a 60 percent wage increase and a six-hour day. As the strike deadline drew near, a White House statement declared that a strike would be "unjustifiable" as well as "unlawful." (The lack of a signed peace agreement meant that technically the war had not yet ended.) Nevertheless, more than four hundred thousand coal miners struck in November 1919. After a preliminary injunction failed to halt the walkout, A. Mitchell Palmer obtained a sweeping injunction forbidding the strike. To the surprise and consternation of many miners, Lewis ordered them to comply with the court edict. But thousands of miners defied their union's president; eventually the government and a special coal commission agreed to healthy wage increases ranging from 20 to 27 percent.

Despite the wage gains, in the immediate postwar period the UMW suffered a string of setbacks in the southern West Virginia coal fields. Once the war was over, operators in this region refused to sign any accord with the union. Relying on private detectives and yellow-dog contracts (which forbade workers from joining a union) to enforce their rule over towns where even the schools and the churches might be owned by the company, employers established a form of industrial autocracy. In one of the most violent incidents in a series of mining wars, the chief of police of Matewan, West Virginia, Sid Hatfield, participated in a May 1920 gun battle during which seven Baldwin-Felts detectives were killed. In retaliation, Hatfield was gunned down. Soon thereafter, in August 1921, armed miners set off on a march to Logan County, only to be halted by federal troops. The events overshadowed the UMW's basic dilemma: without government support, the union could not crack the southern Appalachian fields. The operators began to shift more production to this region, spelling disaster for the UMW and the labor movement in the 1920s.

Despite these setbacks, until the economy dipped in mid-1920, unions continued to build on their wartime gains. Union membership in January 1917 totaled 2.9 million, and in early 1920, it reached an all-time high of 5 million. Progressive garment workers' unions such as the International Ladies Garment Workers Union (ILGWU) and the Amalgamated Clothing Workers of America scored a steady stream of victories throughout 1919; efforts to organize textile and meat-packing workers showed considerable promise; and the building trades, railroads, and many other sectors remained union strongholds. Faced with this reality and anxious to reassert their authority in the workplace, employers set out to perfect antiunion strategies.

The Carrot and the Stick: Welfare Capitalism and the Open Shop

Most large employers knew they could not prevent unionization unless they offered their employees some tangible benefits. As early as the 1880s, Proctor and Gamble and the McCormick Harvesting Machine Company (the core firm of what became International Harvester) made some efforts at industrial betterment. It was not until the World War I era, however, that companies fully embraced the idea of providing a wide range of services, known collectively as welfare capitalism, for their employees. Motivated by a need to attract a labor force and to wean workers away from unions, many large and highly profitable firms greatly expanded such programs in the first year after the war.

Welfare capitalism sought to build ties between employers and employees. Such initiatives included stock-subscription plans, profit sharing, pensions, and group insurance. To discourage strikes and to stem high turnover rates, the benefits depended on continuous service. Programs were established specifically for female employees, a group often neglected by unions. Company cafeterias served low-cost meals in a pleasant atmosphere, and corporate-sponsored sports teams participated in industrial leagues. Glossy, picture-filled magazines publicized company activities and helped build a sense of company identity and loyalty.

Disturbed by the postwar labor unrest, many employers in 1919 and 1920 also established employee representation plans, which sought to provide an alternative to labor unions. Employees desired a means for presenting grievances;

these plans allowed for the election of plant delegates who sat down with company representatives to discuss problems. Their foes dismissed them as meaningless substitutes for real unions, but when they were first established, the plans often garnered considerable support from workers.

In the decade when public relations fully emerged as a field, businessmen received considerable praise for dispensing such largesse. Citing the sharp decline in walkouts after 1922, magazine after magazine touted welfare capitalism as the solution for the "labor problem." The Great Depression would later reveal the shallowness of this claim, but during the 1920s, welfare capitalism set the tone for what many considered a new era of harmonious labor-capital relations.

Welfare capitalism was the soft side of the postwar antiunion offensive. The open-shop movement was the hard side. By declaring themselves in favor of the open shop, employers claimed they only wanted to give their employees a choice whether to join a union. In reality, by declaring for the open shop, employers intended to free themselves entirely of labor unions. The terminology obscured employers' real motivations and made them appear to be fair-minded compared to unions, which, in closed-shop workplaces, restricted employment to union members.

An open-shop drive had been conducted in 1904 and 1905; the second campaign reached even greater proportions. Almost simultaneously in a number of cities in 1919, organizations such as the Seattle Waterfront Employers' Association, the Minneapolis Citizens' Alliance, and the Associated Employers of Indianapolis declared themselves in favor of the open shop. Having enhanced their reputation by directing the five Liberty loan drives, businessmen knew the value of identifying their cause with patriotism and began to refer to the open shop as the American Plan of Employment, or more simply as the American Plan.

The American Plan had great appeal to employers determined to operate without interference from unions. In books and pamphlets and from podiums, employers hammered away at the same themes. Union work rules unnecessarily restricted production; unions' unreasonable wage demands caused the skyrocketing of the cost of living; unions brought all workers down to the level of the least capable. Medium-sized firms belonging to the National Association of Manufacturers—described by Samuel Gompers as a militant "union-hating" organization—most fully embraced the cause, but the open shop also attracted the support of local chambers of commerce and trade associations ranging from the National Metal Trades Association to the National Hairdressers' Association.

The antiunion campaign, devised to stem labor's 1919 organizing drives, began in 1920 to target the more established AFL unions. The fierce vendetta against labor disrupted a second industrial conference, held in January 1920, and caught many complacent AFL leaders off guard. Once the postwar depression began, the campaign gained momentum, and the early 1920s came to be characterized by considerable labor-capital strife.

The Postwar Depression and the 1922 Strikes

The economic collapse that began in mid-1920 was a disaster for labor. In Lawrence, Massachusetts, the giant American Woolen Company closed all of its mills for two months and reopened on a four-day-per-week basis. In the wartime boom town of Akron, Ohio, almost fifty thousand unemployed rubber workers left the city. Most major industrial firms imposed 20 percent wage cuts during 1921; the unemployment rate in manufacturing rose above 20 percent, and cities lacked adequate relief to cope with the mounting suffering.

Between 1916 and 1919, unions had often used labor shortages to extract wage increases and other gains; between 1920 and 1922, employers now used the high unemployment rate to their advantage. Promising industrial union drives in the textile and meat-packing industries were early victims of the severe economic downturn. In textiles, a new union, the Amalgamated Textile Workers of America (ATWA), born amid the 1919 strife, nearly collapsed when workers lost their jobs or became so discouraged that they stopped paying their dues. In meat-packing, organizing efforts in the giant Swift and Armour Companies by an umbrella group called the Stockyards Labor Council (SLC) had already been damaged by the 1919 Chicago race riot. But the SLC did not completely fall apart until the employers, in late 1921, forced a hopeless strike upon diehard union supporters.

Pounded into submission during 1921, labor remained quiet, but when the economy began to rebound in 1922, a new round of walkouts began. These strikes differed markedly from those that had occurred in 1919. Defensive rather than offensive, generally involving craft rather than industrial unions, led by stolid AFL militants, and concentrated in many of the nation's oldest and most labor-intensive industries, the 1922 walkouts lacked the optimistic spirit of the 1919 strikes. From a historical perspective, 1922 marked the end of an era of mass labor unrest and inaugurated an era when capital appeared to have emerged fully triumphant over labor.

Sixty thousand New England textile workers set off the 1922 strike wave when in February they walked off the job in many New Hampshire, Massachusetts, and Rhode Island mills. Employees had accepted a 22.5 percent wage slash in

1921, but a second 20 percent cut announced in January 1922 threatened to eliminate all of their wartime wage gains. New Hampshire and Rhode Island employees also walked picket lines in protest of employers' plans to increase the workweek from forty-eight to fifty-four hours, a move that the manufacturers claimed was necessary because of southern competition.

The nine-month textile walkout typified the 1922 strikes. Workers generated considerable support from local merchants and priests angered by the manufacturers' callousness; employers countered by seeking court injunctions to forbid picketing; faced with declining profits, mill owners had little incentive to settle; gritty and determined, employees showed great resilience in holding out. In the end, the mill owners and the textile unions arranged a compromise settlement. Manufacturers rescinded the 22.5 percent wage cut, but New Hampshire employers went ahead with plans to increase the hours of work. Bled dry by the need to provide relief, the United Textile Workers, an AFL union, emerged from the walkout greatly weakened.

The 1922 coal strike proved even more damaging to the AFL. Ever since the end of the war, large coal companies, including subsidiaries of the U. S. Steel Corporation, had extended their operations in the southern Appalachian field. In 1922, northern companies in the area that had become known as the Central Competitive Field argued that they could no longer compete against nonunion firms, and demanded that separate pacts, rather than a single national agreement, be negotiated.

Since 1898, the UMW had negotiated uniform agreements, and the union could not countenance such a Draconian demand. On 1 April 1922, six hundred thousand miners of anthracite and bituminous coal began what became the most extensive coal strike in American history. Participants included many army veterans who, much like coal miners in Great Britain, France, and Germany, had been victimized by a disaster in coal brought on by the wartime expansion of mining, the emergence of oil as a new fuel source, and the use of coal for reparations.

An incident that occurred in the midst of the walkout indicated the level of bitterness generated by the coal conflict. In June 1922, a coal company in Herrin, Illinois, foolishly began strip-mining operations using nonunion labor and armed private detectives brought in from Ohio. No state had a more devoted UMW membership than Illinois, where the strike had been 100 percent effective. In communities such as Herrin, located in Williamson County (known as "Bloody Williamson" because of its violent history), the union served as a center of social and community life. Soon after their arrival, the private detectives killed three striking union miners. In retaliation, irate local residents captured nineteen of the strikebreakers and massacred them in cold blood. Before killing them, they forced some of the scabs to crawl on their hands and knees to a cemetery and shot them in front of a cheering crowd. Others had their throats slit. To the surprise of no one, no jury in Williamson County ever convicted any of those tried for the cold-blooded slaughter.

Antiunion forces denounced the UMW's complicity in the bloodshed, but the Herrin massacre did not decisively influence the strike's outcome. What did prove decisive was simply that without government support, the UMW could not penetrate the southern Appalachian or other nonunion coal fields. Recognizing this, John L. Lewis cut a deal in mid-1922. He signed an agreement that preserved wages at their 1920 level, but which for the first time since 1898, omitted critical operators in the Central Competitive Field.

Never lacking in hyperbole, the *United Mine Workers' Journal* (the official organ of the UMW) proclaimed the 1922 settlement to be "the greatest victory ever won in an industrial struggle." Astute observers of labor knew better. Not only had the UMW lost some of its northern footholds, but Lewis had abandoned thousands of western Pennsylvania miners fighting for union recognition who were living in tent colonies because they had been expelled from company housing. After 1922, Lewis expelled dissident leaders and locals, red-baited left-wing opponents of his leadership, signed a series of increasingly meaningless agreements, and presided over a union whose membership dipped to one hundred thousand by the late 1920s. Meanwhile, many miners had no choice but to abandon their homes and move to automobile, rubber, and other rising industrial centers, where many of them became spearheads of unionization in the 1930s.

The federal government played a more decisive role in the walkout that became known as the Great Railroad Strike of 1922, the most extensive work stoppage to affect the nation's railroads since 1894. The railroad unions and workers had made great gains during the war when the government operated the railroads. Disappointed by the return of the railroads to private ownership, the unions had hoped for equitable treatment from the Railway Labor Board, established by the 1920 Esch-Cummins Transportation Act. Instead, once the postwar depression began, the board approved a series of wage cuts, endorsed new work rules, and allowed the establishment of employee representation plans.

The board's promanagement slant had little impact on the four operating brotherhoods, which were composed of engineers, conductors, firemen, and trainmen, the true aristocrats of the American labor movement. They were proud of their skills and often contemptuous of those they deemed beneath them, and their strong position remained essentially unchanged. But the Railway Labor Board's decisions riled railroad shop workers—boilermakers, electricians, railway carmen, clerks, sheet-metal workers, and machinists—who ardently defended work rules that management claimed restricted output.

The simmering conflict came to a head on 1 July 1922 when more than four hundred thousand railroad shop workers walked off their jobs at the same time as the coal miners' strike. The simultaneous work stoppages threatened the economic recovery that had just begun. Secretary of Commerce Hoover urged Harding to take a neutral stance, and at first, the president complied. But by the end of August, Attorney General Daugherty had convinced the chief executive that radicals had gained undue influence over the workers. In early September, the Harding administration requested a federal court order to enjoin the strikers, and on 23 September 1922, the court handed down one of the most sweeping injunctions ever issued against labor. Known as the Wilkerson injunction, and modeled on a similar court edict directed against the 1894 railroad strike, the court order forbade workers from engaging in almost any activity that might have aided the walkout.

Lacking the support of the railroad brotherhoods, disheartened by the UMW's failure to come to their aid, and facing the full force of the federal government, the embattled railroad unions had little choice but to give up. Upon the strike's conclusion, the railroads implemented employee representation plans and the railroad unions' membership plummeted. The AFL discussed launching impeachment proceedings against Daugherty, but the Wilkerson injunction highlighted the increasingly hostile political climate. Beset by a highly successful open-shop campaign and stung by a series of defeats, the AFL by the end of 1922 had become a far different organization than the one that had emerged from the war full of confidence about the future.

The Decline of the AFL

Between 1920 and 1923, the AFL's membership declined from a peak of 5 million to 3.6 million. In the case of some unions such as the International Association of Machinists, the success of the open-shop drive accounted almost entirely for the rapid drop in membership. In the case of the brewery workers, Prohibition wiped out a once powerful union.

Manufacturers' desire to shift production from union to nonunion areas also led to a steep drop in membership. The practice had become common in the coal industry, where, in some fiercely antiunion states such as Alabama, a mere 2 percent of all miners belonged to the UMW. The shift of production from union to nonunion areas—known as the runaway shop—also affected the garment industry, where manufacturers in the 1920s began to move production from New York City to the anthracite coal-mining region of northeastern Pennsylvania. This area attracted garment manufacturers because it offered cheap rents, low taxes, and lenient labor laws. The wives and daughters of unemployed coal miners could be employed at wages considerably below those paid to members of the ILGWU, a union that had enjoyed considerable success in organizing New York City garment workers.

The runaway-shop phenomenon had an even more severe impact on textile workers. Ever since the 1880s, advocates of the "New South" had argued that industry could pave the way for progress in America's poorest region. In general, business-oriented southerners had not had much success in attracting northern firms. On the other hand, textile manufacturers had shown considerable interest in a region where state legislatures had little interest in passing laws to protect labor. By World War I, textile towns stretching from Virginia through the Carolinas to Georgia and Alabama dotted the Piedmont. To elevate the status of textile work in the eyes of whites, southern mill owners had rigidly excluded African Americans from all but the most menial jobs. In turn, textile workers had often been scorned as "lint heads" by many southern whites, who viewed industrial work as a form of dependency.

Some valiant efforts to organize southern textile workers had been made in the aftermath of the war, even though they had little chance in a region where authorities considered any union to be radical or red. But the very lack of unions and the lure of profits had led to overexpansion, and by the 1920s, the southern textile industry also faced increased competition from rayon and other synthetic fibers. Southern manufacturers, experiencing a decline in profits, began to require textile workers to tend more machines. Known as the "stretchout," this practice finally led to an explosion of labor unrest in the Piedmont in the late 1920s.

By the 1920s, progress for the South spelled disaster for northern textile workers. Unable to compete against cheap southern labor, mill after mill, often poorly managed and saddled with antiquated machinery, closed its doors in Manchester, Lawrence, Lowell, Fall River, and other New England mill towns. Described by United Textile Workers president Tom McMahon as "sad, sad places," the once vibrant textile centers became so forlorn that the writer Louis Adamic, on his visit to what he called "the tragic towns of New England," interviewed one worker who longed for another war so he could work again.

Massachusetts became the nation's most depressed state; many shoe factories also left Brockton, Lynn, and Haverhill for low-wage areas. By the middle of the decade, textiles, shoes, and coal became known as the "sick" industries, characterized by what labor economists termed structural unemployment. In these areas with shuttered mills and abandoned houses, references to "Coolidge Prosperity" appeared more a mockery than a description of workers' lives.

The success of the open-shop drive, capital flight, and technological change caused the AFL unions in mining, brewing, clothing, and railroads to lose big chunks of their membership in the early 1920s. Many of these organizations had been among the most militant and the most progressive unions in the AFL. At the same time, rising economic giants such as the automobile, rubber, chemical, and electrical industries remained almost totally union-free. As a result, the building trades—one of the few sectors in which the open shop had been stymied—began to play a more prominent role within the AFL.

During the 1920–22 depression, the building trades were subjected to severe attacks by contractors angered by the unions' work rules, restrictions on the use of machinery, control over apprenticeships, and the power given to business agents. Having often engaged in annoying and petty jurisdictional battles, building trades unions such as the carpenters, ironworkers, painters, electricians, and bricklayers made inviting targets for the chambers of commerce and for other business organizations anxious to attack labor. In New York, for example, following a state legislative investigation and criminal trial, building trades czar Bob Brindell ended up in Sing Sing, where one assumes, despite the prison's picturesque Hudson River location, he had little opportunity to practice his original trade, the building of docks and piers. And in some cities, such as San Francisco and Detroit, the use of lockouts, boycotts, and strikebreakers proved so effective that construction became nonunion.

In most other cities, however, the open-shop drive in construction had been halted. In Chicago, for example, American Plan supporters had galvanized their forces in the midst of the postwar depression. A legislative committee had exposed various nefarious practices within the construction industry. Faced with mounting attacks, the building trades had accepted Judge Kennesaw Mountain Landis as an arbitrator in a wage dispute. Landis had handed out harsh sentences to Wobbly leaders after presiding at their 1918 Chicago trial. Because of his reputation for rectitude and for 100 percent Americanism, he had been named commissioner of major league baseball in the wake of the 1919 Black Sox scandal. A stern and uncompromising man, he shocked the Chicago building trades' rank and file when he announced his decision—known as the Landis Award—on 7 September 1921. The decision went far beyond his original mandate and endorsed revisions employers desired in union work rules.

Businessmen, eying an opportunity to rid construction of unions, formed the Citizens Committee to Enforce the Landis Award. But Chicago unionists, bristling with anger at the supposedly impartial umpire's decision, turned to gangsters in mounting a counterattack. Called "sluggers" in labor circles, these professional criminals dynamited work sites and the homes of nonunion contractors. Even the murder of two Chicago policemen did not halt the campaign, which marked the full emergence of labor racketeering, a phenomenon the AFL leadership preferred to ignore. By the end of the 1920s, a decade of great growth for organized crime, mobsters had gained influence in the laborers', bakers', ladies garment workers', and other unions.

In most cities, the building trades' unions triumphed over open-shop forces because once a building boom began in 1923, contractors desperately needed skilled help, but the construction unions' ability to survive the open-shop drive could not mask the sad state of the AFL. Even the return of prosperity in 1923 failed to revive a movement that had lost the will to carry out aggressive organizing campaigns. The postwar onslaught against labor had taken Gompers by surprise; he had calculated that labor's support for the war and its fierce opposition to the IWW and to Bolshevism would win the federation the approval of the employers. Instead, once the radical threat had been removed, Gompers discovered that employers still hated all unions, regardless of ideology.

Although he had not shared the progressives' naiveté, Gompers died in 1924 a disappointed and disillusioned man. AFL chieftains chose an even more cautious and conservative leader, William Green, to replace him. Under Green's direction, AFL conventions began to resemble Rotary Club gatherings more than labor meetings. After its brief flirtation with independent politics in 1924, the AFL retreated to its voluntarist stance, even opposing proposals for unemployment insurance. The only exception that the AFL made to its opposition to state intervention came when it continued to favor protective labor legislation. This it supported because it believed laws protecting female workers could be used to keep women out of the work force. Likewise, the federation supported immigration restriction and continued to admit unions that barred African Americans. To AFL leaders, women, recent immigrants, and blacks represented forms of cheap labor that threatened their members' wages and status. It is not surprising that, having failed to develop any ideology to counter the prevailing business philosophy, the labor movement by mid-decade had shrunk almost into insignificance and the number of strikes dropped to its lowest level in fifty years.

Labor's Initiatives and the New Shape of the American Left

Despite the decline of unions, labor activists initiated a surprising number of innovative projects during the 1920s. Many of the most forward-looking ideas emanated from the Amalgamated Clothing Workers of America, a union founded in 1914 in opposition to the AFL's United Garment Workers. Because it did not belong to the "official" labor movement, the ACWA had room to experiment with new ideas. Also having organized the men's clothing industry, the ACWA had brought large numbers of women and recent immigrants into its ranks. A target of a fierce open-shop drive in 1920–21, the ACWA had survived a six-month New York City lockout and a lawsuit that aimed at its dissolution. The union's ability to withstand the attacks made it more defensive in outlook, but also solidified its role as the principal proponent of what had been termed the "new unionism."

Under the direction of its president, Sidney Hillman, the ACWA sponsored an impressive number of creative projects during the 1920s. In addition to the Russian-American Industrial Corporation, founded to aid in the rehabilitation of Russia, these included establishing its own bank, working with employers to enforce standards of production so as to bring greater efficiency to unionized firms, negotiating an unemployment system funded by both employers and employees, building the first cooperative houses ever constructed by an American trade union, and continuing its efforts in the field of labor education.

Interest in labor education surged during the 1920s. In Boston, Philadelphia, Rochester, Chicago, and many other cities, unionists and college professors cooperated in the establishment of labor colleges, which offered a wide range of courses from economics and history to public speaking. Independent scholars and activists formed the Workers' Education Bureau in 1921 to coordinate the various efforts, but the AFL gained control of it in 1923. Never comfortable with intellectuals, whom it scorned as "sky pilots" and "parlor experimenters," the labor federation kept a close eye on the outsiders who participated in schools under its sponsorship.

Brookwood Labor College proved to be one of the most exciting efforts at workers' education. A product of the conference that led to the establishment of the Workers' Education Bureau and headed by A. J. Muste, a Protestant minister and antiwar leader turned labor activist, Brookwood attracted coal miners, sewing machine operators, steelworkers, and other industrial employees to its idyllic campus in Katonah, New York. The school's structure reflected Muste's idealism. The male and female students shared in the maintenance work and participated in theater and other cooperative activities. Many key leaders of the industrial union battles of the 1930s learned how to become more effective organizers while at Brookwood. But neither Muste nor Brookwood could escape labor's internecine battles. AFL leaders grew increasingly critical of the school, and Muste became involved in conflicts with various factions on the left. By the early 1930s, political wrangling had destroyed much of the original Brookwood spirit.

The Bryn Mawr Summer School for Women Workers provided a unique opportunity for female industrial employees to study and work together. Under the direction of its president, M. Carey Thomas, Bryn Mawr had established itself as one of the most innovative of the women's colleges. Beginning in 1921, a number of women received scholarships to spend the summer there studying academic subjects such as history and economics and developing the self-confidence to assert themselves within the male-dominated labor movement. The experiment flourished until the late 1920s, when the college's board of trustees moved against a program they feared spawned radicalism.

A number of other initiatives sustained militants disappointed by the 1919–22 defeats. Chicago trade unionists sponsored their own radio station; radical filmmakers made labor-oriented films; the Workers' Health Bureau exposed the dangers of mercury and lead poisoning and other industrial diseases; A. Philip Randolph and other African-American activists inaugurated an effort to organize the porters in Pullman sleeping cars; a labor news service, the Federated Press, supplied material to labor and socialist dailies and weeklies; and a new magazine, *Labor Age*, provided a forum for the discussion of the various projects—many of which were supported by the Garland Fund, named for a millionaire who gave away a fortune that he believed he had no right to inherit.

The initiatives kept the hopes of labor radicals alive, but the IWW barely survived the wartime and postwar repression. Founded in 1905, the Wobblies had shared the optimism and the idealism of the prewar era, although they had nothing but contempt for the ameliorative reforms of the progressives. Passionate and spirited, the IWW sought to build a revolutionary industrial union movement that would unite all workers in one big union. Violent in rhetoric but nonviolent in action, it aimed its organizing efforts at recent immigrants, African Americans, and others scorned by the AFL. Fond of bold statements, the Wobblies' songs and cartoons portrayed workers rising up in anger against fat, bloated capitalists. The imagery masked the Wobblies' weaknesses. Far too radical for most workers and lacking a sound organizing strategy, the IWW failed to build a permanent organization in the major industrial centers. On the other hand, it gained a devoted following in the West among "timber beasts," "blanket stiffs," and other migratory workers. For this reason, when the United States entered the war, employers and the governors of western states urged the federal government to crack down on "Imperial Wilhelm's Warriors," as the IWW's enemies liked to call the union.

The federal government complied. In a series of trials in Chicago, Wichita, and Sacramento, the entire Wobbly leadership was convicted of violating the wartime Espionage Act. Practically the only leader to escape imprisonment was Big Bill Heywood, the flamboyant head of the Wobblies, who had jumped bail and fled to the Soviet Union, where he died in 1929, a lonely and disheartened man.

Internal divisions also weakened the Wobblies. Many members bitterly resented Heywood's flight. Others joined the fledgling Communist movement and abandoned the IWW, which found the Soviet exercise of state power abhorrent. Wobblies also disagreed on whether to seek pardons for those they termed "class-war" prisoners. Drained by the constant trials and by the wrangling, the Wobblies bravely fought strikes during the 1920s on the docks of San Pedro, California, in the apple groves of Yakima, Washington, and in the coal fields of Colorado, but the élan and the bravado never returned.

The decline of the IWW led to an important shift on the left. Before the war, members of the Socialist Party and the Wobblies had conducted their debates in full public view. Once the Bolsheviks seized power in Russia, many leftists embraced the Communist model of organizing, which differed from that used by the Socialists and the IWW. Rather than tolerating diverse points of view, the Communists believed that when critical policy decisions had been made, they had to be rigorously followed by all members of the organization.

After healing its own internal divisions, a united Communist Party (known initially as the Workers' Party) emerged in 1923. The Communists ostensibly operated above ground, but they never abandoned their secret ways. As did all of the world's Communist parties, the American party followed the direction set forth by the Comintern, which was based in Moscow. Viewing the proletariat as the agent of revolution, the party tried to bore its way into existing unions. This strategy alienated the heads of practically every major union and caused a deep rift within the ILGWU. The Communists' duplicitous methods even alienated John Fitzpatrick, the highly respected head of the Chicago Federation of Labor, who had at first been willing to work with them.

By the late 1920s, the Communists, following the directive set forth by Moscow, had begun to form unions to rival the AFL. These remained paper organizations, but with the decline of the Wobblies, only the Communists were ready to go to the aid of workers in need of help. This proved particularly true in the textile industry, where workers desperately needed assistance during strikes. In Passaic, New Jersey, in 1926, in New Bedford, Massachusetts, in 1928, and in Gastonia, North Carolina, in 1929, the Communists played a critical role during long, bitter, and eventually unsuccessful strikes. These battles provided experience to the Communists that would be valuable when they later joined forces with the reinvigorated labor movement that emerged by the mid-1930s. But in the midst of "Coolidge Prosperity," the left, outside a few isolated mill towns, had practically disappeared as a vital force on the American scene.

The "Return to Normalcy": The Postwar Experience of Women Workers

During the wartime mobilization when millions of men donned uniforms, women had begun to find forms of employment that had previously been closed to them. For the first time, significant numbers of women began to be employed as welders, drill press operators, machinists, and streetcar conductors. Most of the women who filled these positions had been previously employed in restaurants, laundries, or hotels, or in other service positions. Not surprisingly, many of the working women had jumped at the opportunity to double or even triple their earnings in war-related industries.

The entry of women into new trades encouraged those who had been active in the Women's Trade Union League (WTUL), a unique Progressive Era organization that brought women workers and middle-class reformers together. Members of the WTUL helped working women organize trade unions and win respect from the male trade unionists, who had only grudgingly accepted women into their ranks. With the assistance of the WTUL, women workers won a number of hard-fought garment strikes between 1910 and 1916 and began to gain staff positions (though nowhere near in proportion to their numbers) in the ILGWU and the ACWA.

The immediate postwar period brought some further encouragement to those who hoped that women could play a more prominent role in the labor movement. When more than four thousand New England telephone operators in April 1919 struck the Wire Administration (a federal agency, headed by Postmaster General Albert Burleson, which had taken over operation of the telephone lines), many male trade unionists gave them support. Seeking both wage increases and relief from Burleson's tyrannical rule, the women, who belonged to the International Brotherhood of Electrical Workers, won most of what they demanded, although efforts to organize telephone operators in other parts of the country proved largely futile.

Telephone operators worked in what was seen as the female employment sphere, and thus their activity did not threaten men. But when women tried to maintain their positions in male bastions, they ran into a brick wall. This was best demonstrated in Cleveland, where 173 women fought for more than a year to hold on to jobs as streetcar conductors that they had gained for the first time during the war. The Cleveland local of the Amalgamated Association of Street and Railway Workers had opposed the hiring of women from the beginning. The men had some basis for their position because in some trades, women had been introduced by employers in order to lower wages or to weaken unions. But the women, anxious to fill positions with much to offer compared to work in factories, laundries, or restaurants, had evinced a desire to join the union and had been hired at the same wage rates as the men. Union arguments that this was not a suitable or a proper job for women appeared to some observers to mask a more basic fear: that men would suffer a loss of status if women performed the same jobs they did.

The dispute over whether the women should retain their jobs went before the National War Labor Board, which heard the case in its dying days. AFL unionists, including Samuel Gompers, lined up in support of their brethren fighting to keep streetcar employment a male bastion. The Cleveland Chamber of Commerce and the WTUL, which usually took opposite positions on labor matters, backed the women workers, who were determined to keep their positions. The women also received the support from Cleveland suffragists and feminists and from Frank Walsh, who had resigned from the National War Labor Board when he saw it veering in a promanagement direction. Walsh agreed to represent the women before the labor board and cautioned unionists that they risked alienating women by so vehemently opposing their entry into previously all-male positions.

The National War Labor Board first ruled in favor of the union and then reversed itself, but the outcome was decided on the local level rather than in Washington. Faced with the determined hostility of the AFL and union threats to strike to ensure their firing, the women had no chance of keeping their jobs. Women who had been hired as streetcar conductors in Detroit met the same fate. Even in Kansas City, where the union local proved far more supportive of the women, they were unable to retain their positions—a clear signal that segregation by gender in employment remained unaffected by the temporary wartime changes.

Outraged by the AFL's stance in the Cleveland case, the WTUL had trouble finding allies in a labor movement that became increasingly defensive and inward-looking as the decade wore on. Many female reformers hoped that the Women's Bureau, which had been established in 1920 as a permanent agency within the Department of Labor, would now assume much of the responsibility for representing the interests of women workers. During the 1920s, this department became home to a number of activists who had been members of the WTUL. Headed by Mary Anderson, this agency conducted numerous studies of female workers and assiduously fought efforts to revoke or to nullify legislation that had been passed to protect women.

Both the WTUL and the Women's Bureau focused their attention on women employed in industry. But by the 1920s, most women who worked were not doing factory labor. They were far more likely to be employed as domestic servants, telephone operators, department store clerks, nurses, and clerical employees, or if they filled positions requiring some college education, as teachers, librarians, and social workers.

The basic pattern for female employment had been established during the late nineteenth century. Women were far more likely to work in nonindustrial than in industrial settings. Most women entered the paid work force when they were between the ages of fourteen and sixteen, and worked until they married and had children. This meant that the female work force had been disproportionately young, though unmarried women and many married African-American women (because of the low earnings of African-American men) had remained permanently employed. Jobs defined as female paid lower wages than male jobs that required equivalent training. Women almost never supervised men and had limited opportunities for promotion.

The clerical field best illustrates the extent to which no significant changes occurred during the 1920s. At one time, many men began their employment careers as clerks before being advanced to managerial positions. But with the invention of the typewriter and other new office equipment, clerical employment became far more specialized. One generally began as a secretary, stenographer, or bookkeeper and finished as a secretary, stenographer, or bookkeeper. By 1900, decreasing numbers of men filled these positions, as women—usually after having completed a high school commercial course or having attended a secretarial school—poured into offices.

The 1920s saw a perpetuation of these trends. Because of the improving economy, industrial corporations, banks, insurance companies, and other business firms greatly expanded their office staffs and experienced little difficulty filling these slots. For American-born women from immigrant backgrounds, office work offered a far more pleasant environment than work in a factory. For rural women, it offered an opportunity to move to the city. For women from families of skilled workers, it offered a respectable form of employment.

By the end of the 1920s, office work had become a female employment ghetto; men had practically disappeared from the field. Clerical workers, often employed in large offices, faced the same rigid work discipline as factory employees. The pay remained low, although it compared favorably to the pay for other female jobs. At most, one could hope to be promoted to executive secretary or to head bookkeeper. But the jobs did offer an opportunity to meet a potential spouse holding a managerial position and to dress up for work, no small consideration in an increasingly fashion-conscious society.

The mid-decade economic boom provided jobs for women in many other fields as well. But by the end of the 1920s, there had only been a small increase in the number of married women who worked. Schoolteachers who married still faced automatic firing, and many insurance companies and banks refused to hire married women. Women still faced a stark choice between marriage and a career. Quotas established by universities and barriers erected by professional organizations meant that by 1930, there were fewer women doctors and lawyers than in 1910. Expectations that the war would bring about permanent changes had proven false, and winning the right to vote clearly had no impact in the economic realm. Many of the pioneers of the women's movement expressed disappointment about the frivolity and the lack of career ambitions of women attending college in the 1920s, a decade that saw few significant changes in terms of female employment.

Labor in the New Era

By 1925, many pundits were proclaiming that the United States had entered a new era of labor-capital peace. They had plenty of evidence to support this belief. Welfare capitalism and other initiatives had apparently made labor content. The industrial surge that began in 1923 provided relatively steady work to factory employees. A low inflation rate erased one of labor's sore points. So few strikes or walkouts occurred that the Department of Labor's Mediation and Conciliation Service (established in 1914 to settle disputes) had little to do.

One of the most remarkable signs of change came in 1923 when the U. S. Steel Corporation voluntarily abandoned the twelve-hour day and adopted three eight-hour shifts. In 1919, Judge Elbert Gary had fought this demand tooth and nail, but by 1923, pressures had mounted on U. S. Steel. Engineers produced studies demonstrating that a shift to the eight-hour day would harm neither productivity nor profits; religious leaders harshly criticized the steel firm's labor policies; Secretary of Commerce Herbert Hoover urged U. S. Steel to abandon this relic of a more ruthless era. Finally Judge Gary acted, and the nation's press hailed this evidence that business had become more responsible and more sensitive to workers' needs.

Giving added substance to the belief that the United States had entered a new era, American industry during the 1920s far outpaced any of its international competitors. Mastering the techniques of mass production, investing heavily in new machinery, and making use of scientific management, American firms achieved astonishing gains in productivity. The greatest growth came in the electrical, rubber, automobile, and machine tool industries, all of which were centered in the Great Lakes region stretching from Buffalo through Cleveland and Detroit to Chicago and Milwaukee. Workers poured into these cities, abandoning farms, small towns, and mining communities. Other parts of the nation appeared stagnant compared to the booming urban Midwest, and the cities' new movie palaces, department stores, skyscrapers, and factories indicated that America had entered a new era—one that many referred to as the Machine Age.

Detroit symbolized both the triumph of the machine and the vibrancy of urban life during the Roaring Twenties. The center of the American automobile industry, its factories attracted whites from Appalachia, African Americans from the Deep South, and immigrants from Mexico. Run at a ruthless pace, its assembly lines burned out many a worker. Its employers, staunch proponents of the open shop, blacklisted any employee suspected of union activity. But workers did not engage in overt protest. If they were dissatisfied, they simply quit and took other jobs. With their earnings they could afford to purchase a Model T, the car that Henry Ford had developed for the masses. Workers with families began to purchase their own homes and, for the first time in their lives, experience the luxury of indoor plumbing. Enjoying the latest dances, dressing in the most up-to-date styles, and purchasing liquor supplied by rumrunners, young workers—known as the "suitcase crowd" because they came and went—

gave Detroit a reputation for a lively night life. With money in their pockets, workers flocked to dance halls, ballparks, motion-picture houses, amusement parks, and other places of urban entertainment, and evinced little desire to join labor unions.

Admirers of the business system hailed the decline in labor unrest and boasted that the American standard of living had far outstripped that of any other country in the world. As evidence, they cited not merely the availability of the automobile but the mass production of such new consumer items as the radio, phonograph, refrigerator, and other household appliances, which had be-come available to large numbers of people making use of installment buying. Enjoying its new status, business emerged as a profession in itself, and major universities rushed to establish business schools. Publicists maintained that pro-gressive-minded businessmen had been responsible for the prosperity—a pros-perity that stood out even more because the European economies could not shake off the aftershocks of the Great War.

By mid-decade, labor activists had good reason to despair. Demoralized by the postwar defeats, militants struggled to understand how the passion that had inspired a series of mass walkouts dating back to the late nineteenth century had seemingly disappeared from the labor movement. The AFL, its work confined mainly to industries that were old and sick, inspired no one. In the highly in-fluential book *A Theory of the Labor Movement*, published in 1928, University of Wisconsin labor economist Selig Perlman argued that partly due to the "enor-mous strength of private property in America," the United States had the world's "least class-conscious labor movement." Challenging many of the assumptions of the intellectual supporters of labor, Perlman claimed that a second industrial revolution had brought about a "new" capitalism and that businessmen had proved far more innovative, dynamic, and flexible than labor leaders.

The Great Depression revealed the weaknesses of the system. Without unions, workers had no way to win wage increases or to share in the great pro-ductivity gains. Income distribution remained unequal and 1 percent of the population controlled approximately 30 percent of the nation's wealth. The 1926 Tax Act promoted by Secretary of the Treasury Andrew Mellon put money in the hands of the rich, who invested much of it in the great bull market of the late 1920s. Most workers still lived insecure lives, fearful that layoffs would threaten their survival. In retrospect, the period of prosperity proved brief. But at the time, an impressive number of observers believed that the business cycle had been conquered and that the United States would never again have a major depression. Class conflict had seemingly disappeared from the American scene, although the country was still torn by racial, ethnic, and religious disputes.

5

AFRICAN AMERICANS IN THE POSTWAR PERIOD

AFRICAN AMERICANS had their hopes raised by the war. Between 1916 and 1918, hundreds of thousands of black migrants flocked to northern cities in search of jobs and a freer life. The wartime military service of two hundred thousand African-American men and Wilson's incessant call for democracy furthered expectations for the postwar period. Armed attacks on African Americans in both the North and the South in 1919 shattered many of these dreams. In the wake of the violence, Marcus Garvey's separatist organization, the Universal Negro Improvement Association (UNIA), gained a mass following. The National Association for the Advancement of Colored People, having more faith in the promise of American democracy, committed its resources to winning the passage of a federal antilynching law. In the meantime, moderate reformers sought to bring about change in the South. Despite these efforts, African-American migration to northern cities continued. Distinctive African-American urban institutions began to emerge, until the Great Depression destroyed many of the gains of the 1920s.

The Great Migration and Raised Expectations

Before World War I, almost 90 percent of the African-American population lived in the South. Between 1890 and 1910, ardent racists had gained control of most southern state governments. They had enacted Jim Crow laws requiring segregation and instituted measures denying African Americans the right to vote. A terrifying wave of lynchings was directed at those African Americans who dared to speak out, and the federal government had evinced no inclination to enforce the Fourteenth or the Fifteenth Amendment to the constitution. When he assumed the presidency in 1913, the Virginia-born Woodrow Wilson had instituted segregation in federal departments in Washington, D.C. The nadir came in 1915, when the violently antiblack feature film *The Birth of a Nation* reached a wide audience (including the president), despite efforts to bar its showing.

The year 1916 brought some remarkably sudden changes. Even before the United States entered the conflict, British war orders stimulated an industrial boom and companies faced serious labor shortages because immigration from Europe had almost totally ceased. Between 1905 and 1914, approximately one million immigrants (principally from eastern and southern Europe) had arrived in the United States each year. In 1917, only 110,618 immigrants entered the country. In 1916, employers desperate for a new source of unskilled labor began to send labor agents and recruiters to the South, initiating a process that became known as the Great Migration.

Young African-American men and women readily responded to the labor agents. The generation born after 1890 had known little but poverty, despair, and terror. The sharecropping system had limited their opportunities. Segregated education meant that African-American children attended inferior schools that rarely went beyond the eighth grade. Grandfather clauses, poll taxes, and white primaries severely limited the right to vote. Race baiting had become a staple of demagogic Democratic Party politicians such as South Carolina's "Pitchfork" Ben Tillman and Mississippi's James K. Vardaman. Local law enforcement agents often participated in, or even led, lynch mobs. Humiliations extended to every aspect of daily life, and African Americans, regardless of their age or status, had to address white men as "mister" or "boss" and defer to them at all times.

Labor agents stimulated the migratory process, but it quickly gathered its own momentum. Letters containing money, and return visits by migrants wearing new clothes, offered tangible evidence that one could earn in northern factories cash wages far greater than those paid by southern employers. The *Chicago Defender*, an African-American newspaper widely circulated in the South, contained enticing job advertisements and articles urging southern blacks to make the trek. The *Defender* even designated a single day, 15 May 1917, as marking the beginning of the Great Northern Drive. Headed for the North, migrants spoke of making an "exodus." Filled with the hope that one could live without fear in the North, the approximately five hundred thousand wartime migrants went mainly to the industrial cities of Chicago, Pittsburgh, Cleveland, and Detroit and the East Coast cities of Philadelphia and New York.

Wartime events put a damper on any overly optimistic expectations that the war would revolutionize American race relations. In East St. Louis, Illinois, on 2 July 1917, a rampaging mob killed thirty-nine African Americans and torched numerous homes in the black section of town. In Houston, Texas, in August 1917, African-American troops, angered by the mistreatment of a black corporal, rampaged through the city and killed seventeen whites. In retaliation, following a hastily arranged court-martial, thirteen African-American soldiers were summarily hanged. The United States military remained rigidly segregated, and the army trained African-American officers at a special camp in Des Moines, Iowa. Disproportionately assigned to labor details, African-American soldiers noted the contrast between their situation and the relative lack of segregation in France. In order to put a damper on protests by African-American troops, the Wilson administration sent Dr. Robert Russa Moton—Booker T. Washington's successor as head of Tuskegee Institute—to France to warn black soldiers not to expect the war to bring about any major changes. The final humiliation came when the American military, concerned about the possibility of African-American soldiers fraternizing with French women, prevented black soldiers from participating in the triumphant Bastille Day victory parade held in Paris on 14 July 1919.

Nevertheless, many African Americans remained hopeful as the war drew to a close. For the first time, African Americans had gained a significant foothold in some northern industries. White southerners, fearful of losing their source of cheap labor, had begun to talk about the need for improved race relations. Optimistic that the war would bring about significant social change, W. E. B. Du Bois captured the prevailing mood in a famous editorial entitled "Close Ranks," which he penned for the *Crisis* in July 1918: "Let us not hesitate. Let us, while the war lasts, forget our special grievances and close our ranks shoulder to shoulder with our own fellow white citizens and the allied nations that are fighting for democracy. We make no ordinary sacrifice, but we make it gladly and willingly, with our eyes lifted to the hills." One year later, a far more sober and somber mood would pervade much of black America.

Postwar Racial Violence and the New Negro

The wartime events did not merely raise expectations; they also helped establish a new mood of militancy among many African Americans. Having learned firsthand of the demeaning treatment of African-American troops, Du Bois wrote in the May 1919 issue of the *Crisis*:

We return
We return from fighting
We return fighting

Thousands of spectators cheered as the 369th Infantry, known as Harlem's Hell-fighters, smartly marched through the streets of New York's black community. The NAACP called for a congressional investigation of the discriminatory treatment of African-American soldiers at home and abroad. The year 1919 also marked the tercentenary of the landing of the first African slaves in colonial Virginia. It was an appropriate time for the United States finally to make democracy a reality for all its citizens.

White southerners responded to the end of the war with trepidation. Migration made them uneasy, but the specter of returning African-American soldiers frightened them. During the debate over the draft, Senator Vardaman had opposed universal conscription precisely because it meant that thousands of African Americans would become familiar with firearms. In 1919, the mere presence of an African-American soldier could provoke a violent response. In Chattanooga, Tennessee, crowds tried to stop black veterans from wearing their uniforms. In the small southwestern Georgia town of Blakely, a mob killed an African-American solider. In Vicksburg and other Mississippi communities, attacks on African-American soldiers became common during 1919.

Lynchings had been gradually declining since the turn of the century, but in the first year after the war, they took a sharp turn upward. The seventy-six African Americans lynched in the South represented the highest number since 1908, and some of the victims were military veterans. In response, the NAACP decided to press its campaign for a federal antilynching bill. The president's response was telling. Just as he had remained silent during the widespread violations of civil liberties and during the intense labor-capital conflict, Woodrow Wilson chose not to speak out about the mistreatment of returning African-American soldiers. For all of his florid talk about democracy, he did not even suggest that some of the voting restrictions on African Americans be eased. Evidently, the concept of self-determination did not apply to Asia, Africa, or the American South.

The violence peaked during the summer of 1919, which became known as the Red Summer because of the many bloody racial conflicts that occurred. The majority of these battles took place in the small towns and cities of the South, where whites feared African-American army veterans might challenge the tightly woven racial caste system. Unlike the midsummer racial conflict in Chicago, the southern violence had little to do with job competition. It grew out of uneasiness on the part of whites who felt that African Americans had been contaminated by foreign ideas during their sojourn in army camps in the North or in France. During the 1919 racial confrontations, African Americans showed a new determination to fight back. For example, when whites attacked blacks in

Charleston, South Carolina, Longview, Texas, Knoxville, Tennessee, and Washington, D.C., pitched battles resulted. Because of the bias of all-white police forces, African Americans suffered a disproportionate share of the casualties, but the bloodshed demonstrated that whites could no longer attack blacks with impunity.

Nothing disturbed southern whites more than the idea that African Americans might organize to demand their economic and political rights. Southern fears became most evident during a violent racial conflict that took place in October 1919 in the Mississippi Delta town of Elaine, Arkansas, located in Phillips County. As was typical in Deep South cotton regions, African Americans made up more than 70 percent of the population of Phillips County. Whites had maintained their control through terror and through the denial of the franchise. Most African Americans—men, women, and children—labored as sharecroppers, and by 1900 they had become trapped in a form of bondage known as debt peonage. The furnishing system by which planters (more properly thought of as planter-merchants) supplied goods to sharecroppers over the course of the year stood at the core of this form of servitude. The sharecroppers never saw an itemized statement of their accounts, for which the planters charged exorbitant rates of interest. After marketing their cotton through the planters, those who did the backbreaking work on the land usually ended up in debt.

Believing that they were not receiving their fair share of the wartime price increases for cotton, Phillips County sharecroppers formed an organization called the Progressive Farmers and Householders Union. Seeking an accurate statement of their accounts and a fair market price for their cotton, the members of the fledgling union began to meet in secret. Local whites, however, found out about the organization and attacked one of the gatherings held in a church in Hoop Spur, Arkansas. In response, armed sharecroppers killed a special agent and wounded a deputy sheriff. To whites, this action amounted to an insurrection. In retaliation, white mobs hunted down African Americans, beating hundreds and killing at least twenty-five (some estimates went as high as one hundred), many of whom had no involvement in the union.

A grand jury that was convened immediately following the incident indicted only African Americans, even though whites had been responsible for almost all of the violence. Following farcical trials, more than ninety African Americans were convicted of various "crimes" and twelve were sentenced to be executed. Only the ardent efforts of the NAACP, antilynching crusader Ida B. Wells, and other supporters eventually saved their lives. But the short-lived organization had been crushed, and the *Crisis* said that blacks in the Mississippi Delta had been left "demoralized, discouraged and depressed."

The Chicago riot that raged for a week in late July and early August 1919 received far more national attention than the events in Phillips County. The bloody street-fighting between whites and blacks shocked the nation, but it did not come as a surprise to residents of the city called by Carl Sandburg the "hog butcher for the world," where tensions had built steadily during the war.

Chicago had served as a magnet for more than fifty thousand African-American migrants between 1916 and 1919—the greatest number to arrive in any city except New York. The rough-and-tumble Midwest metropolis attracted migrants for a number of reasons. The *Chicago Defender* had urged southern blacks to make the trek. The city's steel mills and meat-packing plants desperately needed workers to replace the immigrants who could no longer make the voyage across the Atlantic. The city served as a terminal point for a number of railroads, the mode of transportation used by most migrants.

Racial tensions had simmered in all of the cities that had received significant numbers of black migrants, but in Chicago those tensions had reached the boiling point. Housing and jobs had emerged as the principal areas of conflict. Even before the wartime migration, African Americans had been confined to a section of the city known as the Black Belt. Restricted in their choice of housing, African Americans, unlike immigrants, had not been able to rent homes close to the factories where they were employed, and thus had to travel considerable distances to work. The limited housing market meant that African Americans often paid exorbitant rents for dilapidated living quarters. To enforce segregation, groups euphemistically calling themselves "neighborhood improvement associations" had sprung up in areas bordering the steadily expanding ghetto. By 1918, bombings of homes and attacks on African Americans who dared to try to move into white neighborhoods had become common.

Employment provided a second area of tension in the combustible city. During the war, many African-American men had taken jobs in Chicago-area steel mills; by 1919 they constituted approximately 12 percent of the steel work force. The meat-packers, including the giant firms Armour and Swift, had hired African-American men for dangerous jobs on the loading docks, cold-storage areas, and killing floors. Black women had also been hired for some of the most difficult jobs, although the canning and wrapping positions remained staffed entirely by whites. The twelve thousand black employees filled about 20 percent of the jobs in the meat-packing industry.

By 1919, no union could hope to organize either the steel or the meat-packing industry without the support of African-American workers. The twenty-four AFL unions that had joined in the steel drive had made almost no effort to recruit African-American employees. On the other hand, the AFL unions that constituted the Stockyards Labor Council, which sought to organize the packing houses, had reached out to black workers and had won the backing of many veteran African-American employees, although recent migrants, more suspicious of unions, were reluctant to sign up. By July 1919, the union effort had garnered tremendous support from Poles, Lithuanians, and other immigrants who worked in the plants, but the organizing drive had to be conducted against the backdrop of fears concerning layoffs and growing tensions between whites and blacks on the factory floor.

In a city seething with tensions, it took just one incident to touch off a racial conflagration. This occurred in late July when a fourteen-year-old black youth was stoned to death after his raft had drifted into an area that whites had designated for their own use. Over the next two weeks, whites and blacks fought one another in pitched battles that spread to many areas of the city. Gangs invaded black neighborhoods, shooting at random. African Americans responded to fire with fire. Whites randomly assaulted blacks, who responded in kind. An entire block of homes inhabited by Polish and Lithuanian families went up in flames. When the Illinois National Guard restored order, twenty-three blacks and fifteen whites had been killed and hundreds had been injured or assaulted.

Following the riot, Governor Frank Lowden of Illinois appointed the Chicago Commission on Race Relations, composed of an equal number of whites and blacks, which heard considerable testimony from African-American witnesses. Its massive report, however, had almost no impact; it served more as a salve than as a basis for change. Of more immediate significance, bombings of homes occupied by African Americans who tried to move into white areas continued without letup. Blacks found it almost impossible to move out of the Black Belt, which continued to expand as new migrants arrived.

The racial conflict also had long-term repercussions for Chicago's labor movement. Even though most of the violence had occurred outside the meatpacking district, the hostile climate made it impossible for the Stockyards Labor Council to recruit African-American workers. In the aftermath of the violence, few African Americans evinced any desire to join the union, especially because the packers took steps to portray themselves as the protectors of the African-American workers. After the disastrous 1921 strike, the organizing effort fell apart, although it would eventually be revived with far more success in the late 1930s.

The hellish events revealed the intensity of white racism in the North. Southern newspapers gleefully reported the attacks and suggested that migrants might be better off if they returned home. But no other northern city experienced a riot of such dimensions (although there were some ferocious assaults on African Americans in Omaha, Nebraska, also a meat-packing center, in September 1919). W. E. B. Du Bois and other black leaders urged African Americans to leave the South, and the northward migratory movement continued.

The violent incidents declined as 1919 drew to a close, and the 1920s did not see a repeat of the wartime and postwar bloodshed. This is not surprising; racial violence in the United States has often peaked during periods of warfare. But there was one major exception to the pattern. One of the nation's most destructive riots took place in Tulsa, Oklahoma, in 1921—a riot that began when armed African Americans tried to prevent a lynching.

Tulsa had experienced a boom ever since the discovery of oil in Oklahoma. The city attracted black migrants who established successful businesses in the Greenwood district of town. One day in late May 1921, a young white female elevator operator claimed that a black man, Dick Rowland, had molested her. In response, the police jailed Rowland. When a white mob gathered outside the courthouse, armed blacks, including military veterans, showed up to protect the accused, and the two sides exchanged gunfire. This so enraged Tulsa's whites that over the next twenty-four hours, hundreds of them invaded the black area, destroyed Greenwood's homes and businesses, and killed at least thirty-five blacks. African Americans managed to shoot some of the white invaders, but most of the black population had no choice but to flee the city. Nevertheless, a grand jury refused to indict any whites and blamed the riot on "the presence of the armed negroes" and "agitation among the negroes of social equality."

A new mood of militancy became apparent in much of black America during the postwar period. The defiant spirit became associated with the New Negro, a phrase used throughout the 1920s that captured the willingness of blacks to stand up for their rights. Claude McKay, a Jamaican immigrant to the United States who had traveled much of the country, expressed the mood in a poem entitled "If We Must Die." Written a few months before the Chicago conflagration, it almost predicted the subsequent events:

> If we must die, let it not be like hogs
> Hunted and penned in an inglorious spot
> While round us bark the mad and hungry dogs,
> Making their mock at our accursed lot.
> If we must die, O let us nobly die,
> So that our precious blood may not be shed
> In vain, then even the monsters we defy

Shall be constrained to honor us though dead;
O kinsmen! we must meet the common foe
Though far outnumbered let us show us brave;
And for their thousand blows deal one deathblow,
What though before us lies the open grave,
Like men we'll face the murderous, cowardly pack
Pressed to the wall, dying, but fighting back.

Northern black leaders such as Marcus Garvey and W. E. B. Du Bois voiced similar sentiments, but they disagreed in their goals. The disputes led to bitter divisions in the black community in the 1920s.

"Up You Mighty Race": Marcus Garvey and the Universal Negro Improvement Association

More than any other black leader, Marcus Garvey captured the attention of the African-American masses in the immediate postwar period. A charismatic, colorful, and flamboyant personality, Garvey appealed to many blacks who had been disappointed that victory in the war had brought so little in terms of positive change. But by 1922, Garvey had become a cause of division in the black community, and practically every major African-American leader had come out in opposition to him.

Garvey's early travels had shaped his perspective. Born in Jamaica, he had learned the printer's trade before being employed as a timekeeper on a United Fruit Company plantation in Costa Rica. He had then journeyed through much of Central and Latin America before settling in London, where, for the first time, he met advocates of Pan-Africanism. Upon his return to Jamaica in 1914, he founded the UNIA, the organization he headed for the rest of his life. In 1916, he joined numerous other Jamaicans in moving to Harlem, which was gaining a reputation as the "Negro Capital of the World."

Harlem provided the ideal milieu for Garvey. Home to a number of West Indian radicals, its streets teemed with ferment during the war years. On warm summer evenings, hundreds of residents would gather to hear speakers suggest solutions to America's race problem. Garvey, often mounting a soapbox at 135th Street and Lenox Avenue, quickly became one of the best known and most effective of these "stepladder" orators.

By 1919, Garvey had developed his principal themes. He emphasized that African Americans should take pride in being black and should avoid miscegenation in order to maintain the purity of the race. He criticized members of the light-skinned elite for exercising a disproportionate influence in the African-American community. He condemned organizations such as the NAACP that relied on white funding or had white members. He preached the need for African Americans to remain separate from whites and to develop their own institutions, businesses, and enterprises. He argued that whites would never accept blacks on an equal basis. He extolled the richness of past African civilizations and stated that blacks in the diaspora would never be truly safe until a strong, independent African nation existed to protect them. He suggested that American blacks consider returning to Africa. Much of Garvey's thinking mirrored ideas current in the United States and in other areas of the world. The nationalist emphasis, for example, paralleled the postwar rise of movements such as the Irish Sinn Fein and the Italian Fascisti. The belief in the need for people to have their own nation echoed the Zionists, who sought to establish a Jewish homeland in Palestine. The emphasis on racial purity sounded similar to the importance given this idea by advocates of immigration restriction such as Madison Grant and Lothrop Stoddard. The idealization of African civilization reflected the emergence of leaders in Asia and Africa who had become bolder in challenging notions of Western superiority. The stress on the need to study black history came soon after the black scholar Carter G. Woodson had founded the Association for the Study of Negro Life and History.

Garvey made use of all of these ideas and themes, and historians have debated how to describe him in ideological terms. But to his supporters and admirers, Garvey represented one idea above all: pride of race. The emphasis he placed on racial consciousness was not new, but no African-American leader had ever preached this theme so effectively and with such force. This resonated with African Americans, who had been subjected to negative stereotypes in advertisements, films, minstrel shows, and children's stories, which portrayed blacks in a degrading way. To those who may have absorbed the negative images, or who used products to lighten their skin or to straighten their hair, Garvey asked one simple question: Why do you have so little self-respect?

The UNIA gained thousands of new members in 1919 and 1920. Its principal base of support remained in Harlem, where it attracted many West Indian immigrants as well as other residents. But it also established chapters in all northern cities with a significant black population, as well as in smaller communities such as Norfolk, Virginia, and Gary, Indiana. To aid in the recruitment of members, the organization sponsored its own bands, held parades, and established affiliates such as the Black Cross Nurses. The weekly the *Negro World* had one of the highest circulation figures of any African-American newspaper in the country. The capstone to this period of rapid growth came in August 1920, when more than twenty thousand supporters packed Madison Square Garden for the first International Convention of the Negro Peoples of the World. This gathering named Garvey the Provisional President of Africa and adopted the colors red, green, and black for the UNIA's emblem.

Garvey's ambitions, however, ran far ahead of his ability to implement his plans. Consistent with Garvey's belief in the need to establish black-owned businesses, the UNIA in 1919 founded its own shipping company, which it named the Black Star Line. As a propaganda device, this was a brilliant stroke because it highlighted the need to develop connections among blacks living in various nations. On a practical level, it promised to aid black travelers who suffered indignities on white-owned ships and to create jobs for black seamen. To raise capital, UNIA agents, in the style of wartime Liberty loan salesmen, sold thousands of five-dollar shares to African-American investors.

But the enterprise was a massive failure, and the business fiasco greatly damaged Garvey's reputation. None of the three ships that the Black Star Line eventually launched was particularly seaworthy, although the ships received an enthusiastic reception when docking in various Caribbean ports. The shareholders lost all of their hard-earned funds, and Garvey lacked an adequate explanation for those who had been asked to invest as an act of racial solidarity.

The UNIA encountered other problems. The 1920–22 depression made it difficult for African-American workers, who sustained a disproportionate share of the layoffs, to maintain their dues payments. A well-publicized plan for investments in Liberia never got off the ground. Surrounding himself with acolytes, Garvey created his own cult of personality; members of the UNIA were referred to as Garveyites. Reversing the status hierarchy of the African-American elite, Garvey increasingly stressed the need for racial purity, which led W. E. B. Du Bois (one of Garvey's principal targets) to accuse him of creating needless divisions within the African-American community.

By 1922, no African-American leader could ignore Garvey. Many of them made harsh attacks on a man they viewed as a clown, a charlatan, or simply an embarrassment to the black community. Some opponents may also have been jealous of the only man to gain a mass following among African Americans during the postwar period.

The real opportunity to strike at Garvey came when he met in Atlanta in June

1922 with Edward Clarke, a leader of the revived Ku Klux Klan. Garvey never made it clear why he chose to confer with one of the most prominent figures in the white supremacist organization, and his motivation can only be surmised. He evidently believed that the Klan's seal of approval would enable the UNIA to organize chapters in the South, a region that had proved more difficult to penetrate than the North. He may also have thought the meeting would be a good way to generate publicity for the UNIA, which was beginning to lose members. But a more basic calculation also influenced Garvey's thinking. He had scorned the quest for racial equality and integration. He had preached that all whites were Klansmen at heart. Why not, then, meet with a man who simply happened to be more honest about his opinions than other whites?

The Klan meeting galvanized Garvey's opponents, who could not understand how any African-American leader could meet with someone who so explicitly believed in black inferiority. Gathering under the "Garvey Must Go" banner, his enemies began to match Garvey's invective and insults.

Dislike and fear of Garvey created some unusual bedfellows. Ever since Garvey's emergence as a mass leader, the federal government had monitored his activities. By 1921, federal officials had received the cooperation of a number of Harlem activists who had become disillusioned with the UNIA. In 1922, Garvey was indicted for mail fraud. When the Justice Department delayed in bringing him to trial, eight prominent African Americans who belonged to a group calling itself the Friends of Negro Freedom urged the federal government to act swiftly to eliminate the UNIA. In 1923, Garvey was finally brought to trial and convicted by an all-white jury. He entered the Atlanta federal penitentiary in 1925. Upon his release, Garvey, who had never become a citizen, was deported as an undesirable alien in 1927.

Chapters of the UNIA survived Garvey's deportation, but the organization never again displayed the same verve it had evidenced between 1919 and 1922. Even at its peak, the UNIA's bravado had disguised its failings, and only in New York had it emerged as a true mass movement. Garvey had articulated the anger of African Americans. He had captured the disillusionment with the outcome of the war experienced by many blacks. He had spoken to the need for racial pride. He had challenged the idea that blacks should seek to work with whites. He had affected the consciousness of many people. But neither he nor his followers had succeeded in building a permanent organization. In contrast, the NAACP continued its steady pursuit of racial justice while developing new initiatives in response to the postwar lynchings and waves of violence.

The NAACP Campaign against Lynching

Founded in 1909, the NAACP expressed far more faith than had the UNIA in the potential of American democracy. A product of the Progressive Era, it had attracted the support of a number of prominent social reformers. Committed to fighting for integration and social equality, it sought full citizenship rights for African Americans. Although whites filled many of the executive positions and provided most of the funds, African Americans constituted the bulk of the membership of the various chapters.

The Great War energized the NAACP. Two prominent African Americans, James Weldon Johnson and Walter White, had joined its national staff, and the civil-rights organization aggressively set out to establish chapters in the South, a region where whites viewed any challenge to Jim Crow policies as subversive. By 1919, the NAACP had close to ninety thousand members and had become the one organization that spoke out whenever injustices to blacks occurred.

Since its founding, the NAACP had been identified with W. E. B. Du Bois, who edited its journal, the *Crisis*. Under Du Bois's direction, the *Crisis*, which appeared monthly, had become the leading magazine of black opinion in the United States. Although it carried a great deal of organizational news about the NAACP, its contents also reflected Du Bois's cosmopolitan interests, which ranged from international affairs and politics to literature, music, art, and history. Volatile in his opinions, Du Bois often reacted with eloquence and emotion to immediate events, but the major effect of his editorship was to keep the NAACP on a more aggressive course than it might have otherwise taken.

Encouraged by the wartime jump in its membership and distressed by the outbursts of violence against blacks in the South, the NAACP decided to focus its energies on gaining the passage of a bill making lynching a federal crime. To build public support for its campaign, in April 1919 the NAACP sponsored an antilynching conference and released a study, *Thirty Years of Lynching in the United States, 1889–1918*, which documented the circumstances surrounding the murder of more than twenty-five hundred African Americans in the South.

To bolster its campaign, the NAACP challenged the mythology that surrounded lynching. According to white southerners, the vast majority of lynchings occurred following sexual attacks by black men on white women. This accusation had become common during the late nineteenth century, a period when virulent racists portrayed African-American men as beasts and brutes waiting to prey on white women. The NAACP revealed that only 20 percent of all lynchings even involved accusations of sexual assault; the others occurred for a variety of reasons, including white anger at the failure of blacks to show proper deference to southern racial codes.

Lynching had thus become a means to enforce the caste system, particularly in areas of the South where blacks outnumbered whites. Quite often, African Americans had been murdered by mobs who, in a sadistic frenzy, tortured and mutilated their victims. Celebratory crowds would gather to view the corpses, which were left dangling on ropes, photographs would be taken, and postcards might even be distributed of the grisly display. In the 1890s, Ida B. Wells, who had been born in slavery, began an often lonely crusade against lynching. In the postwar period, she was joined by a number of black and white women who began to challenge southern racial mores.

On the national level, the huge Republican victory in the 1920 elections greatly encouraged the NAACP. Ever since Reconstruction, the Republicans had received the support of those African Americans who could vote. Following the disappointments of the Wilson years, African Americans had hopes for the party of Lincoln. The 1920 Republican Party platform had at least mentioned the need to end lynching. President Harding had been willing to meet with NAACP leaders; in an April 1921 message to Congress, the new chief executive had called on the legislators "to wipe the stain of barbaric lynching from the banners of a free and orderly representative democracy."

To muster support for its "Lynch Law Must Go" campaign, the NAACP sponsored rallies and demonstrations, including a silent parade that passed the White House. The chief sponsor of the antilynching bill in the House of Representatives (which had no African-American members) was Leonidas C. Dyer, a Republican and a member of the NAACP, who represented a constituency in St. Louis, Missouri, with a large black population. Congress had not seriously considered any civil rights legislation since the late nineteenth century. Southern Democrats objected to the Dyer bill (as it became known) on the grounds that it infringed on states' rights, although many of the same congressmen had favored the Prohibition amendment, which had greatly extended the jurisdiction of the federal government over the states.

Despite southern opposition, and following diligent lobbying by the NAACP, the House of Representatives in January 1922 passed the Dyer bill by a decisive 232 to 119 margin. But when the bill reached the Senate floor, southern Democrats began a filibuster that threatened a ship-subsidy measure strongly favored by the Harding administration; in order to gain action on the ship bill, the Republicans withdrew the antilynching measure from consideration.

Furious NAACP members—already upset over the Harding administration's failure to appoint African Americans to traditional "Negro positions"—believed they had been betrayed. Du Bois and black newspaper editors such as the *Chicago Defender*'s Robert S. Abbott suspected that the Republicans had sold them out in order to woo potential white supporters in the South. Both Dyer and the NAACP continued to champion the bill, but in the 1920s it never again came so close to passage.

Despite the bill's defeat, the NAACP could be proud that it had launched the effort to make lynching a federal crime. But with the decline of reform senti- ment, the NAACP found it more and more difficult to sustain enthusiasm for campaigns such as the anti-lynching effort. Flush with excitement, the NAACP in 1919 had announced that it sought to achieve a membership of 250,000. In- stead, by 1929, the organization had lost more than half of its 1919 membership. The loss of chapters was particularly severe in the South, where many of the branches established in the immediate postwar period disappeared by 1923. Nev- ertheless, the NAACP remained ready to pick up the cudgels for African Amer- icans who had been wronged. And in the South, its chapters (located mainly in urban areas) stood in the forefront of efforts to bring change to a region where segregation and white supremacy had become a way of life.

Halting Change in the South and the Renewal of Mass Migration to the North

Not all white southerners reacted to the postwar wave of violence and lynchings with equanimity. Concerned about the changes brought about by the war, in December 1918 a number of Atlanta-area residents—calling themselves the Committee on After-War Cooperation—began to meet on a regular basis. By 1920, the organization had become known as the Commission on Interracial Cooperation (CIC), and had taken on the daunting task of improving race re- lations in the South. A number of Atlanta's leading citizens had invited the NAACP to hold its 1920 national convention in the city; this was the first time the organization had ever met in the South.

During the early 1920s, the CIC established state chapters and branches in a number of southern cities. It attracted businessmen concerned about the con- tinued outflow of black labor and reformers anxious to establish lines of com- munication with blacks. Will Winton Alexander, its founder, was a Methodist minister, and many of the men and women who joined had been active in the Young Men's Christian Association, the Young Women's Christian Association,

and other Protestant-influenced groups. A number of African-American edu-
cators, who preferred the CIC's more moderate approach to the militancy of the
NAACP, also became members of the interracial organization.

The CIC provided a forum that allowed whites and blacks to establish a dialogue. In addition, it conducted research, campaigned for state antilynching
laws, and sponsored black speakers who lectured to white college audiences. But
many of the CIC's white members retained a paternalistic approach in their
dealings with blacks, and much of the early enthusiasm for the organization had
faded by the late 1920s.

Prodding by the CIC did lead to the publication of one remarkable pamphlet. In 1921, the group convinced outgoing Georgia governor Hugh M. Dorsey
to release a study of the physical abuse of Georgia's blacks. It documented 135
cases of white terror, violence, and forced servitude. Historian John Dittmer
described it as "probably the most candid and courageous attack on racial in-
justice issued by an American governor." The NAACP and other black organizations warmly welcomed its publication, but most Georgia whites scorned its
findings, and the new governor paid little attention to it.

Efforts to stem lynching did have some impact. A number of white women
who belonged to the CIC's women's committees took the lead in this endeavor.
Refuting the elaborate mythology that surrounded lynching, these southern
women challenged the idea that helpless southern ladies needed white men to
protect them against black rapists. Resenting an ideology that placed them on
a pedestal, they argued that southern notions of manhood had been used to oppress both white women and black men. Their efforts, along with those of the
NAACP, made a difference. Southern officials during the 1920s began to disperse
lynch mobs and in some cases even got indictments against their leaders. The
number of lynchings steadily declined from seventy-six in 1919 to sixteen in
1924, leading W. E. B. Du Bois to declare that a decisive change had occurred
in the South.

The early 1920s also saw some stirrings of black protest in the South. The
most notable example involved the controversy surrounding a hospital for
African-American veterans that opened in Tuskegee, Alabama, in 1923. Although
most black leaders opposed segregation, they consented to the construction of
a separate institution because African-American veterans had received dis-
graceful treatment when confined to Jim Crow wings of southern hospitals.
They also agreed to its construction because they had been led to believe that
black doctors and nurses would staff it, ensuring proper care for African-American veterans and providing positions for black medical personnel, who for once

would have an opportunity to practice in an up-to-date facility. But when the institution opened, the Veterans' Bureau, reneging on its prior promises, hired white medical personnel for all the top positions.

The failure to appoint a black staff was a clarion call to African Americans, who viewed the hospital as a means of recognizing their contributions to the war effort. Groups ranging from the National Medical Association (an organization of black doctors) to the NAACP mounted a protest. The president of the Tuskegee Institute, Robert Russa Moton, whose institution had donated land for the hospital, stood up to the Ku Klux Klan when it mounted a huge demonstration demanding that the hospital maintain an all-white staff. After a complicated series of maneuvers and some compromises (which caused the NAACP to withdraw from the controversy), Moton and his allies accomplished their central goal. Tuskegee Veterans' Hospital became a black-run facility, fulfilling the *Chicago Defender*'s dream that it would become "a moral fortress of the Negro race."

Dissent also began to be voiced on southern black college campuses. For example, students at Fisk University, one of the most prestigious of the black colleges, protested the tyrannical rule of their white president, Fayette Avery McKenzie, who strictly monitored every aspect of campus life. In November 1924, students demanding McKenzie's firing interrupted a board of trustees' meeting and received the support of Du Bois (a Fisk graduate whose daughter attended the institution) and many members of Nashville's black community. Faced with unrelenting pressure, McKenzie resigned, and the new president, Thomas Elsa Jones, who was also white, instituted a series of reforms that eliminated the most onerous regulations and that greatly improved Fisk's academic standing.

The more assertive mood associated with the New Negro also affected Virginia's Hampton Institute, where students engaged in a series of protests. Some of their goals involved permission to establish fraternities and sororities, whose popularity was increasing on many college campuses during the 1920s. But students also took umbrage at the school's focus on vocational programs rather than on the liberal arts, and the college's practice of having the glee club perform spirituals and plantation songs before approving white audiences. Like the students at Fisk, they received the support of Du Bois and accomplished many of their goals even though a 1927 student strike had been unsuccessful.

Tuskegee, Fisk, and Hampton indicated that the new mood of militancy was not confined to the North. In much of the South, however, protest still carried the threat of violent retaliation, and African Americans remained fearful of speaking out. Only in a few southern cities did African-American women have any success when they attempted to register to vote following the passage of the Nineteenth Amendment. Legal executions continued with regularity, and a number of southern states had merely replaced the notorious convict lease system (by which prisoners had worked for private employers) with the chain gang. Spasms of violence still occurred. In Ocoee, Florida, in 1920, whites massacred blacks attempting to vote; in Rosewood, Florida, in 1923, whites burned the entire black community to the ground. Particularly in rural areas, despite talk that the fear of losing their labor supply would force change upon the South, the rhythms of daily life remained much the same.

The South remained a poor and overwhelmingly agricultural region dependent on sugar, rice, tobacco, and above all cotton, which was grown in a broad swath stretching from North Carolina through eastern Texas. The wartime rise in cotton prices had ended abruptly in 1920; prices for cotton, like those for other crops, remained low throughout the decade. White and black farmers alike, whether sharecroppers or tenants, remained entrapped in what novelist Richard Wright called in *Black Boy* the "hateful web of cotton culture" that caused them to plant more and more in a desperate effort to survive. The hoe remained an essential tool, and in contrast to the North, where tractors had become common, sharecroppers and tenants still relied on mule-drawn plows. For a short time in the 1920s, some landlords, in an effort to prevent the loss of labor, supplied cash advances, but this experiment did not last long, and most sharecroppers had to wait until the end of the year for their accounts to be settled. Living in one-room or two-room shacks, often drinking contaminated well water, consuming a "white food" diet consisting of fat pork, cornmeal, grits, and molasses, sharecroppers suffered from extremely high rates of diseases such as tuberculosis, hookworm, and pellagra. Adding to cotton farmers' woes, the boll weevil, which came from Mexico and which had eaten its way across the South, finally reached the Atlantic Coast states between 1917 and 1921.

Not surprisingly, many sharecroppers throughout the 1920s abandoned cotton. Some African Americans moved to southern cities, where they lived in neighborhoods lacking urban conveniences such as running water, electricity, and paved streets. They also faced intensified job competition from whites, who began to replace African Americans as truck drivers, building tradesmen, and street cleaners. African Americans remained barred from all but the most menial jobs in textile factories and confined to the most tedious tasks in tobacco factories. Black men worked mainly as hospital orderlies, elevator operators, janitors, and porters; black women worked mainly as cooks, washerwomen, and

domestics. Probably the major gain came in the area of education; many southern cities began to provide high schools for the first time for African Americans.

Many urban and rural residents moved to the North. During the industrial
depression in 1920 and 1921, a number of blacks who lost their jobs returned
to the South. But a second massive wave of migration to the North, which began
in 1922 and picked up steam in 1923, marked a major turning point and demonstrated that the North had not lost its appeal to those fed up with life in Dixie.

The 1923 "rush to the North" stunned many white southerners. The magnitude of the outward migration destroyed any illusion that the wartime movement had been an aberration and served as proof that many migrants had found
life in the North superior to that in the South. The hardest-hit states turned out
to be those that had been most affected by the boll weevil. Georgia suffered the
highest loss of population; one report claimed that sixty-cight thousand blacks
left the state in a single four-month period. Approximately twenty-four thousand blacks abandoned South Carolina in the first seven months of 1923, and
North Carolina could not complete its highway projects because of the shortage of labor. The outward migration affected all of the southern states, and so
many farm laborers left the cotton fields of the Mississippi-Arkansas Delta that
landlords feared the harvest might be threatened.

The sudden jump in migration was caused by two interrelated factors. The
industrial boom that began in 1923 created a vast number of new jobs; the decision of U. S. Steel to switch from the twelve-hour day to the eight-hour day almost overnight opened up thousands of positions. And Congress in 1921 had
restricted immigration, a restriction made far more severe by another law enacted in 1924. Since 1916, whenever immigration from Europe declined, migration from the South increased, and this proved true for the rest of the decade as
northern industry continued to tap the African-American labor reserve in the
South. To put it more bluntly, immigration restriction opened up jobs for African
Americans—a point made by a number of observers at the time.

Disproportionately young and often more ambitious than those who remained behind, African Americans moved north with a sense of purpose and
hope. Some migrants, making use of kin networks, joined relatives. The *Chicago
Defender* (which ran a "Come Out of the South" department) reported that large
crowds gathered to greet arriving trains. Others sought a better education or decided that if they could not vote in the South, they would vote with their feet.
Many might have asked, as Richard Wright did, "What kind of life was possible under that hate?" and decided to take their chances with a region that represented "all" they had "not felt and seen."

African Americans made it clear that they considered migration a form of protest against conditions in the South. At a 1923 conference of black leaders in Georgia, those who gathered cited "lack of credit facilities for Negro farmers," "bad working conditions on plantations managed by overseers in the absence of owners," and "poor accommodations for Negroes while traveling" among the factors causing blacks to leave. A similar 1923 meeting in Mississippi mentioned the paucity of spending for black schools, exclusion of blacks from juries, and southern opposition to the Dyer antilynching bill as reasons for the mass departure. Emboldened by landlords' fears of labor shortages, some southern blacks became more forthright in stating their grievances. In Mississippi—the most repressive of all southern states—a 1923 African-American convention prepared a twenty-one-point bill of grievances.

The demands led to only minor adjustments in the South, and the northward movement continued for the rest of the decade. Following the same routes as the wartime migrants, African Americans concentrated in the major industrial cities of the Midwest, the smaller steel towns, and the East Coast cities. By 1929, approximately two million African Americans lived in the North, which became the area where the swiftest and most dynamic changes occurred.

Making a Place for Themselves: Work and Community Formation in the North during the 1920s

The top priority of most migrants remained finding a job, and the basic employment pattern that had been established during the war remained in place. Black men and women had far more success obtaining jobs in open-shop industries than in sectors of the economy that had been unionized. Employers paid black workers the same wages as white workers for performing the same jobs, but African Americans almost never were promoted into the more skilled positions. The availability of industrial jobs signified progress in the black community and was an indication that a permanent African-American working class was beginning to emerge. With skilled jobs such as those in the building trades closed to them, those who worked for the United States Post Office or as Pullman porters held some of the most prestigious positions, but African-American men who labored in industry also were proud of their status.

The steel, automobile, and meat-packing industries became the largest employers of black men. Beginning in 1916, the steel industry had hired large numbers of black workers, and it had flagrantly used African-American strikebreakers during the 1919 steel strike. Many black employees had lost their jobs during the 1920–21 depression, but the industrial boom and the switch from the twelve-hour day to the eight-hour day created more than fifty thousand new jobs. African Americans continued to find employment in large steel centers such as Buffalo, Cleveland, Pittsburgh, and Chicago, and in smaller steel cities such as Youngstown, Ohio, and Gary, Indiana. By the mid-1920s, they filled approximately 20 percent of all steel jobs. Whether employed by U. S. Steel, Jones and Laughlin, Republic, or any of the other large steel producers, African Americans generally found themselves confined to the dangerous "hot jobs" around coke ovens, open hearths, and blast furnaces.

Tens of thousands of new jobs also opened up in the burgeoning automobile industry. In automobile manufacturing, far more than in steel, employers' racial hiring policies varied. General Motors hired a minimal number of African-American workers. But the Ford Motor Company made a concerted effort to hire African Americans, and as a result, Detroit's black population swelled from 40,000 in 1920 to 120,000 in 1930.

Ford's hiring policies reflected the idiosyncrasies of the firm's president, Henry Ford. A virulent anti-Semite, Ford devoted much of his own newspaper, the *Dearborn Independent*, to denunciations of the "International Jew." In general, he distrusted immigrants from southern and eastern Europe. By contrast, he believed that African Americans would be loyal and devoted employees, unlikely to support either radical causes or trade unions. Ford believed that church members would make the most dependable employees, and when hiring workers, he relied heavily on the recommendations of some of Detroit's leading ministers. He became known as a benefactor in the black community, especially because he had hired ten thousand black workers for the firm's enormous River Rouge complex. Other automobile manufacturers such as Packard and Dodge employed black workers almost exclusively in the least-desirable jobs, but Ford gave them the opportunity to work in various assembly operations, to be trained for skilled positions, and even to supervise white employees, a rare occurrence in any industry.

Bitter about the AFL's discriminatory policies and aware of labor's rapid decline, many African-American leaders believed that black workers had little to gain by joining the struggle for trade unions. In a widely read 1925 *American Mercury* article, "The Negro as a Workingman," Kelly Miller, the dean of Howard University's College of Arts and Sciences, argued that the "white laboring man" had "nothing to give" black workers, who should instead "stand shoulder to shoulder with the captains of industry."

A. Philip Randolph, for one, dissented. This Florida-born labor leader had emerged during World War I as one of Harlem's leading radicals. Seeing the decline of the left in the early 1920s, Randolph had moderated his views, but he remained firm in his belief that African Americans needed to ally themselves with the trade-union movement. In 1925, along with other activists, he founded the Brotherhood of Sleeping Car Porters, which began to challenge the paternalistic rule of the Pullman Palace Car Company, one of the largest employers of African-American labor in the country. Pullman porters, who often worked eighty-hour weeks, and who were subjected to a demeaning tipping system and forced to join an employee representation plan, had good reason to join a union. The effort did not fully succeed until the mid-1930s, but even by the late 1920s, it had gained considerable support from Pullman porters moved by a new spirit of independence.

Black women had fewer employment choices than black men. In northern cities, they found it almost impossible to obtain any jobs that involved dealing with the public. Telephone companies and department stores refused to hire African-American women as operators and clerks. Even when they obtained jobs in the meat-packing plants, black women were not allowed to handle the finished products. Employers claimed that their white female employees opposed working with African-American women. They also refused to hire African-American women for positions in the rapidly expanding clerical field. Some black women became schoolteachers or nurses, but it was not unusual to find highly educated African-American women (like black men) doing jobs requiring little formal education.

The discriminatory policies meant that employment patterns for black women in the North did not vary much from those in the South. A higher percentage of married black women than married white women worked, and domestic service became the most common form of employment for African-American women. Domestic service required far more day-to-day deference than industrial work. Daughters of immigrant parents sought any job other than this. To replace them, well-to-do northern families increasingly hired African-American women, although they often refused to live in, preferring to return to their own homes at night.

Migrants to the North in the late 1920s began to experience difficulty in finding jobs. As the industrial boom slowed down, the unemployment rate of black workers in 1927 and 1928 rose. Nevertheless, wages earned by black employees fueled the growth of a number of autonomous black institutions that flourished during the 1920s.

The church stood out as the paramount institution in the black community.

But the churches also perpetuated preexisting divisions. In cities such as New York, Philadelphia, Cleveland, and Chicago that had small but well-established African-American populations dating back to the nineteenth century, older black residents usually attended Episcopalian or Presbyterian churches. This color-conscious, light-skinned elite, which Garvey so scorned, had been extremely critical of the customs and mores of the wartime migrants, and often blamed them for the rise in discrimination that began to affect all blacks living in northern cities. Embarrassed by the migrants' behavior, they had no desire to welcome them to their churches, which, even when led by charismatic ministers, had a well-defined sense of decorum.

In any case, the migrants did not necessarily want to join such churches. Retaining many elements of a distinctive southern black culture, they often joined Holiness, Pentecostal, Baptist, or other congregations that made more use of the shouting tradition or of the call-and-response pattern of worship that was a distinctive element of black Christianity. The storefront churches, often led by dynamic preachers who could whip their congregations into a frenzy, provided great comfort to those who had not necessarily shed their superstitions or their country ways just because they had moved to the city.

Churches filled a number of important functions. Ministers found jobs for parishioners; congregations sponsored clubs that brought people together for fellowship and outings. For women in particular, the church served as an important social outlet and provided one of the few gathering places outside the home. Most of all, churches gave parishioners a space of their own where they could share a few hours of prayer, hope, and togetherness each week.

For the most part, African Americans in the North did not have to be so humble or so deferential on a day-to-day basis as they did in the South. Northern cities did not have signs reading For Colored Only and For Whites Only. Some communities, such as Indianapolis, Indiana, and Cincinnati, Ohio, required blacks to attend segregated schools, although this was not typical. But despite laws that had been passed in a number of northern states guaranteeing access to public accommodations, blacks found that many hotels and restaurants would not serve them, theaters required them to sit in balconies, and amusement parks only admitted them on special Jim Crow days. The *Chicago Defender*, which could be extremely harsh in its condemnation of the conduct of the recent migrants, blamed "vile and loud talking men" and "howling mobs of blatant buzzards" for causing the restrictions, but informal segregation became common in all northern cities because of whites' racist reaction to the growing black population.

Hospitals also discriminated against African Americans. Patients often found that northern hospitals would not admit them at all, or confined them to segregated wings. Only a few hospitals granted black doctors admitting privileges. In response, the National Medical Association and its sister organization, the National Hospital Association, launched a black hospital movement, which took a twofold approach. With the aid of black politicians and community activists, they fought for the appointment of African-American doctors to staff positions, a battle they won at institutions such as Harlem Hospital and Cleveland City Hospital. Although some African Americans believed that the fight for integration should not be abandoned, other leaders sought to establish black-controlled hospitals that would provide African-American patients with first-class facilities and understanding care. Chicago's Provident Hospital, a source of considerable pride in the black community, became such an institution. Even as late as the 1950s, a black hospital opened in Cleveland.

Baseball, the national pastime, forced blacks to establish their own parallel institutions. Sparked by the astounding home run exploits of Babe Ruth, interest in major league baseball increased rapidly in the 1920s. Traditionally, the "American game" had provided an opportunity for immigrants, and by the 1920s, Italian, Polish, and Jewish players began to appear on major league rosters along with those from Irish and German backgrounds. African Americans had been barred from organized baseball since 1887, although a few Cubans had managed to pass. No explicit edict had banned black ballplayers; their exclusion had been accomplished by a gentlemen's agreement. By the early 1900s, blacks had begun to organize their own teams, and in 1920, Rube Foster, a pitcher for the Chicago American Giants, played a key role in the organization of the first formal Negro League, whose teams usually played in midwestern cities and often used big-league ballparks. Black fans, with money in their pockets, flocked to the games, and despite the efforts of baseball's czar, Kennesaw Mountain Landis, to prevent it, black and white players began to face off against one another during postseason barnstorming tours.

The mainstream press rarely carried any news about the Negro Leagues— or any other news about African Americans, for that matter. The African-American newspapers filled the gap, and examples such as the *Chicago Defender, Pittsburgh Courier,* and *Baltimore Afro-American* enjoyed a wide circulation. Some papers, emulating the tabloids, gave sensationalist coverage to crime, and given the difficulty migrants had in adjusting to the hard city streets, there were many murders and robberies to report. The papers also contained a great deal of information about the solid achievements of African Americans, however, and they played an indispensable role in an era when people still relied on the press for their news.

Cities also provided African-American musicians and filmmakers with a growing audience during the 1920s. Southern blacks had often packed juke joints and honky-tonks, enjoying a lively nightlife. In northern cities, they filled cabarets, dance halls, and after-hours clubs where bootleg liquor flowed and the police generally looked the other way. Mississippi Delta migrants brought the blues to Chicago, and this music found a new home while undergoing numerous transformations. Theaters in the black community showed "race films" produced for and by blacks, before the development of "talkies" made production costs prohibitive. And for those who stayed at home, "race records" produced by major studios allowed them to listen to such greats as Bessie Smith and Ma Rainey on the radio or the Victrola.

Harlem became the cultural capital of black America during the 1920s. Located in uptown Manhattan, it attracted African-American writers, poets, artists, and musicians who sought the stimulation, energy, and excitement that the district offered. Harlem differed in many ways from other northern black communities. Most of its male residents worked in the service sector rather than in industry. Developed initially as a residential area for middle-class whites, Harlem contained some of New York City's finest brownstones. It was home to many West Indian immigrants and had become an area of considerable ethnic diversity; it was also home to a number of African-American organizations and to publications with a national circulation.

During the 1920s, the community became identified with a cultural movement known as the Harlem Renaissance. Some of the writers identified with the Harlem Renaissance, such as Langston Hughes, were embarking on long and distinguished writing careers; others, such as Jean Toomer, author of the poetic novel *Cane*, never wrote another significant work; some, such as Zora Neale Hurston, fell into obscurity, only to be rediscovered by later generations. Earthy, colorful, and often sensual, their works lacked the cynicism or existential angst of such Lost Generation writers as Sinclair Lewis, F. Scott Fitzgerald, and Ernest Hemingway. Participants in the Harlem Renaissance had an exaggerated sense of their ability to affect the black population. But at the time, novelists and poets received considerable support from the broader community. Both the *Crisis* and the *Opportunity* published fiction and poetry and sponsored prizes to encourage aspiring African-American writers. The writers received further encouragement from wealthy white patrons and from H. L. Mencken, the nation's most brilliant and caustic critic and a student of the English language who admired good writers, especially those who stood outside the mainstream.

A tone of optimism pervaded the Harlem Renaissance. This was best captured in a 1925 anthology entitled *The New Negro*, edited by the Howard University scholar Alain Locke. Dedicated to "the Younger Generation," the volume contained short stories, poetry, music, analytical essays, and artwork, including reproductions of African art. Many of the authors implicitly acknowledged that the burst of creativity would not have been possible in the more closed atmosphere of the South. Far less defensive than in the past, many of the essayists celebrated joyful aspects of African-American life, and most of the contributors probably would have agreed with historian J. A. Rogers's observation in the volume that "those who laugh and dance and sing are better off even in their vices than those who do not."

Sharing in the optimistic mood, the African-American press had begun by mid-decade to give prominent coverage to the successes of African-American business. In many cases, the successes were exaggerated; for all the efforts of the UNIA and others who pushed for the founding of "race enterprises," the number of black-owned businesses grew slowly. In response to the discrimination that African Americans faced, black businessmen founded a number of insurance and real-estate agencies. Undertakers had traditionally played an important role in the black community, and black-owned barber shops, always a popular gathering place, dotted the ghetto, while black women ran restaurants, beauty shops, and rooming houses. In Chicago, black businessman Jesse Binga established his own bank and became a powerful political and economic force in that community.

But only Harlem, where West Indian immigrants established a number of small enterprises, had a thriving black retail sector. In contrast, migrants from the South, much like the Slavic immigrants, lacked the tradition, experience, and capital required for initiating such enterprises. As a result, whites owned a majority of the stores in the black community, which led to complaints about profiteers. Despite their dependence on black shoppers, many of the businesses hired African Americans for only the most menial positions. In protest, a "spend your money where you work" movement emerged in Chicago and spread to a number of black communities during the 1930s.

Politics provided a means of advancement for a small number of ambitious men. African Americans made up only about 7 to 15 percent of the population in large cities such as New York, Philadelphia, Detroit, and Chicago, and blacks thus played a secondary role in the political machine. When Chicago's Oscar de Priest won election to Congress in 1929, he became the first northern black ever elected to that body, and the first African American in the House of Representatives since 1901. Their lack of clout meant that black politicians could only obtain a limited number of city positions for their constituents, in contrast to the Irish, who often placed new arrivals in jobs almost as soon as they got off the boat.

Machine politics, by its very nature, encouraged tunnel vision, and African-American urban politicians generally had little interest in national issues. Even those ward or precinct bosses who on the surface appeared to be militant "race men" followed the dictates of the machine. "Clientage politics" also had an unsavory side, and the black community often became a center for gambling, prostitution, and other illegal activities in which politicians had a stake.

During the 1920s, the urban areas where African Americans lived began to be commonly referred to as ghettos, a term derived from the word for the walled quarters of Italian cities where Jews had been forced to live. Whatever optimism African Americans expressed about the positive aspects of moving north was tempered by the harsh reality that, regardless of income, they could only live in certain sections of the city. In most cities, the ghetto consisted of one area, although in a few communities, such as Pittsburgh, blacks lived in widely scattered sections.

Throughout the decade, most ghettos expanded as the black population moved into adjoining areas. Real-estate agents, using a practice known as blockbusting, often induced panic selling by whites, forcing them to sell their homes at below market value, and then reselling or renting the houses to African Americans at a considerable profit. In many white residential areas, homeowners began to employ restrictive covenants that forbade the owner of a home from selling to African Americans or to Jews. The National Association of Real Estate Boards actually included restrictive covenants as part of its code of ethics, and in a 1926 decision, the deeply conservative Supreme Court upheld their legality.

When African Americans managed to buy houses outside the ghetto, organized mobs or firebombings might force them to abandon their homes. Clashes over housing became most common in cities experiencing rapid population growth, and by the middle of the 1920s, Detroit's racial tensions rivaled those of Chicago. In one of the decade's most notorious incidents, Dr. Ossian Sweet and his family became the target of unruly crowds when they attempted to move into an all-white area. In September 1925, Dr. Sweet killed a member of one of these mobs, which had gathered outside his home at midnight. In response, Detroit mayor John Smith, who had been elected with black support, commented: "I believe that any colored person who endangers life and property, simply to gratify his personal pride, is an enemy of his race as well as an incitant of riot and murder," and a grand jury indicted Dr. Sweet on a charge of premeditated murder. With the aid of the brilliant defense attorney Clarence Darrow, Dr. Sweet won an acquittal after his first trial ended in a hung jury. But Dr. Sweet never recovered from the painful experience, and he later committed suicide.

Dr. Sweet's ordeal symbolized the trauma that African Americans suffered in their search for housing. Forced to live a considerable distance from their place of employment, African Americans often had little choice but to take in lodgers to help pay the excessive rents. The black population, living in crowded quarters, suffered from extremely high rates of tuberculosis and other communicable diseases. Although recent immigrants during the 1920s began to buy homes outside their original areas of settlement, African Americans remained tightly confined in some of the most densely populated sections of northern cities.

The sorry housing situation demonstrated the harsh limitations that African Americans faced in their search for a better life in the North. Most likely, members of the African-American community would have disagreed among themselves if asked to assess how much they had gained by moving from the South to the North. It is reasonable to believe that the freer atmosphere of the North and the industrial boom between 1923 and 1928 had given many African Americans a glimpse at a better life and had confirmed W. E. B. Du Bois's prediction that migration would serve as a vehicle for advancement. In retrospect, although the 1920s could hardly be considered a new era for northern blacks, it represented a period of hope and of institution building.

Tragically, many of the gains quickly disappeared once the Great Depression began. Blacks were the first workers laid off, housing conditions seriously deteriorated, and a large percentage of the northern black population became dependent on the meager relief allotments of cities and of private agencies. As a sign of the devastation, Chicago's Binga State Bank, the nation's most successful black-owned financial institution, collapsed in 1930, and many depositors lost their life savings. By the early 1930s, numbers racketeers had become some of the most successful "businessmen" in the black community, and they owned a number of the Negro League teams. Nevertheless, most of the migrants remained in the North, where their presence added to the mixed population that so disturbed those who viewed themselves as the defenders of tradition.

6

THE RAPID RISE AND THE SWIFT DECLINE OF THE KU KLUX KLAN

DURING THE EARLY 1920s, the Ku Klux Klan rose to a position of influence in many areas of the country. Appealing to Protestants' anti-Catholicism, emphasizing the need to enforce Prohibition, and capitalizing on the sour, antiforeign mood, the Klan became a lightning rod for many of the postwar fears and resentments. By 1923, it had become a force to reckon with in states such as Texas, Indiana, Colorado, and Oregon, and the source of great national controversy. But the Klan also provoked widespread opposition and faced a number of internal difficulties; amid the mid-decade prosperity, it fell into insignificance.

The Reborn Klan

The original Ku Klux Klan was a terrorist organization that used violence in an effort to overthrow the Reconstruction governments that had been established in the South following the Civil War. Disguised in long flowing robes, hooded Klansmen had assassinated a number of African Americans and their white supporters, and targeted schoolteachers and African-American officeholders. Klansmen included some of the South's leading citizens. In 1871, the federal government suppressed the Klan, although a number of similar organizations continued its work until the final overthrow of Reconstruction in 1877.

Interest in the Klan revived with the appearance of *The Birth of a Nation* in 1915. A movie based on a 1905 novel, *The Clansman* by Thomas Dixon, it has been described by historian Fred Silva as "the most controversial American film ever made." The first half of the motion picture depicted Civil War battle scenes so graphic that they might have convinced many Americans not to participate in the slaughter then taking place in Europe. The second half of the film, however, which portrayed the heroic Ku Klux Klan rescuing southern white women

from brutal and bestial blacks and their northern allies, captured the most attention and helped account for the record-breaking audiences that saw the
movie.

Hoping to capitalize on the film's popularity, an obscure circuit-riding
Methodist Episcopal minister and Spanish-American War veteran by the name
of William J. Simmons decided that the time had come to revive the Klan. On
Thanksgiving Eve in 1915, Simmons and about fifteen of his friends climbed to
the peak of Stone Mountain near Atlanta and set fire to a cross, signaling the rebirth of the Klan. Although this second Klan had no direct connection to the first,
it claimed to be its successor and adopted its rituals, language, and costumes.

The new Klan limited membership to native-born, white Protestants; it excluded Catholics and Jews as well as African Americans. Between 1915 and 1920,
despite the use of *The Birth of a Nation* as a recruiting tool, it attracted only a
few supporters. But in 1920, Colonel Simmons (the title had been conferred by
a fraternal organization, the Woodmen of the World) hired two publicists,
Edward Clarke and Elizabeth Tyler, who had raised money for groups such as
the Red Cross, the YMCA, and the Anti-Saloon League. During the war, Clarke
and Tyler had been impressed by the power of propaganda and advertising.
They typified the opportunists that the Klan attracted in that these two "salesmen of hate" viewed the hooded order mainly as a moneymaking scheme.
Clarke and Tyler convinced Simmons that the Klan needed to adopt modern
sales techniques, and they instituted a system by which each local recruiter received four dollars of the ten-dollar initiation fee. Appealing to the heightened
sense of nationalism engendered by the war, the Red Scare, and the League of
Nations debate, they began to advertise the Klan as a 100 percent American organization that would clamp down on African Americans, foreigners, Catholics,
Jews, law violators, immoral men and women, and a host of other evil forces.

Making use of Clarke's and Tyler's marketing techniques, during the depression years of 1920 and 1921 the Klan began to gain members throughout
Georgia and in Alabama, Louisiana, Oklahoma, and Texas. Even in the Deep
South states, the Klan did not focus on African Americans; its rise coincided
with the decline in lynchings. It primarily aimed its fire at Prohibition violators
and at those who transgressed its own moral standards. Portraying itself as the
defender of "pure womanhood" and expressing the belief that the war had led
to a loosening of morals, the Klan voiced concern with evils such as "loose danc-
ing," "petting parties," and "roadside parking." Particularly in Texas and Oklahoma, the Klan began to mete out its own version of rough justice to those it
accused of being adulterers, joyriders, wife-beaters, and abortionists. Violators

of the Victorian moral code might be kidnapped, whipped, flogged, branded, mutilated, tarred and feathered, or simply warned by signs with messages such as "Wife-beaters, family-deserters, home-wreckers, we have no room for you," "Go joy riding with your own wife," or "Fooling around the other fellow's home is not wise." Most of the victims were white men and women, although the Klan also used violence against African Americans whom it viewed as stepping out of line or accused of cohabiting with whites.

Reports of Klan activities alarmed many liberal-minded Americans already concerned by the extent to which wartime hatreds had been perpetuated in the postwar period. In September 1921, the *New York World* published a series of articles exposing the Klan that a number of other leading newspapers reprinted. Partly because of the publicity that the *New York World* series received, the House of Representatives initiated an investigation of the Klan. To the disappointment of the Klan's opponents, this inquiry backfired, and according to John Moffatt Mecklin, a critic of the KKK, it provided the Klan with "a vast amount of gratuitous and invaluable advertising." William J. Simmons, appearing before a congressional committee, gave a masterful performance. Fighting to restrain his tears, he disavowed all acts of violence committed in the Klan's name. Faced with a counterthreat to investigate the Knights of Columbus, an embarrassed House of Representatives dropped the investigation on 17 October 1921.

The congressional hearings brought the Klan helpful publicity, and during 1922 the Klan began to expand into the North. But many Klansmen were disturbed by the negative publicity that Clarke and Tyler brought to the organization. The *New York World* had reported that a partially clad Clarke and Tyler had been arrested by Atlanta police in 1919 and charged with disorderly conduct, and that Clarke had deserted his wife. In September 1922, shortly after having delivered a speech calling for the enforcement of Prohibition, Clarke was arrested and charged with possession of alcohol. Colonel Simmons, who also had a fondness for the bottle, stood by his comrades, but other Klansmen demanded that the organization be cleaned up.

In November 1922, a Dallas dentist, Hiram Wesley Evans, seized control of the Klan, expelled Simmons, Clarke, and Tyler, and proclaimed himself the new imperial wizard of the KKK. (The takeover occurred soon after Clarke's much-publicized meeting with Marcus Garvey, but this was not an issue in the Klan infighting.) Evans set out to reform the Klan. He tried to make the Klan more respectable by stressing its belief in "education, temperance, the flag, Protestantism and charity." A strong advocate of Nordic superiority and fearful of those he labeled the mongrel races, he stressed the danger that immigrants posed to the nation. The Klan made great use of local recruiters and expanded into many areas of the country. According to some estimates, it gained more than two million new members. It attracted many of those who belonged to the Masons and other fraternal groups. The Klan won its greatest support in heavily Protestant areas of Michigan, Ohio, Indiana, Illinois, Colorado, and Oregon, but it also developed pockets of support in areas as diverse as Worcester, Massachusetts, southern New Jersey, and Anaheim, California.

The Klan's burst of growth surprised many people. A number of observers at the time blamed it on the aftereffects of the war. According to this interpretation, the war had unleashed hatreds that needed a new focus. Some columnists suggested that the military conflict had ended so abruptly that the extreme anti-German feeling that the government had stimulated needed new targets. Other pundits pointed out that the war had accustomed people to propaganda and exaggeration and to spying on their neighbors. In addition, many Americans had been frustrated by events since the armistice. The Senate's rejection of the treaty made it appear that the war had been fought for nothing. The request of the European nations for debt relief made the beneficiaries of American aid appear ungrateful. Despite the passage of the 1921 quota bill, immigrants continued to arrive in large numbers. Conflicts between labor and capital tore at the country, and the depression led to large-scale unemployment. Prohibition had been enacted but it had been openly violated. And perhaps the cruelest blow of all fell when the American public, in the autumn of 1920, learned that the 1919 World Series had been fixed. To some disillusioned Americans, the Klan appeared to provide a cure for the postwar malaise. That it continued to grow in 1923 indicated that it also spoke to some deeper concerns of native-born, white, Protestant Americans.

The Klan's Appeals

Wherever it appeared, the Klan made use of local prejudices and concerns. This could mean focusing on the supposed menace posed by Japanese, Mexicans, Italians, Greeks, or some other immigrant group, or exposing the peccadilloes of a corrupt political machine. But all Klansmen shared certain core concerns. The two causes that received the most attention from them were the alleged power and subversive intentions of the Roman Catholic church and the failure of authorities to enforce Prohibition.

Anti-Catholicism had deep roots in the United States dating back to the colonial period. Most early settlers brought a hatred of Catholicism with them, and had little respect for a religion that they often scornfully referred to as popery. Those who wrote the Constitution viewed the United States as a Protestant nation and identified Protestantism with progress and self-government and Catholicism with medievalism and backwardness. Most Protestants in the United States and in Europe grew up disliking Catholic ceremonies and rituals and even thinking of Catholics as representatives of the Antichrist. But anti-Catholicism as a social movement did not surface until the 1840s, when large numbers of German Catholic and especially Irish Catholic immigrants arrived in the United States. People hostile to Catholicism began to distribute salacious tracts and pamphlets containing tantalizing accounts of debaucheries that supposedly took place behind convent walls or in confessionals, a type of literature that enjoyed wide circulation well into the twentieth century. Antebellum reformers also voiced strong criticism of the Catholic church because most Roman Catholics were hostile to the antislavery and temperance movements. To these nineteenth-century anti-Catholics, Protestantism was identified with independence, self-reliance, and freedom. Briefly in the 1850s, an anti-Catholic political party flourished until issues dividing northerners from southerners replaced those dividing Protestants from Catholics as uppermost in the public mind.

Anti-Catholicism resurfaced in the late 1880s, when the American Protective Association (APA) gained considerable support in the midwestern states. The APA had faded by the mid-1890s, although anti-Catholic newspapers such as the *Menace*, founded in 1911, carried on the cause. But with the growth of the Klan, militant Protestantism once again emerged as a mass movement. Not all those hostile to Catholicism joined the Klan, but all Klansmen were anti-Catholic. Marching to the tune of "Onward Christian Soldiers," the KKK identified itself as a Protestant-American organization and referred to the United States as a "Protestant-Christian nation." To many people at the time, the Klan appeared to represent a rebirth of the APA, especially because it attracted members in many areas of the country where the APA had once been strong.

Klan newspapers, speakers, and publications aired all the standard anti-Catholic themes and added a number of twists of their own. They voiced contempt for Catholic practices such as celibacy and the refusal to eat meat on Fridays. They circulated anti-Catholic standbys such as *Maria Monk's Awful Disclosures of the Hotel Dieu Nunnery of Montreal*, first published in 1836, and new tracts such as *Convent Cruelties* by Helen Jackson, who claimed to be a former nun. Making frequent use of the slogan "One flag, one school, one Bible," they criticized Catholics for sending their children to parochial schools and for launching campaigns to remove the Protestant Bible from the public schools.

They accused Catholics of engaging in bloc voting and of marching voters to the polls to select handpicked candidates. They charged that Catholics did not properly respect the Sabbath and that they defied the blue laws.

The Klan also claimed that Catholics could never be good citizens because they owed their primary loyalty to the pope. During the war, immigrants had been accused of having dual loyalties, and this charge still resonated during the postwar period. Hatred of the pope seemed to exceed the wartime hatred for the kaiser, possibly because the pope, to whom the Klan referred as "that dago on the Tiber," was Italian, a nationality the Klan identified with crime, bootlegging, vice, and dirt.

The Klan also targeted the Knights of Columbus, a Catholic fraternal organization founded in 1882. Although it was heavily dominated by Irish Catholics, it had been named for Christopher Columbus in order to make it sound more patriotic. The Klan, however, believed that it constituted the pope's standing army in the United States and that the organization held secret military drills in preparation for a takeover by the "dirty papists." Klan members circulated a bogus Knights of Columbus oath, and the KKK claimed that whenever a male child was born to a Catholic family, the Knights of Columbus buried a rifle under the local Catholic church. Prone to belief in conspiracies, Klansmen gave credence to a number of other wild stories connected to what they considered a Catholic effort to take over the United States. At various times, they circulated rumors that the pope planned to move to Washington, D.C., or to Indiana; on one occasion, a traveling shoe salesman received the surprise of his life when a crowd, believing he was the pope, gathered as he disembarked from a train.

Gullible Klansmen evidently believed many of these far-fetched rumors. But the Klan also criticized the Catholic church on the same grounds that liberals and socialists criticized Catholics. For example, Klansmen argued that Catholic nations remained far more backward than Protestant nations; they pointed out that Catholic-dominated countries such as Spain failed to extend religious toleration to minorities; they warned that the Catholic church had lobbied to send American troops to overthrow the anticlerical Mexican government; they noted that the Catholic church opposed women's suffrage and other reforms intended to grant women more rights; and they strongly supported the Towner-Sterling bill, which would have established a federal department of education, a measure the Catholic church opposed.

On the other hand, Klansmen remained blind to a central aspect of Catholic life in the United States: Catholics recognized that they were a minority, and their church was a strong defender of pluralism and of minority rights. Even if the Catholic church favored mandatory religious instruction in public schools in other nations, this did not hold true for the United States, where the church hierarchy strongly supported the separation of church and state (a position the Klan also claimed to favor). More-sophisticated observers had been bothered by what they perceived to be the Catholic church's expedient stance. A 1923 editorial in the Protestant weekly the *Christian Century* noted that "it is a little hard to have satisfactory reciprocal relations with an organization which claims equal rights where it is in a minority and exclusive rights where it has the power to enforce them."

Ironically, leaders of the Ku Klux Klan and the Catholic church agreed on many issues. The Klan stood for the flag and the Bible; the Catholic church called for support of God and country. Both the Klan and the Catholic church condemned behavior associated with the free expression of sexuality and new fashions. Both the Klan and the Catholic church spoke out about the evils of divorce and the modern motion picture. Klansmen and Catholic church leaders were uneasy with the pace of change during the 1920s and responded defensively as they saw their way of life under attack. But the intense hostility directed at Catholics by militant Protestants in this era prevented either side from acknowledging these common concerns.

Some observers at the time connected the reemergence of anti-Catholicism to the rise of fundamentalism, but the Klan said little about the teaching of evolution in the public schools, an issue that riled the fundamentalists. In many areas, the KKK received more support from evangelical Protestants than from fundamentalists. Rather than being based in fundamentalism, the renewed hostility to a church governed from Rome stemmed from the same postwar distrust of foreign forces that influenced the Red Scare, opposition to the Treaty of Versailles, Harding's 1920 campaign, and passage of high-tariff and immigration-restriction legislation.

Wherever it appeared, the Klan referred to itself as a law-and-order organization. Although it called for the enforcement of laws against gambling and prostitution, it focused most of all on the need for Prohibition to be enforced. Widespread violations of Prohibition had begun as soon as the constitutional amendment and the Volstead Act had been passed. In the early 1920s, many Americans were concerned about a crime wave, a condition they were at first prone to blame on the unsettling effects of the war. But by 1922 and 1923, it had become quite clear that Prohibition, rather than the war, had been the cause of the growth in crime.

Prohibition violations were common in some heavily Protestant areas such as Appalachia, where moonshiners and home stills had been part of the social landscape since the first white settlers crossed the Blue Ridge. But in much of the country, immigrants from Catholic and Jewish backgrounds were the most visible offenders. Some immigrants had gotten involved in crime on their arrival in the United States. Prohibition gave them an opportunity to expand their criminal activities beyond their own ethnic communities. Chicago gained the most notoriety, but during the 1920s, organized criminal networks and syndicates expanded their operations in almost all large and medium-sized cities.

The Klan aimed to halt the activities of the rumrunners. Viewing itself as an agent of moral reform, the KKK gained members in the same Protestant areas where there had been substantial support for the Prohibition amendment. The KKK, often working hand in hand with agents of the Anti-Saloon League, gathered information on "dance halls," "road houses," and "pool rooms" selling "white mule," "rot gut," and other illegal beverages. Bristling with anger at the complacence of local officials, the Klan conducted its own "clean up your town" campaigns. The KKK felt this was necessary because there were hundreds of towns and cities where local police, city officials, and mayors took bribes from mobsters. Where corruption flourished, the Klan argued that it had no choice but to carry out its own vice raids to enforce Prohibition. This earned it the support of local dry forces who appreciated the Klan's exposure of Prohibition violators. But the Klan's antivice campaigns also led to some extremely violent confrontations with those who did not take kindly to being described in the Indiana Klan organ, the *Fiery Cross*, as "dregs from putrefied vomit" or as "thugs, degenerates and social parasites" and who did not appreciate having their operations exposed by the KKK.

The Klan had a long list of other dislikes. From its inception, the KKK, as part of its campaign for "pure Americanism," had targeted immigrants. The Klansman's Creed concluded with these two pledges:

I believe in the limitation of foreign immigration.

I am a native-born American citizen and I believe my rights in this country are superior to those of foreigners.

The hostility to foreigners received far more attention from the Klan after Hiram Evans became the head of the Invisible Empire. The Dallas dentist admired the writings of Madison Grant, Lothrop Stoddard, and other racist foes of the new immigrants. Just as the congressional debate concerning a new quota law reached a climax in 1924, he wrote a widely circulated booklet, *The Menace of Modern Immigration*.

The Klan's arguments for immigration restriction differed little from those made by mainstream organizations and politicians at the time. Along with many other Americans, Klansmen believed that the recent arrivals from eastern and southern Europe were of inferior racial stock and incapable of assimilation. The Klan's belief that the United States was becoming the "dumping ground" for the "scum," "dirt," and "filth" of Europe resembled ideas advocated by leading academic critics of immigration. The Klan appeared more extreme only in its demand that all immigration be halted for ten years.

The criticism of foreigners posed a dilemma for the Klan. By restricting membership to native-born Americans, they risked losing potential supporters among strongly anti-Catholic, Protestant immigrants. Many of the evangelical Protestants who had been the APA's biggest backers came from Scandinavian, German, and Welsh backgrounds. Immigrants from these groups brought a fierce anti-Catholicism with them to the United States, although few could match the ferocious anti-Catholicism of the Scotch-Irish. Alert to this dilemma, the Klan came up with a compromise solution; it founded an auxiliary called the "Royal Riders of the Red Robe" for Protestant immigrants.

Jews came in for their share of abuse from the Klan, although anti-Semitism was secondary to anti-Catholicism. Following the lead of Henry Ford, the KKK aimed its fire at "money grasping Jews" and suggested that Jewish financiers had been responsible for World War I. Klan newspapers frequently carried reprints from the *Dearborn Independent* and reported favorably about the Detroit automobile manufacturer's crusade against the "International Jew." Jewish organizations showed far more concern about Henry Ford than they did about the Klan; they did not view the Klan as a serious threat, despite reports of scattered physical attacks on Jews.

The Klan billed itself as a white supremacist organization that believed in the need to preserve racial purity. In cities such as Indianapolis, Indiana, Springfield, Ohio, and Coffeyville, Kansas, the Klan joined campaigns for segregated schools while claiming to be "the friend of the Negro." As proof of its good intentions, the Klan made financial contributions to black churches. In response, incredulous African-American newspaper editors heaped scorn on ministers who "betrayed" their congregations for "paltry" dollars. Blacks living in the heart of Klan country openly defied the hooded order. In Columbus, Ohio, black leaders sought a court injunction against Klan activities and organized a boycott of Klan stores; in Dayton, Ohio, black residents organized a countermarch over the same route that a Klan parade had taken the day before; in Indianapolis, African Americans held numerous meetings protesting the activities of the

KKK. Klansmen in the South put far more emphasis on the dangers that African Americans' new aspirations resulting from the war posed to the status quo, and the KKK's racist appeals carried more of a threat of violence in Dixie than in the North. There were instances in the South where Klansmen whipped African Americans for voting, for refusing to enter Jim Crow railroad cars, for being "too free" with hotel guests, and for demanding more pay for picking cotton.

Uneasy with manifestations of female sexuality such as open necking and petting, "suggestive dances," and "immodest dress," the Klan also called for the protection of "pure womanhood." Many of the Klan's concerns dealt with changes in female behavior that had begun to be apparent in the prewar era, although contemporaries blamed the war for the "unloosening" of morals. During the 1920s, these new forms of conduct became associated with the flapper, whom the Klan viewed as little more than a vamp. Klansmen, like other Americans, were made uncomfortable by young women bobbing their hair, smoking, drinking, wearing less-constrictive clothing, enjoying leisure-time pursuits with male companions, and using the automobile to escape the watchful eyes of their parents.

In searching for the cause of the decline in morals, the Klan targeted the film industry, and it blamed "aliens" (Jews) for the "stream of pollution" it saw emanating from the new Hollywood studios. By the early 1920s, movies had become a highly affordable and popular form of entertainment. Catholic church leaders and many other Americans had begun, like the Klan, to express concern about brazen displays of female sexuality on the screen (and perhaps about what happened in the theaters when the lights went out). A number of cities and states had formed their own censorship boards; in an effort to head off further government intervention, the Motion Picture Producers and Distributors of America hired Will Hays to police the motion-picture industry.

In the year after Hays assumed his new position (at the munificent salary of one hundred thousand dollars a year), the Klan responded with indignation when Charlie Chaplin played a Protestant minister in a film entitled *The Pilgrim*, a movie that ridiculed small-town life. Films in which "the wife" was "always shown as inferior" and "the mistress as a heroine" continued to raise their ire. The *Fiery Cross*, fed up with Hays's alleged kowtowing to Hollywood producers, called upon the Hollywood film czar to resign. Merging with the Klan's call for "pure womanhood," the demand for cleaner films had less success in the 1920s than it would in the 1930s, when the Catholic Legion of Decency began to exercise influence.

Bitter, humorless, and fearful of all things foreign, the Klan seized on an astonishing array of issues as it extended its reach across much of the United States. Klan supporters knew something was wrong but they were not sure what it was. In addition to lashing out at "thugs," "home wreckers," "shyster lawyers," and a host of other enemies, the Klan campaigned for cleaner government, improved schools, and freedom of speech and the press. The Klan said little about Communism, because the Red Scare fears had receded by the early 1920s and the Klan's enemy across the seas resided in Rome rather than in Moscow. The Klan's creed called for "a closer relationship between capital and labor" and for "the prevention of unwanted strikes by foreign labor agitators," but the KKK said little about the labor question; a few Klaverns (local Klan organizations) even supported the 1922 railroad strike.

Although it took some positions that could be considered progressive, the Klan appeals indicate that it was an intensely nationalistic, xenophobic Protestant reform organization that captured the resentments and grievances of Americans upset by the changes brought about by the war, disturbed by the government's failure to enforce Prohibition, and fearful of an increasingly urban and racially mixed society.

The Klan Organizes

During 1923, the "Protestant American giant" (as the Klan described itself) appeared to be on the march. The KKK steadily expanded its reach until it had branches in practically every state in the nation. It began to receive considerable publicity from journalists amazed by its mushrooming growth during a year when the economy had fully rebounded from the postwar depression.

By 1923, the Klan had perfected its recruiting techniques. It usually announced its presence by burning a twenty- or thirty-foot cross on a local hillside. Next, hooded and robed Klansmen singing "Onward Christian Soldiers" would show up at a local Protestant church and present the congregation with a contribution, flowers, and a Bible. Usually, these visits had been prearranged with a sympathetic minister, who might allow one of the Klan representatives to speak from the pulpit. Additional members would be recruited by word of mouth or at Klan-sponsored band concerts, picnics, barbecues, and rallies. The Klan further burnished its image by making contributions to local hospitals or charities, presenting food baskets to deserving families, and donating Bibles and flags to public schools.

When large numbers of new members had been enlisted, the Klan would hold a nighttime initiation ceremony at a local farm or park. At the largest of these ceremonies, hundreds or even thousands of Klansmen would arrive by automobile, and the cars, with their headlights turned on, would form a circle around those being "naturalized." Each new enrollee would swear fealty to the Klan, usually by kissing an American flag and repeating some of the hooded order's mumbo jumbo. As a further demonstration of the organization's strength, flag-bearing Klansmen would then stage a parade through the center of town, a procession that might include floats and a marching band. Some Klan rallies resembled county fairs; one Indiana Klan Homecoming and May Festival advertised a "dazzling day of diversified delight" including twenty brass bands, a "big barbecue," and circus acts. Much like revival meetings, these mass assemblies relieved the monotony of small-town life and provided a spark of excitement in people's lives.

Huge crowds gathered for some of the most spectacular rallies. On 4 July 1923, approximately a hundred thousand Klan members and sympathizers, many arriving on special excursion trains, filled a park in Kokomo, Indiana, for a day of feasting and celebration, capped by the dramatic aerial arrival of the Indiana grand dragon, D. C. Stephenson. Verbal pyrotechnics and real fireworks filled the air when Hiram Evans and seventy-five thousand other Klansmen attended Ku Klux Klan Day at the Texas State Fair in Dallas on 24 October 1923.

Who joined the Klan? In many ways its membership in the northern and western states resembled that of the Anti-Saloon League. Klansmen were most likely to be longtime supporters of the dry cause and middle-aged members of the Republican Party, the Methodist Church, and fraternal organizations such as the Masons. Many members had been involved in previous attempts to protect the Protestant Sabbath by campaigning to outlaw Sunday films and baseball, and had been active in various crusades against gambling, prostitution, and crime. They rarely came from the upper classes, and often voiced resentment at the power exercised by local elites. A large percentage of Klansmen lived in medium-sized cities, and membership in the KKK evidently provided many recent arrivals in urban areas with a sense of community and companionship with people of similar backgrounds. Often, Klan members had family roots in the Midwest even if they had moved on to other areas. They were employed as businessmen in small concerns, retailers, skilled workers, lawyers, and ministers. As Oscar Ameringer, a shrewd German-born socialist leader, noted, Klan strength appeared to be drawn from "the county-seat towns and smaller trading centers of the South and the Middle West," where native-born shopkeepers faced competition from "a sprinkling of Greek, Italian and Jewish merchants." Many Klansmen appear to have felt that they were falling behind, and the shopkeepers blamed foreigners for the difficulties that stemmed from inroads made by chain stores. Despite hard times on the land, few farmers joined; even in Texas and Oklahoma, the bulk of the KKK members came from cities such as Dallas, El Paso, and Tulsa. Few industrial workers joined the hooded order, although coal miners enrolled in large numbers, causing a number of UMW locals to become divided into pro- and anti-Klan factions.

To urban sophisticates, these were the "booboisie," as H. L. Mencken called smug, unthinking Americans. Hiram Evans appeared to agree when, in an article in the *North American Review*, he noted that Klansmen had been accused of being "rubes," "hicks," and "drivers of second hand Fords" and he replied: "We admit it." Neither rich nor poor, neither members of the elite nor members of the working class, the Klan appeared strikingly average in its makeup.

The Klan reached its apogee in 1923 and 1924 in the midwestern states of Michigan, Ohio, Indiana, and Illinois. Ohio and Indiana—which the Klan referred to as the Central West—had the most members, and mayors sympathetic to the KKK had been elected in several cities in those states. Only Gary, South Bend (home to the University of Notre Dame), and some smaller towns in southern Indiana where moonshiners had long held sway seemed immune to the Klan's advance in the Hoosier state. The Klan also gained significant numbers of recruits in overwhelmingly Protestant states such as Maine, Texas, Oklahoma, Colorado, and Oregon, which had received few immigrants. In cities with large Catholic populations, the Klan made inroads in outlying areas such as Norwood (near Cincinnati), Wilkinsberg (near Pittsburgh), and Long Island towns located close to New York City. It gained some recruits in Detroit and Chicago, but had almost no members in Boston, Philadelphia, Baltimore, or Cleveland.

Frequently, the Klan operated through front organizations bearing such names as the Denver Doers Club, the Youngstown Civic League, and the Public School Defense League of Michigan. In areas where the Klan had considerable strength, its supporters could be open about their membership. This could mean parading unmasked, advertising their businesses in Klan newspapers, or putting KIGY (Klansmen, I Greet You) signs in their store windows. As part of the push for what Hiram Evans termed vocational Klannishness, Klansmen patronized shops that displayed TWK (Trade with Klansmen) signs, and women often took the lead in organizing boycotts of businesses owned by foreigners.

Defining the proper role for women in the organization posed a problem for

Klansmen. From its inception, the Klan viewed itself as a fraternal organization and drew many of its members from preexisting fraternal networks. But as the KKK gained influence, many women, emboldened by the passage of the suffrage amendment, questioned why they had not been included in the crusade to clean up America. After all, the Klan dealt with issues—ranging from abuse of alcohol to the need to improve the public schools—that had historically concerned women. Women from Protestant backgrounds had led the drive for the vote, and many of them, aware that Catholic countries had been some of the most resistant to granting women full citizenship rights, could be as intensely anti-Catholic as men.

Wives of Klansmen resented being left out of the organization and chafed at having to remain at home while their husbands went out to attend meetings. One woman writing to the *Fiery Cross* even queried: "Are you treating us fair? Are we counted with the K of C's, Jews or negroes?" Faced with criticism of this type, Evans relented and allowed for the establishment of a separate organization known as the Women of the Ku Klux Klan. (A splinter Klan faction, headed by Simmons, set up a female organization known as the Kamelia.) The *Fiery Cross* boasted that Klan ranks would now be filled with "women of social and business standing," but Evans and most Klansmen thought that the Women of the Ku Klux Klan would serve as an auxiliary to the parent organization. Female KKK members had other ideas, however, and the Klan became torn by an internal dispute between women anxious to assert a leadership role and men uncomfortable with that notion.

As the Klan grew beyond all expectations (some historians have claimed that at its peak, it enrolled more than five million members), its leaders developed political ambitions. Angry that politicians catered to, among other things, "the Catholic vote, the Jewish vote, the Italian vote, the vice vote," the Klan sought to force political leaders "to pay some attention to the American vote, the Protestant Christian vote, and the decent, God-fearing, law-abiding vote." In other words, just as they called for the separation of church and state and then pushed for Bible reading in public schools, these opponents of bloc voting called upon white Protestants to vote as a bloc. But because the Klan lacked central direction, the organization left it up to local Klaverns to develop their own political agendas and to decide which candidates to support.

Education and the call for law and order stood out as the Klan's foremost political concerns. In many towns and cities, the hooded order backed reform-minded school board candidates, who, despite their talk about the need for change, did little other than seek the ouster of Catholic schoolteachers. The

Klan-influenced legislature in Ohio in 1925 passed bills making it illegal for Catholics to teach in the public schools and requiring the daily reading of ten verses from the Bible, but the governor vetoed both measures because they violated the separation of church and state.

In Oregon, a state where the KKK for a while exercised considerable political influence, voters in 1922 passed a Klan-backed initiative that required all children between the ages of eight and sixteen to attend public schools. The measure struck at Lutheran, Seventh-Day Adventist, and Catholic parochial schools, and may well have cost the Klan potential supporters. A 1924 effort to enact a similar measure by referendum in Michigan went down to a resounding defeat, and the next year, the Supreme Court ruled the Oregon law, which was not due to take effect until 1926, unconstitutional.

The Klan exercised its greatest political influence in Texas and Indiana. In Texas, Earle Mayfield, who probably had joined the Klan and whose newspaper spewed forth hate-filled diatribes against Catholics and Jews, had been elected to the United States Senate in 1922. After a long investigation of his campaign finances and his Klan connections, in 1925 he had finally been allowed to take his seat, where he joined Alabama's Tom Heflin as the august body's most explicitly anti-Catholic senators. In Indiana, a Klan-backed candidate had been elected governor in 1925, but he accomplished little while in office. In retrospect, the Klan's political forays appear to have been less than an overwhelming success. They alienated people who believed a secret organization had no business in politics, and they exposed the weaknesses of a group uncertain about how to define itself. They also galvanized the Klan's opponents, who at first had been prone not to take the KKK seriously.

Opposing the Klan

If a social movement gains support and influence, it is bound to provoke a countermovement opposed to its goals. As the fierce debate at the Democratic convention revealed, the Klan's enemies by 1924 had become angry and vocal. According to calling cards issued by the Indiana Klan, its opponents included "every criminal, every gambler, every thug, every libertine, every girl ruiner, every home wrecker, every wife beater, every dope peddler, every moonshiner, every crooked politician, every pagan priest, every shyster lawyer, every K. of C., every white slaver, every brothel madam, every Rome controlled newspaper." In reality, the anti-Klan forces included diverse groups who for their own reasons had become determined to halt the hooded order's progress.

Opposition emerged from some surprising sources, including members of a predominantly Irish gang, Ragen's Colts, who had assaulted blacks during the 1919 Chicago race riots but who took offense at the Klan's anti-Catholicism; Thomas Dixon, the author of *The Clansman*, who resented the Klan's claim that it was the successor to the original KKK; and numerous chapters of the American Legion, whose definition of 100 percent Americanism did not exclude African Americans, Catholics, or Jews.

Roman Catholics took the lead in organizing opposition to the Klan. Some Catholic leaders had initially believed that the KKK would quickly pass from the scene, but the passage of the 1922 Oregon initiative jolted them into action. If the Oregon measure had gone into effect, the parochial school, the bedrock of Catholic education, would have been outlawed. This was of special importance because the meeting of the church's Third Plenary Council in Baltimore in 1884 had held that Catholic parents were "duty bound" to send their children to parochial schools. In any case, Catholic parents wanted their children to learn a fourth R, religion.

The Catholic church that the Klan attacked was no longer the diffident church of the mid-nineteenth century. Instead, the "church militant" of the 1920s made no apologies for its ties to Rome or for its determination to defend its own interests. To attack the church also meant to attack Irish Americans, who played the predominant role in church affairs. So intertwined were the Irish with the church that some diocesan newspapers sounded as if they were Irish publications. Angered by Wilson's Paris betrayal and inspired by the 1919 tour of the United States by Eamon de Valera, the Irish were in no mood to hear some Protestant secret order question their patriotism.

Irish-Catholic officials did not hesitate to ban Klan gatherings and to outlaw Klan activities. Chicago chief of police Charles Fitzmorris barred the Klan from parading, and New York City mayor John Hylan ordered the police to run the Klan out of town. Cleveland mayor W. S. Fitzgerald supported a city council ordinance providing a five-hundred-dollar fine and six months' imprisonment for anyone belonging to a society "tending to promote racial hatred and religious bigotry," and told the council: "This is a city of many different nationalities, many different creeds and colors. . . . There is no place here for such an order." Boston mayor James Michael Curley exaggerated the Klan's presence for his own purposes. Curley had earlier barred birth-control advocate Margaret Sanger from speaking, and he jumped at the opportunity to issue a similar ban on the Klan. While running for governor of Massachusetts in 1924, he pledged to run the Klan out of the state and arranged for his campaign workers to burn crosses when he spoke so he could appear brave in condemning the KKK.

Some state legislatures passed laws making it a crime for anyone to appear in public wearing a mask, hood, robe, or other disguise. New York passed the nation's most drastic anti-Klan law, which was named the Walker Bill after New York City assemblyman (soon to be mayor) Jimmy Walker. Al Smith signed the measure in May 1923, which ensured the Klan's hostility to Smith when he sought the Democratic presidential nomination in 1924. Specifically exempting labor unions, the law required each unincorporated oath-bound organization to file a list of its members, constitution, oaths, bylaws, and rules with the secretary of state. It attached penalties for the sending of anonymous documents or letters. The bill did not specifically mention the Klan, but everyone knew that it was aimed at the KKK, which vociferously protested its passage and attempted to evade its provisions by incorporating as a fraternity, Alpha Pi Sigma.

Wherever it appeared the Klan faced opposition. The *Fiery Cross* noted this in a special column entitled "The Penalty of Protestantism." In Kansas, after the Klan horsewhipped a mayor who barred its meetings, Governor Henry Allen launched an ouster suit against the hooded order. The United Mine Workers, a union that since its founding had welcomed immigrants and African Americans to its ranks, voted to expel any member who joined the KKK, although this proved difficult to impose on the rank and file. At the risk of losing southern support in his bid for the 1924 Democratic presidential nomination, Alabama senator Oscar Underwood chastised the Klan; Louisiana governor John Parker toured the country in order to lambaste the KKK. A crusading juvenile court judge from Denver, Ben Lindsey, risked his career to speak out against the hate-mongers, and the outspoken opposition of Utah's Mormon leaders helped block the advance of the Klan in that state. In Anaheim, anti-Klan forces paid cash in order to obtain the names of Klan members and then handed the list over to a local prosecutor. In El Paso, an attorney petitioned to have Klan-backed candidates removed from the ballot on the grounds that by joining the KKK they had forsworn allegiance to the United States. In Indiana, a number of officeholders and newspaper editors condemned the Klan when it was at its peak.

The African-American press denounced the KKK and ridiculed Marcus Garvey for his June 1922 meeting with Edward Clarke. But some editors also responded cynically to the sudden focus on the KKK. The *Cleveland Gazette* pointed out that the city's mayor evinced little concern about the Klan until "Catholics and Jews were hit"; the *Pittsburgh Courier* noted that "no one objected to the crime of mob violence as long as the Negro was the victim"; and the *Chicago Defender* commented that "little attention was paid to these things when members of our group were the sole sufferers." Nevertheless, African-American leaders welcomed the opportunity to work with Catholics and Jews in combating prejudice, and participated in a number of meetings with representatives of both groups.

Militant opponents of the Klan formed organizations to combat it. The most effective proved to be the Chicago-based American Unity League (AUL), headed by Patrick O'Donnell. O'Donnell typified the second- and third-generation Irish Catholics who were well positioned to combat the resurgence of anti-Catholicism. An upwardly mobile, eloquent criminal lawyer, O'Donnell had been active in a number of Irish nationalist organizations. Known as an aggressive attorney, he had developed a reputation for stretching the law (and maybe even breaking it) to win a case.

O'Donnell brought this combativeness to the American Unity League. Proclaiming in its newspaper *Tolerance* that "we HATE the Ku Klux Klan and everything it stands for," the AUL declared that it "sought to smash the Invisible Empire." Although it was primarily Irish in leadership and membership, the AUL gained strong endorsements from Jesse Binga and from the *Chicago Defender*'s editor, Robert Abbott, who called on African Americans "to join Catholics, Jews and the Irish in the war against the Klan."

In confronting the Klan, the AUL developed its own version of multiculturalism, and the celebration of a mixed-race America flew in the face of the highly nationalistic, antiforeign mood that in 1924 led to the severe restriction of immigration. When it launched its national campaign in February 1923, the AUL sponsored a six-day "All Nations" rally that featured presentations by a variety of speakers. Stating in *Tolerance* that it sought a "truer appreciation of those great groups whose desirability as American citizens is denied by the Ku Klux Klan viz. the Catholic, the Jew, the foreign born and the Negro," the AUL advocated "true Americanism" to counter the Klan's "pure Americanism." It called its organ *Tolerance*; citing Abraham Lincoln's stand against the Know-Nothings, it held up the former president as its exemplar of Americanism.

The AUL also demonstrated tactical ingenuity. Recognizing that Klan members in many areas did not want their membership known, the AUL knew that the hooded order's emphasis on secrecy made it vulnerable to exposure. To obtain the names of Klan members, the AUL infiltrated the Klan, staged break-ins at various Klan offices, and gathered information supplied by disillusioned former Klansmen. It then published extensive lists of Klan members in *Tolerance*.

The names appeared under the heading "Who's Who in Nightgowns" and covered towns and cities in Illinois, Indiana, Ohio, and Michigan. In Youngstown, Ohio, where the AUL staged a break-in with the compliance of local police, the names appeared in a booklet entitled "Is Your Neighbor a Kluxer?" By July 1923, the AUL claimed that it had exposed more than twenty-three thousand Klan members in Indiana and Illinois alone. But publication of names in *Tolerance* made the AUL vulnerable to lawsuits. In the most notorious case, the AUL was forced to apologize to Chicago chewing-gum magnate William Wrigley for falsely stating that he was a Klan member.

AUL attacks in *Tolerance* on the "nightie-clad koo koos" upset the Klan. Soon after the American Unity League's founding, the *Fiery Cross* filled its columns with articles condemning "mad Patrick O'Donnell" and the "scandal sheet" *Tolerance*, which the Klan termed the "official hate organ of the American Unity League." Mocking the AUL's founders as "Chicago criminals" and "jury fixers," the *Fiery Cross* scornfully noted that the "Unamerican Unity League" drew its support from "swarthy Jews, Negroes and foreigners."

For all the verbal jousting, the AUL had only a limited impact on the Klan. Within a year of its founding, the American Unity League faced serious financial difficulties because of the many lawsuits against it. The Klan still appeared to be on the march and it remained confident about the prospects for continued expansion.

Having gained considerable strength in the overwhelmingly Protestant areas of central Ohio and Indiana, the Klan faced a major dilemma. If it was to expand beyond the Protestant core, it would have to recruit new members in areas where many Catholics also lived. Once it attempted to move into industrial districts where workers had often engaged in violent strikes, the Klan found that it could not operate so freely as it had in its secure bastions. The Klan quickly discovered that, particularly in the tristate area of the West Virginia panhandle, eastern Ohio, and western Pennsylvania, the opponents of the Klan, often with the connivance of the local police, were prepared to use considerable violence against the KKK. In 1923 and 1924, anti-Klan forces used far more violence than the Klan had ever employed in the North.

The string of incidents began in April 1923, when a bomb destroyed the office of *Dawn*, the chief organ of the Chicago-area Klan. The next month, an angry crowd forced five hundred frightened Klansmen to take refuge in a church in Bound Brook, New Jersey, before they could be rescued by state police. Then in August and September 1923, a series of extremely violent attacks on the Klan took place in quick succession in Steubenville, Ohio, Carnegie, Pennsylvania,

Perth Amboy, New Jersey, and New Castle, Delaware. The attacks continued in 1924, when mobs assaulted Klansmen in Waukesha, Wisconsin, and Niles, Ohio; forced Klansmen to flee South Bend, Indiana; ran the Klan out of the coal-mining town of Lilly, Pennsylvania (killing two Klan members); and skirmished with the Klan in Herrin, Illinois, a town in which violence appeared to be endemic.

In all of these incidents, the Klan got the worst of the encounters. It demonstrated a curious lack of will to engage in battle with its enemies on city streets. In Steubenville, the mob severely beat Klansmen, forcing them to call off a planned march. Thousands of local citizens in Carnegie disrupted a "Karnegie Day celebration," killing one Klansman, destroying a ten-foot-high electric cross, and forcing Klan members to retreat under a hail of bricks. In Perth Amboy, six thousand counterdemonstrators forced Klan members to seek refuge in an Odd Fellows hall. A New Castle crowd pelted Klansmen after an initiation ceremony. In Waukesha, a crowd shouting "The meeting is off" stormed a hotel where the Klan had gathered. Crowds administered a terrible beating to Klan members in Niles. In El Paso, fear of facing an armed mob caused the Klan to call off a planned parade. Retreating Klansmen in South Bend fled a crowd composed primarily of college students.

The counterdemonstrations required planning; they did not occur spontaneously. On some occasions, shadowy groups known as the "Knights of the Blazing Ring" and the "Knights of the Flaming Circle," which liked to mock the Klan, became involved. Bootleggers, no strangers to violence, also participated in many of the mobs. Gangsters had good reason to oppose the Klan, because the hooded order had so often worked with Anti-Saloon League agents in gathering information about illegal drinking establishments and in trying to secure stricter enforcement of Prohibition. In Steubenville, a wide-open river town that the *Fiery Cross* characterized as a "dump hole of moral pollution and degeneracy" filled with "brothels, blind tigers [illegal saloons] and gambling dives," anti-Klan elements shot the leader of the local dry forces. In Atlantic City, Perth Amboy, Youngstown, and Herrin, anti-Klan mobs included those opposed to KKK efforts to clamp down on prostitution, gambling, and rumrunning.

The Klan attempted to use these incidents to reinforce its call for "one country, one flag, one language." Portraying themselves as "free born American citizens," they claimed that "dirty papists" and "aliens" had been responsible for disrupting their parades and meetings. In particular, the KKK tried to capitalize on the Carnegie riot because a Klansman had been killed and Hiram Evans had been present at the scene of attack. Shortly after the incident, the Klan issued a ninety-page booklet, *The Martyred Klansman*, which used the attack to try to recruit new members. Likewise, after the South Bend rout, the Klan responded by printing a pamphlet, *The Truth about the Notre Dame Riot at South Bend, Indiana.*

The Klan's timid response is revealing. The organization attracted its share of hatemongers, but for the most part, its rank and file consisted of ordinary, naive, fearful, gullible citizens. These were not the American equivalent of Blackshirts or Brownshirts; these were not Fascists or even proto-Fascists anxious to spill blood in the streets. The United States during the 1920s bore little resemblance to European societies in which a weak commitment to liberal democracy and fears of the left spawned Fascist movements. Intimidated by the violence and unprepared to respond in kind, the Klan discovered that it could not hope to organize in any community where a significant number of those ineligible to join the KKK had decided to take the law into their own hands.

The incidents did not merely block the Klan's advance; they played a role in its decline. Although the Klan did not want to be viewed as violent, the string of confrontations associated the Klan with violence and made it easier for enemies of the KKK to attack it as disruptive and as an enemy of law and order.

The Decline of the Klan

By mid-1923, the Klan appeared to be on the rise, but by early 1925, many members who had rushed to join were rushing to get out. Even by the time of the great Democratic Party debate of 1924, the KKK was beginning to lose strength. What happened?

None of the Klan's leaders was prepared for its sudden growth. Hiram Evans was a small-town dentist, devoid of charisma, incapable of providing direction to an organization with some three to five million members. By 1923 and 1924, local Klansmen essentially made their own decisions, and the Dallas central office had little control over them.

Even if Evans and his associates had exercised leadership, they were not sure themselves what they wanted the Klan to be. It was not strictly a fraternal organization, although it had the trappings of one. The KKK backed political candidates but it did not claim to be a political organization, and hooded Klansmen were certainly in no position to act as lobbyists. It worked with local officials in enforcing Prohibition, but it was not prepared to take over their responsibilities. In the North, it could not be considered a terrorist group, and even in the South, the use of violence lessened after Evans's takeover. A strange hybrid, the Klan never fully understood what direction it wanted to take. Journalist Robert Duffus's 1923 description of it in *World's Work* as a "cumbersome monster of an organization, ill-planned in every way except as a means of raising money" proved correct.

Money could be made in the Klan. Even after the ouster of Simmons, Clarke, and Tyler, the KKK continued to attract a steady stream of opportunists who had no particular belief in the Klan's principles, and who often engaged in precisely the type of conduct the Klan condemned. As a series of messy scandals hit the Klan in 1924 and 1925, those who had joined the KKK thinking it genuinely intended to combat vice quickly left the organization.

The Klan attracted some peculiar characters, but none caused the organization more embarrassment than D. C. Stephenson. A pathological liar, a drifter, a heavy drinker who had abandoned his wife, Stephenson was also a master hustler. In 1923, he had become the grand dragon of the Indiana Klan; he used that position to acquire a small fortune and an ornate Indianapolis mansion. He was known to fellow Klansmen by the code name "Old Man." The *Fiery Cross* had hailed his "unselfish devotion, sterling integrity, honor and loving personality," but his behind-the-scenes activity conflicted with this benign image. In 1923 and 1924, he was involved in a number of sexual attacks and was arrested for public intoxication. Stephenson managed to cover up these incidents until March 1925, when he kidnapped and raped an Indiana government employee named Madge Oberholzer, leaving human bite marks all over her body. Shortly thereafter, Oberholzer committed suicide. During the summer and fall of 1925, just as a Klan-backed governor took office, these facts became public. Stephenson was soon convicted of second-degree murder and the Indiana Klan never recovered from its disgrace.

Stephenson was an extreme example of the hustlers and hypocrites who latched on to the Klan. In Buffalo in September 1924, a Klan leader, the Reverend Charles C. Penfold, was arrested, caught in "an improper position" in an automobile with a woman who was not his wife. Dubbed the "parking parson" by the Buffalo press, the minister's "indiscretion" subjected the organization, which had been campaigning for higher moral standards, to ridicule. In Youngstown, Ohio, Evan A. Watkins, a "driving force" behind the local Klavern, was "exposed as a charlatan" and fled the community. In Denver, Colorado, vice raids resulted in the arrest of a number of Klansmen, and when Klan head John Galen Locke became involved in a number of scandals, Evans forced him to resign. Evans appeared to be one of the few true believers in the top ranks of the organization, which had been continuously embroiled in personal rivalries and disputes over money. By mid-decade, the Klan had been exposed to many as a moneymaking racket that enriched its leaders at the expense of its followers.

Even without the scandals, the Klan had trouble maintaining its member-ship. By 1925, the postwar tensions had largely faded as the United States truly entered a new era in which automobiles, radio, and films filled people's leisure time and fraternal organizations began to appear old-fashioned. As Americans relaxed, the Klan's stridency seemed out of place. The enactment of the 1924 quota bill fulfilled one of the Klan's most sought-after goals and eased the fear of immigrants. Many Americans had come to accept that Prohibition could never be fully enforced. Frustrated by its inability to gain complete implemen-tation, the leadership of the Anti-Saloon League became increasingly sour dur-ing the decade of its greatest triumph. Anti-Catholicism persisted, but anti-Catholic movements had never been able to sustain themselves.

The Klan's rapid demise fulfilled the predictions of those who had warned against taking the hooded order seriously. When thousands of unmasked Klans-men marched down Pennsylvania Avenue in August 1925, the event marked the Klan's last hurrah rather than a revival. By that time, even President Coolidge, who had refused to denounce the Klan during the 1924 presidential campaign, had decided it was time to speak out against the KKK. The Klan could still cause mischief (the "radio priest," Father Charles Coughlin, first took to the airwaves in 1926 after a cross-burning outside his church), but even the huge outcry over Al Smith's 1928 nomination could not revive the dormant Klan. For commu-nities whose normal life had been disrupted, the damage had already been done, and some people never forgot the sight of a burning cross, or who among their neighbors had been a "Kluxer."

Deep-seated and powerful social movements do not generally fall apart overnight. The Klan's rapid demise suggests how shallow much of the support for this sometimes ridiculous, sometimes scary organization had been. In ret-rospect, André Siegfried appears to have been quite correct in his observation that the Klan was more significant for "the atmosphere it expresse[d]" than for the power it possessed. A catchall for postwar disappointments and frustrations, the Klan expressed the hatreds of many people confused by a world that ap-peared so different from the Victorian America they fondly remembered.

Finally, the Klan collapsed because it had taken on too many enemies. In con-trast, the anti-immigrant movement that had been gaining strength since the 1890s had one clear goal: to restrict the number of eastern and southern Euro-pean immigrants coming to the United States. When the 1924 quota bill became law, the Klan celebrated and took some of the credit for the accomplishment. But the KKK played only a limited role in the enactment of a piece of legisla-tion that resulted from a groundswell of anti-immigrant sentiment.

7

NORDICS TO THE FRONT

THE 1924 NATIONAL ORIGINS ACT

BETWEEN 1890 AND 1914, Americans began to reassess their attitudes toward immigrants. Many old-stock Americans (the term includes descendants of immigrants from northwestern Europe and Canada, but not Native Americans or African Americans) became disturbed by the arrival of millions of immigrants from eastern and southern Europe, whom they deemed to be inferior to those who had arrived before 1890. On the West Coast, a virulent anti-Japanese movement had emerged. Despite the growing opposition, before the war no significant restrictionist legislation had been passed. The Great War marked a turning point. In 1917, Congress, overriding Wilson's veto, enacted a literacy test requirement for new arrivals. Anti-immigrant attitudes, fed by racial theories, hardened in the immediate postwar years, leading to passage of the Emergency Immigration Act in 1921. In 1924, Congress passed the National Origins Act, a law that favored so-called Nordic immigrants and that stood out as one of the most significant pieces of legislation enacted during the entire decade.

The Emergence of Anti-Immigrant Sentiment, 1890–1914

Before 1890, most immigrants to the United States came from northwestern Europe, Canada, and China. Massive immigration to the United States began in the 1840s and the 1850s, when more than three million German and Irish immigrants arrived. The Germans, who often settled on farmland or in western cities such as Cincinnati, Milwaukee, and St. Louis, had generally been welcomed, but the Irish had met fierce hostility. Even before the arrival of those fleeing the devastation of the 1845–50 famine, critics had charged the Irish with undermining American wage rates, voting as a bloc, and causing a rise in crime. The Irish also faced hostility because most of them were Catholic. With the arrival of the famine refugees, a full-blown nativist movement emerged, although it lost intensity in the years immediately before and after the Civil War.

The gold rush brought the first Chinese to California; between 1850 and 1882, more than three hundred thousand Chinese immigrants, almost all of them men from the Canton region, arrived in the United States. The Chinese worked in the mines and on the railroads, where they sustained a frightful death toll laying track through the Sierra Nevada and Rocky Mountains. By the 1870s, many of the Chinese had settled in San Francisco. Their presence evoked an anti-Chinese movement that accused the Chinese of working for "coolie wages," bringing diseases, and being heathens. But the Chinese also evoked fears of a Yellow Peril among those who prided themselves on living in a white man's country. The Chinese who lived in isolated mining camps frequently became victims of massacres by racially charged mobs. In 1882, the Chinese became the first group ever excluded from the United States by Congress, an exclusion extended in 1902 and which remained in force until 1943.

In the 1870s and the 1880s, many Irish and German immigrants, along with their British, Norwegian, Swedish, Dutch, and French Canadian counterparts, continued to arrive in the United States. In the decade of the 1880s alone, approximately eight million immigrants made the trip. By the 1890s, however, new groups began to emigrate; German immigration, in particular, sharply declined.

The post-1890 immigrants changed the face of America. The Slavs, Italians (almost all of whom came from southern Italy), and eastern European Jews were the three largest groups, but significant numbers of Portuguese, Hungarians, Finns, Lithuanians, Rumanians, and Greeks came as well. By 1910, many Lebanese, Syrians, Armenians, and Cape Verdeans arrived as "American fever" reached the eastern Mediterranean and islands off the west coast of Africa. Ellis Island had been opened in 1892 to process the new arrivals, and by 1914, approximately seventeen million immigrants had passed through its doors. Well aware that the South offered few opportunities for them to earn cash wages, almost all of those who made the voyage settled in the North. After 1900, more than a million immigrants arrived in peak years. By 1910, the foreign born constituted approximately 13 percent of the total population, and the foreign stock (immigrants and their children) represented 40 to 50 percent of the population in a number of northern cities.

Many of the new arrivals intended to remain in the United States only a few years before using their accumulated savings to purchase land in their native regions. They eagerly sought employment in mines and mills, where increased use of machinery opened up millions of unskilled and semiskilled jobs. New and improved steamships cut the transatlantic voyage to ten days, and many of the "birds of passage," as they became known, crisscrossed the ocean several times.

But whatever their original intentions, many of the immigrants decided to remain permanently in the United States and sent for their families to join them.

Eastern European Jews offered a major exception to this pattern. Coming primarily from areas of Poland and Lithuania that had fallen under the control of czarist Russia, they began to flee to the United States in the 1880s. The victims of pogroms and discriminatory laws, few of these Yiddish-speaking immigrants intended to return; entire families traveled to America together. Even more eastern European Jews made the decision to emigrate following the failed Russian Revolution of 1905, and by 1914, they far outnumbered the Sephardic and German Jews who had arrived earlier.

By 1905, Americans were well aware that their population was undergoing a dramatic change. Photographs of exotic-looking immigrants filled the mass-circulation magazines, which printed articles describing the arrival of the immigrant "hordes." A number of popular books called attention to the "peril" resulting from the "invasion" from Europe. Anti-immigrant sentiment fed the war on the saloons and the effort to ban leisure-time activities on Sunday. Even sympathetic journalists referred to the immigrants as a problem. Those less charitable began to refer to them as "dirt," "filth," and "scum," and the association of immigrants with dirt and disease became a standard theme in the anti-immigrant press. On the streets, bigots referred to the Slavs, Italians, and Jews as "hunkies," "dagoes," and "sheenies." Although it did not match the level of violence directed against the Chinese, the lynching of eleven Sicilians taken from their New Orleans prison cells in 1891 and the killing of nineteen striking Slavic and Hungarian mine workers in Lattimer, Pennsylvania, in 1897 demonstrated the vulnerability of the immigrants. Clearly, many Americans did not consider the recent arrivals from southern and eastern Europe to be "white."

Beginning in 1894, the Immigration Restriction League (IRL) took a stand against the immigrants. Mainly composed of Boston Brahmins (descended from old Boston families), the new organization attracted a number of Harvard professors and alumni to the cause. They were advocates of Anglo-Saxonism, and their belief in the superiority of people descended from English stock led them to advocate immigration restriction. Influenced by the new science of eugenics (which in their hands became a pseudoscience), they argued that immigrants from southern and eastern Europe possessed germ plasm of an inferior quality. The IRL's leaders, noting the high birth rates of those they referred to as "beaten men from beaten races," feared that old-stock Americans were having fewer children so as not to compete with the inferior breeds. Known as race suicide, this idea, which gained currency on both sides of the Atlantic, captivated a number of Americans, including Theodore Roosevelt. Indeed, by the 1920s, eugenics was in vogue among the educated classes; André Siegfried suggested that one needed to take a "treatise on eugenics," along with a Bible, when visiting the United States.

Henry Cabot Lodge became the leading proponent of immigration restriction in Congress. Elected to his first term in 1892, Lodge crusaded for this cause in the Senate until he witnessed its triumph in 1924, shortly before his death. He was an ardent advocate of Anglo-Saxonism, and he felt that Slavs, Italians, and Jews were inferior "races." Like many Boston Brahmins, Lodge harbored a strong dislike for the Irish, but as a politician, he needed to mask his disdain for a group with considerable voting power in Massachusetts. He therefore included the Irish among the English-speaking races and suggested that the Irish had benefited from one thousand years of contact with the English, although he failed to mention that much of this contact had been at gunpoint.

Acting on behalf of the Immigration Restriction League, Lodge urged Congress to pass a literacy test requirement, which was the organization's preferred method for limiting immigration. The IRL favored the measure because it believed that many immigrants from southern and eastern Europe were illiterate and could not pass a simple test conducted in their own native languages, a belief based on the nativists' misinformation and ignorance. In 1897, Congress had passed a law requiring all immigrants to pass a literacy test, but the outgoing president, Grover Cleveland, became the first of three presidents to veto it.

The restrictionist movement gained momentum after 1900. Southern congressmen coming from the nation's most race-conscious region—one that prided itself on the purity of its Anglo-Saxon stock—favored limiting the entry of groups they considered nonwhite. On the West Coast, the arrival of approximately a hundred thousand Japanese immigrants caused alarmists, motivated both by racial fears and by resentment of the Japanese immigrants' economic success, to warn of a new Yellow Peril.

With anti-immigrant sentiment growing, it appeared that once again the literacy test stood a good chance of being passed. To stave off legislation, the immigrants' defenders in 1907 convinced Congress to form a national commission to study the immigration problem. Commissions of this type had become common during the Progressive Era, a time when many middle class Americans looked to experts to resolve complex issues.

The United States Immigration Commission, which became known as the Dillingham Commission (named for Senator Dillingham, its chairman), spent more than a million dollars on an exhaustive three-year study of immigrants.

In 1911, it published a massive forty-two-volume report that contained information on the immigrants' impact on various industrial communities throughout the North. The charts and statistics appeared objective, but the report also made casual generalizations about the abilities of various "races" that reflected the prejudices of the commission's members.

The Dillingham Commission's conclusions were contained in a summary report that established the terms of the debate until the passage of the 1924 legislation. It termed groups that arrived before 1890 the old immigrants (a category that included the Irish but not the Chinese) and termed groups that arrived in large numbers after 1890 the new immigrants. Throughout, it implied that the old immigrants were more desirable than the new. It asserted that the new immigrants failed to assimilate as easily as the old, tended to be more clannish, concentrated more in cities, and lowered the American standard of living. Some of the conclusions had an element of truth to them, but they sounded like a series of accusations, and they became staples in the anti-immigrant arsenal. Nevertheless, despite the implication that the new immigrants were inferior to the old, the report recommended no restrictionist legislation other than the literacy test, which Congress again passed in 1913, only to have it vetoed by President William Howard Taft.

Restrictionists generally welcomed the Dillingham Commission's conclusions. Before the war, they included the organized-labor movement and a number of progressive-minded academics. Ever since the depression of the early 1890s, the AFL had been moving into the anti-immigrant camp, and the success of the 1904–5 open-shop campaign convinced the labor federation's leadership that cheap foreign labor threatened their interests. Although a federal statute made it illegal for corporations to recruit labor overseas, many workers believed industrialists brought in "hordes" of immigrants to lower their wages. Highly skilled "aristocrats of labor" often expressed contempt for semiskilled and unskilled workers, especially when they were of a different nationality. The labor movement did not embrace the pseudoscientific notions of the IRL, but Samuel Gompers, an English-born Jew, held prejudicial attitudes toward the recent immigrants, a perspective he shared with many trade unionists from British backgrounds.

John R. Commons, a professor of political economy at the University of Wisconsin and a pioneer in the academic study of labor, voiced similar opinions. In a volume entitled *Races and Immigrants in America*, published in 1908, Commons stated that "peasants" from "Catholic Europe" had "become almost a distinct race, drained of those superior qualities which are the foundation of a democratic republic." Reinforcing the AFL's position, Commons blamed the influx of "backward races" on corporations and steamship companies eager to increase profits at labor's expense.

The sociologist E. A. Ross, a colleague of Commons' at the University of Wisconsin, held racial opinions that were even more extreme. A native of Iowa, Ross had become convinced that the arrival of immigrants from southern and eastern Europe endangered the nation's racial stock. In 1911, he traveled across the country on behalf of *Century* magazine, for which he wrote a series of articles eventually published as a book entitled *The Old World in the New* (1914), a work that bristled with malicious stereotypes of the new immigrants and warned: "Not until the twenty-first century will . . . the historian be able to declare with scientific certitude that the cause of the mysterious decline that came upon the American people in the early twentieth century was the deterioration of popular intelligence by the admission of great numbers of backward immigrants."

Unlike the conservatives who dominated the IRL, Commons and Ross had supported a number of reform causes. But both of the public-minded academics put the same stress on heredity as did the advocates of Anglo-Saxonism. Before the war, however, most progressives still expressed faith in the meliorative effects of the environment. Moreover, the defenders of the immigrants still could make their voices heard in a society open to divergent views concerning the new arrivals.

The Immigrants' Defenders

Defenders of the immigrants faced a difficult task, especially because many of the accusations against the recent arrivals had some legitimate basis to them. Many immigrants did not plan on becoming citizens and intended to return to Europe; many put up with long hours and onerous working conditions because they viewed their status as temporary; large amounts of money had been sent out of the country in the form of remittances; few immigrants had settled on the land; they had clustered together in urban areas; immigration had led to some increase in crime. Moreover, it did not appear unreasonable for critics to argue that any nation receiving diverse nationalities, speaking various languages, found its own sense of national identity and unity threatened.

Some immigrants attempted to speak out in their own defense. For example, *Outlook* magazine published a series of immigrant memoirs that its editor, Hamilton Holt, included in a 1906 anthology, *The Life Stories of Undistinguished Americans.* Jewish immigrants, quicker to learn English than many others, wrote autobiographies, including Mary Antin's *From Plotsk to Boston* (1899) and *The Promised Land* (1912), Marcus Ravage's *An American in the Making* (1917), and Rose Cohen's *Out of the Shadow* (1918). In another book by Mary Antin entitled *They Who Knock at Our Gates* (1914), she explicitly took on the restrictionists and pungently observed: "When we watch the procession of cripples hobbling back to their native village, it looks more as if America is exploiting Europe." On the other hand, filiopietistic efforts to establish a substantial immigrant contribution dating back to the colonial period appeared pathetic and probably convinced no one.

For the most part, immigrants had to rely on sympathetic progressives to present their case to the public. Hutchins Hapgood's *The Spirit of the Ghetto* (1902), for example, captured the richness of Jewish life on New York City's Lower East Side. Lewis Hine's photographs evoked pity for the travail of the immigrants, as did Upton Sinclair's *The Jungle* (1906). The *Survey*, the same magazine that sponsored the 1925 New Negro anthology, published articles describing the harsh working and housing conditions of immigrants.

Emily Greene Balch, a descendant of an old Boston family, wrote the most informative book dealing with the lives of the recent arrivals. Balch, who had worked in a settlement house and taught at Wellesley College, spent much of 1905 traveling through Slovakia, Galicia, Croatia, and other Slavic regions ruled by the Austro-Hungarian Empire. She had then visited several Slavic communities in the United States. Her study was unique in its use of this dual approach. When she published her work in 1910, she called it *Our Slavic Fellow Citizens*, a title that may have made her wealthy Boston neighbors choke on their afternoon sherry. The book, more than four hundred pages long, contains innumerable insights about immigrant life, and it anticipated many observations made by subsequent historians. It remains one of the best books ever written about immigrants, although Balch romanticized peasant life and so completely absorbed the Slavic perspective that she filled her book with negative references to "commercial-minded Jews."

Women reformers emerged as the principal defenders of the immigrants. As was true during the postwar campaign against lynching, women appeared less skittish than men about openly expressing humanitarian sympathies for the oppressed. Many women during the early twentieth century became familiar with the lives of immigrants while residing at settlement houses. Scorning eugenics and the scientific approach to immigration, settlement house workers clung to the historic conception of America as a refuge for the oppressed, and stressed the immigrants' contributions to music, art, and dance that could benefit more-materialistic old-stock Americans.

The settlement house workers and their allies failed to develop an organizational vehicle to rival the Immigration Restriction League. In 1906, Chicago-based reformers founded the Immigrant Protective League, but it mainly provided services for the new arrivals. The National Liberal Immigration League, which hoped to bring all the opponents of restriction together, remained a paper organization. As a result, once the postwar onslaught against immigrants began, the defenders did not have an umbrella organization to present their case.

The American Jewish Committee (AJC), almost by default, became the principal defender of the immigrants from southern and eastern Europe. The AJC had been founded in 1906 by German Jews, a group that had frequently expressed disdain for the Yiddish-speaking Jews from eastern Europe. But the arrival of the eastern European Jews in the late nineteenth century had led to an increase in anti-Semitism, and many of the German Jews, who had previously sought to assimilate or even to disguise their religious backgrounds, had become more conscious of their Jewish identity. A wave of pogroms in Russian Poland and Rumania between 1903 and 1905 highlighted the need for the United States to maintain an open door for their coreligionists. Although it was formed to represent Jewish interests, the AJC spoke out in defense of all immigrants, and the organization secretly financed a study by the economist Isaac Hourwich, *Immigration and Labor: The Economic Aspects* (1911), which challenged the Dillingham Commission's contention that immigrants lowered the wages of American workers and hampered trade-union organizing efforts.

Jewish trade unionists and academics were also outspoken defenders of the immigrants. The International Ladies Garment Workers Union, which had a predominantly Jewish membership, was one of the few unions to oppose the AFL's restrictionist stance, and the very success of the Amalgamated Clothing Workers of America, which had organized a wide variety of nationalities, refuted the notion that immigrants resisted unionization efforts. Franz Boas, a German-Jewish immigrant, was one of the first anthropologists to challenge the idea that genetically superior and inferior races existed, and Horace Kallen, an American-Jewish philosopher, argued that ethnic diversity strengthened democracy, an idea that became known as cultural pluralism.

Near-unanimous Jewish opinion on the issue contrasted with the ambivalent posture of the American Catholic church. In 1900, the church was dominated by leaders from Irish backgrounds who had first appeared to welcome the additions to their flocks. Both James Cardinal Gibbons of Baltimore and Archbishop John Ireland of New York had condemned the prejudicial attitude of old-stock Americans. On the other hand, the Irish bishops had faced demands from

Polish, Slovakian, Lithuanian, Hungarian, and other Catholics for clergy who spoke their languages and were familiar with their national customs. Only reluctantly had the American church leadership agreed to the formation of nationality parishes, a concept that challenged notions of catholicity. Some of the fiercest conflicts had been with southern Italians, whose custom of celebrating festas honoring various patron saints, appeared almost pagan to the Irish-American clergy. Many church leaders were uncertain whether the arrival of so many eastern and southern European immigrants aided or damaged the church. In any case, it is unlikely that a church identified as foreign in the minds of so many Protestants could have done much to impede the restrictionist movement.

By the time of the war, a major national debate had been in progress for more than twenty years. Restrictionists had gained a sympathetic ear, but many Americans still believed their nation should continue to provide an asylum for the oppressed. This and many similar notions fell victim to the wartime patriotic campaigns, the Red Scare, and the postwar suspicion of all things foreign.

The War and the Postwar Onslaught against the Immigrant

The Great War, which led to a heightened emphasis on conformity, made Americans far more aware of the immigrant presence in their midst. Despite the recession, a near-record two million immigrants passed through Ellis Island during 1913 and 1914. Many Americans wondered whether recent arrivals could forgo their own national loyalties and demonstrate allegiance to their adopted country.

Woodrow Wilson and Theodore Roosevelt had their doubts. Although in 1915 he had become the third president to veto the literacy test, Wilson had warned about the dangers of the "hyphenate" vote during his 1916 campaign. With Theodore Roosevelt crisscrossing the country in 1915 and 1916 calling for preparedness and 100 percent Americanism, even before America's entry into the war, a patriotic mood swept the land.

In February 1917, Congress passed the literacy test over Wilson's veto. With war on the horizon, the measure indicated that the tide had turned decisively in favor of the restrictionists. Part of an omnibus immigration bill that included other restrictionist provisions, the law was approved amid nativist warnings that the postwar period would bring a new deluge of immigrants.

Once Congress declared war, anti-German sentiment seized much of the country. No matter when they had arrived in the United States, all German Americans appeared suspect, and Oscar Ameringer, in his autobiography, later recalled the war years as a time when Americans "broke Beethoven's records, boycotted Wagner's music, burned German books, painted German Lutheran churches and Goethe's monument in Chicago the color of Shell filling stations." Although the anti-German hysteria had passed by 1920, the rich array of German social, cultural, educational, and athletic institutions never fully recovered from the wartime assault. By 1918, Hungarians also had been declared by the government to be alien enemies. On the surface, some groups such as the Poles, Czechs, and Slovaks could appear to be loyal both to the United States and their homelands because by 1918, it appeared likely that an Allied victory in the war would lead to the breakup of the Austro-Hungarian Empire and the establishment of new, independent nations in East Central Europe. But Americans did not always distinguish between "friendly" and "unfriendly" foreigners, and during the war, one needed to be circumspect when reading a foreign-language newspaper or speaking in a foreign tongue. Evidently, many Americans agreed with Senator Kenneth McKellar of Tennessee, who declared in April 1917, "From now on there can be but two classes of people in the country—Americans and traitors."

The wartime use of intelligence tests bolstered anti-immigrant sentiment. These tests, which had first been developed by the French psychologist Alfred Binet, had never been extensively used in the United States until 1917, when the army began to test draftees. The tests supposedly measured innate intelligence, but a person with more formal education would likely have a higher score. Race-conscious restrictionists welcomed the results because many recent immigrants scored below normal, thus supporting their contention that immigrants from southern and eastern Europe threatened to dilute America's racial stock.

The Russian Revolution further fueled the animosity toward immigrants. During the Red Scare, Bolshevism became identified in the minds of many Americans with Slavs and Jews—the two groups that bore the brunt of the Palmer Raids. Cartoonists portrayed radicals as whiskered foreigners holding bombs in their hands; business, religious, and patriotic organizations pushed their pet Americanization schemes as the "cure" for Bolshevism; and employers used the steel strike to further Americans' fears of "dirty" Bolsheviks in their midst. In 1919, Frederic Howe, the liberal commissioner of immigration was forced to resign when a special House of Representatives investigation concluded that he had not been assiduous enough in deporting alien radicals. And in the last letter he wrote before his death, Theodore Roosevelt warned that "there must be no sagging back in the fight for Americanism merely because the war is over."

Also in 1919, stimulated in part by resentment over Japanese demands at Versailles, a new wave of anti-Japanese sentiment spread up and down the West Coast. The Japanese, many of whom had emigrated from Hawaii, had never been accepted by those determined to keep Washington, Oregon, and California "white." The Japanese immigrants were classified by the federal government as aliens ineligible ever to become citizens; their small numbers made them vulnerable to attack by bigots. Condemned more for their "virtues" than for their "vices," the Japanese were targeted by many Californians resentful of their success in agriculture. The American Legion and the Hearst press, motivated by jealousy and racism, pushed a 1920 ballot measure that sought to toughen the restrictions of a law limiting alien land ownership that had first been enacted in 1913. The 1920 measure, which proved ineffectual, was adopted by a three-to-one margin in a referendum—a device favored by the progressives in order to give the people more voice in government.

The Sacco and Vanzetti case highlighted the vulnerability of immigrants to nativist and antiradical crusades. Nicola Sacco and Bartolomeo Vanzetti were arrested in May 1920 and accused of killing a paymaster and a payroll guard during a robbery of a shoe company in South Braintree, Massachusetts, on 15 April 1920. Not the naive fishmonger and shoe worker that their defense committee later portrayed to the American public, Sacco and Vanzetti had been militant anarchists for a number of years. Before the war, the anarchists had considerable influence within the Italian-American working-class movement, but by 1920, they had been reduced to small, isolated cells. Believers in a doctrine known as "propaganda by the deed," anarchists had been responsible for a number of bombings and assassinations on both sides of the Atlantic. Sacco and Vanzetti, burning with indignation at the injustices of capitalism, remained devoted to the cause despite the imprisonment of many of their comrades.

No one will ever know for sure whether either Sacco or Vanzetti had participated in the South Braintree robbery. But the trial judge, Webster Thayer, exhibited extreme bias against the two Italian immigrant defendants when he presided over the case in the spring and summer of 1921. Following their convictions, the imprisonment of Sacco and Vanzetti became a cause célèbre among the leftists, but it also became a cause célèbre in the Italian-American community, which had long resented the negative stereotypes and derogatory treatment of Italian immigrants. When Massachusetts executed Sacco and Vanzetti in 1927, demonstrations in the United States and in many other countries protested the refusal of Massachusetts governor Alvan T. Fuller to grant clemency. The case symbolized the polarization between defenders and critics of immigrants during the postwar period.

The 1921 Emergency Immigration Act

Restrictionists had warned that as soon as the war was over, a flood of poverty-stricken immigrants would inundate the United States. But in 1919, to the surprise of many, the anticipated deluge failed to materialize, in part because ships departing from Europe were used to transport American troops back home. Emigration from the United States apparently outpaced immigration in 1919. Some of those who left had not seen their families in years; some hoped to use their wartime savings in order to purchase land; others anticipated more opportunity in the newly independent European nations. Concerned Cleveland employers belonging to the Chamber of Commerce, fearing labor shortages during the 1919 boom, even admonished prospective emigrants not to engage in a "wild goose chase" and cautioned them about the dangers of returning to "the war-ravaged, famine-haunted lands" of their birth.

But by the summer of 1920, immigration once again began to reach prewar levels. Despite the onset of the depression, between June and December 1920 more than fifty thousand immigrants arrived each month, and the numbers increased in early 1921. There was a sharp rise in Jewish immigration. Polish Jews had been the victims of pogroms in 1919 and thousands of Jews had been harmed by warring armies in Ukraine in 1919 and 1920. Many Jews hoped to find refuge in the United States, leading Wilbur Carr, the head of the United States Consular Service, to predict that the Polish ghettos were about to empty their population on American shores.

Like the open-shop employers who used the 1920–22 depression to break labor unions, restrictionists used the economic downturn of the early 1920s to press for the closing of the American gates. No longer, they said, were the immigrants coming to fill jobs and to perform much-needed labor. Instead, they claimed, America was becoming a "dumping ground" for Europe's "refuse," and few of the arriving immigrants even expected to do productive work.

By 1920, Albert Johnson emerged as the leader of the ultrarestrictionist forces in Congress. A former newspaper publisher in Hoquiam, Washington, Johnson had been elected to the House of Representatives in 1912. His extreme hostility to immigrants emerged from three distinct influences. He despised the IWW, an organization that, despite its considerable native-born membership, he (like many others) associated with foreigners; he belonged to the Asiatic Exclusion League and had soaked up the anti-Japanese sentiment that permeated his home state; and he had developed close ties with a number of intellectuals who believed immigrants from southern and eastern Europe were members of inferior races. When the Republicans regained a House majority in the 1918 elections, Johnson became head of the Committee on Immigration, a position that allowed him to exercise considerable influence over legislation. The House had become home to some of the most rabid nativists, and Johnson's raw style made the Boston Brahmin Lodge look almost tepid by comparison.

Restrictionists believed additional legislation was necessary because the literacy test, which required prospective immigrants to read forty words in any language, had failed to accomplish its goal. In 1904, Robert DeCourcy Ward, a founder of the Immigration Restriction League, had predicted that if the literacy test became law, the immigration problem would dissapear. John R. Commons had anticipated that 30 to 40 percent of all Slavs and 50 percent of all southern Italians would fail such an exam. Both men underestimated the spread of literacy in southern and eastern Europe; almost all new arrivals had passed the test.

Those hostile to the immigrants argued that Congress needed to act immediately or else millions of immigrants fleeing war-stricken Europe would descend on the United States. The scare tactics worked. Early in 1921, the House adopted Johnson's proposal for a two-year suspension of all immigration. The Senate, more willing to listen to those opposed to restriction, adopted a proposal to limit immigration to "five percent of the number of foreign-born of each nationality" residing in the United States at the time of the 1910 census. Senator Dillingham, in particular, had been an advocate of a quota for a number of years. A proposal by Hiram Johnson to exempt those fleeing religious or political persecution (favored by those sympathetic to the plight of the Jews) failed by a wide margin. A joint House and Senate committee cut the final quota to 3 percent of each nationality and specified that a maximum of 357,803 immigrants from Europe could enter the United States each year.

The policy favored the old immigrants, who would receive approximately 200,000 of the 357,000 slots, and considerably reduced the numbers of immigrants from southern and eastern Europe. Great Britain and Ireland (combined until the establishment of the Irish Free State), for example, received a quota allotment of 77,342, and Germany an allotment of 67,607, while Italy had 42,057 slots and Poland 30,979. Congress intended the law, entitled the Emergency Immigration Act (reflecting the stark warnings of the restrictionists), to remain in effect for one year, but in May 1922 the House and the Senate extended it for two more years. President Wilson, remaining true to his urban, Democratic constituents, refused to sign it, but Warren Harding, flush from his America First campaign, eagerly affixed his signature when he took office.

The ease with which the legislation had been enacted caught the immigrants' defenders by surprise. Some thought the bill would turn out to be a "temporary expedient" and anticipated that once the economy rebounded, a more liberal measure would be passed. But the law failed to satisfy the extreme restrictionists, who remained determined to have their way in 1924 when the emergency bill expired.

The One-Sided Debate, 1921–24

The campaign against immigrants peaked in the years leading up to the passage of the climactic 1924 law. During this period, which coincided with the Klan's growth, many Americans questioned the idea that their nation should serve as an asylum for Europe's oppressed and scorned the immigrants' advocates as sentimentalists. The idea that Europe wanted to make the United States a "dumping ground" for its "scum" and "vermin" became commonly accepted, and many old-stock residents believed the nation was about to become a cesspool rather than a melting pot—not that they were comfortable with that idea either. New racial theories justified the harsher tone, theories that elevated Nordics above the "mongrel" races and that raised fears that "streams of foreign blood" threatened to "pollute the race."

Madison Grant did much to popularize notions of Nordic superiority. Grant was the chairman of the New York Zoological Society and a trustee of the American Museum of Natural History. Grant's magnum opus, *The Passing of the Great Race, or the Racial Basis of European History* had been published in 1916, but it did not receive extensive attention until the postwar period. Greatly influenced by European thinkers such as Count J. A. de Gobineau of France, Grant emphasized the importance of heredity and criticized the "widespread and fatuous belief in the power of environment." Many of his ideas resembled those of the eugenicists. Grant favored sterilization to prevent "the perpetuation of worthless types." (Involuntary sterilization of the feeble-minded became legal in many states in the early twentieth century.) He viewed the Great War as a racial tragedy because the "loss of life" fell "more heavily" on the "blond giant than on the little brunette." Alarmed by the arrival of "the weak, the broken and the mentally crippled . . . from the lower stratum of the Mediterranean Basin and the Balkans," along with "the hordes of the wretched, submerged populations of the Polish ghettos," Grant warned that a lax immigration policy would lead to the "survival of the unfit."

Grant's tripartite division of European races made the deepest impression on the popular mind. To the Nordics, a "race of soldiers, sailors, adventurers and explorers but above all, of rulers, organizers and aristocrats," he ascribed superior qualities, although he cautioned that the race would degenerate if it lived outside its natural habitat. (This explained the poor quality of southern whites.) The Alpines, a central European people, he considered "a sturdy and persistent stock," and all others he grouped together as Mediterraneans, a genetically inferior type. Deeply pessimistic, Grant feared that improvements in transportation had made it too easy for inferior peoples to come to the United States, an idea that found considerable support in Congress when the 1924 law came up for debate.

Lothrop Stoddard, a Harvard Ph.D., stressed similar racial themes in two books, *The Rising Tide of Color against White World-Supremacy* (1920) and *The Revolt against Civilization: The Menace of the Under Man* (1923). Although Stoddard offered a worldwide focus in contrast to Grant's European-centered work, Grant wrote the introduction to *The Rising Tide of Color*, and the two men became coupled in the public mind. According to Stoddard, who sounded even more fearful than Grant, the United States faced a threat from the yellow, brown, and black races as well as from the inferior Mediterranean germ plasm. Bolshevism represented the ultimate menace because it sought "to enlist the colored races in the grand assault on civilization," and Stoddard believed the Russian Communists needed to be "crushed . . . no matter what the cost." Stoddard became popular reading on college campuses during the early 1920s. In F. Scott Fitzgerald's *Great Gatsby*, the empty-headed Yale graduate Tom Buchanan reports that he has been reading "Goddard," and comments: "It's all scientific stuff; it's been proved . . . we're Nordics . . . and we've produced all the things that go to make civilization."

Few people had even heard of the Nordic race until Grant wrote his book, but the term had great appeal to the restrictionists because it included far more nationalities than could be fit under the rubric of Anglo-Saxonism. Along with the British, the Scandinavians, Germans, Dutch, and possibly even the Irish could qualify. By the early 1920s, the supposedly superior immigrants from northwestern Europe began to be commonly referred to as Nordics, which remained a favored term among the old stock, until the near-extermination of the European Jews and fifty million dead in World War II discredited it.

The *Saturday Evening Post* and the *World's Work* spread the Nordic idea and the anti-immigrant perspective to a much wider audience. In 1920, the *Post*, which had the largest circulation of any weekly in the United States, sponsored a European tour by Kenneth Roberts, one of its staff writers, which led to a series that in 1922 appeared as a book, *Why Europe Leaves Home*. Roberts's articles contained a good deal of factual information but they also contained some extreme anti-immigrant invective. Fearful of the spread of diseases such as typhoid and cholera, Roberts warned Americans of the dangers of being used as a "dumping ground" for "congenital slum material." The more highbrow *World's Work* published two series of articles dealing with immigrants. One, written by the magazine's editor, Burton J. Hendrick, made many of the standard accusations against Jews and appeared as a book, *The Jews in America* (1923); the other, written by Gino Speranza, an Italian American whose background gave the series more credibility, appeared in 1923 and 1924, under the overall title "The Immigration Peril."

Anti-Semitism, which had been steadily growing since the 1880s, fed the restrictionist movement. Anti-Semitism in the United States had been based on hostility to the Jews' religion and "race," as well as resentment of their economic success, and it found supporters among midwestern farmers, southerners, skilled workers, and Catholic immigrants, but it may have been most pervasive among the British-dominated elite. A number of anti-Semites filled key posts in the State Department, and many leading banks, insurance companies, and corporations refused to hire any Jews at all. In 1922, Harvard president A. Lawrence Lowell attempted to institute a Jewish quota, and many other eastern colleges strictly limited the number of Jews they admitted.

Henry Ford emerged as the nation's leading anti-Semite. In 1919, Ford had purchased a small weekly newspaper, the *Dearborn Independent*, which he soon turned into an anti-Semitic organ. In 1922 and 1923, Ford was almost consumed by his hostility to Jews; his views were well known to Adolf Hitler and other German and Austrian anti-Semites. To Ford, Jews represented all that he disliked: trade unions, films, financiers, jazz, Bolsheviks, gamblers. Ironically, the man whose assembly line did so much to destroy traditional skills held Jews responsible for the ills of modern life. Jews and many other Americans condemned his bigotry, but Ford's anti-Semitism did not prevent him from being prominently mentioned as a potential Democratic candidate in the 1924 presidential election. (He ended up endorsing Calvin Coolidge.)

Some industrialists strongly opposed the restrictionists. Immigrants, after all, had provided most of the labor in coal mines, steel mills, meat-packing plants, textile factories, and countless other industries. American industrial power, so evident during the war, would have been inconceivable without the contributions of immigrant workers. Steel producers in particular claimed that they could not adopt three eight-hour shifts unless the country maintained an open door for immigrants. U. S. Steel chairman Elbert Gary even told his company's shareholders in 1923 that he considered the emergency law "one of the worst things this country has ever done for itself economically," a statement that the restrictionists seized upon to support their contention that big business favored an open-door policy so as to drive down the wages of American workers.

Most businessmen, however, had begun to reevaluate their attitudes toward immigration. Business organizations such as the United States Chamber of Commerce and the National Association of Manufacturers had favored a liberal policy in the past and had opposed the 1921 quota law. But many industrialists came to believe that machines could do much of the work previously done by unskilled and semiskilled labor. More importantly, by 1923, the renewal of massive African-American migration had relieved labor shortages in several industries. Moreover, Mexican immigrants, who were not affected by the 1921 law, had begun to fill many jobs in midwestern steel and automobile plants during the 1923 industrial boom. As a result, most business interests wanted Congress to adopt an immigration policy that allowed for flexibility depending on economic conditions, but they did not press the issue.

Increasingly defensive in outlook, the AFL in the early 1920s fully embraced the restrictionist cause and joined many congressmen in calling for a moratorium on immigration. Pottery workers, coal miners, shoe employees, and others who labored in the sick industries believed that their difficulties might be relieved if America closed its doors. They received strong support for their position from Secretary of Labor James J. Davis, whose department supervised the Bureau of Immigration. A Welsh immigrant who had become a staunch advocate of the Nordic racial theory, Davis was the chief proponent of immigration restriction in the Harding and Coolidge administrations. In his 1922 autobiography *The Iron Puddler*, he favorably contrasted the nation's earliest settlers, whom he called the "beaver type," with the recent immigrants, whom he termed the "rat people."

Most African-American leaders by 1922 and 1923 had also become supporters of the restrictionist cause. Ever since the arrival of the Irish in the 1840s and 1850s, African-American longshoremen, waiters, barbers, hotel employees, and even bootblacks had been replaced by successive waves of European immigrants. World War I had highlighted the close connection between European immigration and African-American migration, and African Americans feared losing their foothold in industry if large-scale immigration resumed. The 1919 Chicago race riot demonstrated how quickly some recent immigrants had become openly racist, and the 1921 quota law had appeared to open thousands of steel, meat-packing, and automobile industry jobs to the 1923 migrants. In that year, Emmett J. Scott, the secretary-treasurer of Howard University, wrote to Elbert Gary, urging him to hire black workers and noting that "it seems unnecessary to look for foreign shores to supply any labor shortage that may exist in American industries when there is this large and sympathetic group within reach. These Colored Americans are not aliens, they have never sought to disrupt the government nor do they harbor Bolshevistic or anarchistic ideals. They are ready and willing to help develop the resources of their country." Other black leaders shared the negative stereotypes of southern and eastern European immigrants, although, because they had nary a representative in Congress, their opinions counted for little in the determination of policy.

With so many groups lined up against them, defenders of immigrants stood almost no chance of winning the postwar debate. Even George Norris and Robert La Follette, so bold on other issues, never challenged the new racial theories. By 1922 and 1923, anti-immigrant sentiments had become part of the normal American discourse, and journals that defended the immigrants reached a tiny audience compared to the *Saturday Evening Post* and *World's Work*. No pro-immigrant spokesperson became so well known as Madison Grant and Lothrop Stoddard, or even gained the prominence of John R. Commons and E. A. Ross. Put on the defensive, some advocates of the immigrants now accepted the idea that the United States needed a more selective policy, that immigrants needed to be better distributed throughout the country, and that immigrants had not become Americanized quickly enough in the past.

Jewish organizations were in a delicate situation. If they spoke out too boldly, they risked calling attention to themselves. This, they feared, would stimulate anti-Semitism. If they admitted that hundreds of thousands of eastern European Jews hoped to emigrate to the United States, they risked giving credence to the restrictionists' claim that the Polish ghettos were about to empty their population on American shores. For these and other reasons, the American Jewish Committee favored a cautious approach and did not push for a policy that would grant special exemptions for groups facing religious persecution. Some Jewish newspapers, however, showed less restraint and strongly condemned the "Nordic supremacy legislation" aimed at "practically barring Hebrew, Slavic and Latin peoples."

Armenians had vociferously denounced the 1921 law, and they too feared the effect that further restriction would have on their community. During the Great War, Armenians had suffered horribly at the hands of the Turks. Like the Jews, many Armenians hoped to find refuge in the United States. But the Armenians, like the Slavs and Italians, lacked any influence and could do little but send petitions to Congress calling for a liberal and nondiscriminatory policy.

Irish politicians, who often represented constituencies with many recent immigrants, generally opposed the restrictionist effort. Al Smith, for example, had become known as a friend of the immigrants and had expressed the view that an illiterate could be as good a citizen as a descendant of an old New England family. Instinctively anti-English, the Irish ridiculed racial theories that elevated the Anglo-Saxons. In the early 1920s, the Knights of Columbus sponsored a series of books praising the contributions of various racial groups and challenging the notion that people of Anglo-Saxon descent were solely responsible for establishing the nation's institutions.

On the other hand, because they often served as parish priests, factory foremen, schoolteachers, and policemen, the Irish had more direct contact with the recent immigrants than any other old immigrant group. Relations had not always been friendly, and conflicts, such as the one that tore at the church, had resulted. Many residents of Ireland still grew up expecting to emigrate to America, and because of the instability of the Irish Free State, established in 1922, the outward flow continued. Many Irish Americans were uncertain how the 1921 law and the proposed changes in it would affect them, and they stood on the sidelines during the debate.

By 1923, the chaotic operation of the emergency law contributed to the pressures building on Congress to enact an even more restrictive measure. Hurriedly written and poorly thought out, the 1921 bill had provided that no more than 20 percent of a nation's quota could be used in a single month. This meant that ships carrying immigrants to Ellis Island began to race so as to be the first to arrive just after midnight on the first day of the month. Theoretically, if a ship arrived a few seconds before midnight and some passengers came from a nation whose monthly or yearly quota had been exhausted, the immigrants in excess of the quota could be forced to return to Europe. Even after a May 1922 amendment to the law required companies to reimburse passengers for the return trip, what newspapers referred to as the "first of the month stampede in the harbor of New York" continued.

Most of the southern and eastern European nations used up their quotas during the first six months of the fiscal year, and Ellis Island officials had little choice but to enforce a law that some of them considered objectionable. Great personal tragedies resulted. Dr. S. H. Abkarian, president of the United Armenian Immigration and Welfare Societies, observed: "When you send these Armenians back, where do you send them? You send them back to Turkey simply to be butchered." The severe limitation in numbers also stirred ethnic tensions, and Poles accused Jews of receiving the lion's share of Poland's quota. Secretary of Labor James J. Davis had the discretionary authority to admit "excess quota" immigrants—a power he exercised on a number of occasions, although the Jewish press expressed little faith in the ability of "Nordic Mr. Davis" to be fair.

Restrictionists used the confusion at the ports of arrival to their advantage and argued that Congress needed to write a totally new immigration law. Advocates of Nordic superiority remained unhappy that approximately 150,000 Italians, Slavs, Jews, and people of other "inferior" nationalities could still emigrate to the United States. Anti-immigration forces remained determined to get Congress to adopt a tougher law when the 1921 measure expired. The only question by 1924 was how tough the new law would be.

Closing the Doors: The 1924 National Origins Act and Its Consequences

Since the passage of the 1921 quota bill, Albert Johnson and his nativist colleagues on the House Immigration Committee had set out to find a way further to reduce the numbers of immigrants from southern and eastern Europe. Although some of them favored a complete moratorium on immigration, they knew such a drastic measure could not pass Congress. They faced a dilemma. How could they continue to admit British, Scandinavian, and German immigrants while excluding the "undesirables," without appearing to be discriminatory?

Fortunately for Johnson, supporters of restriction developed a brilliant ploy by which they could disarm their opponents. Working closely with the committee, a number of college professors and eugenicists argued that basing quotas on the foreign-born population residing in the United States in 1910 or 1920 favored the most-recent immigrants. Instead, they contended that the fairest policy would be to establish quotas based on the foreign-born population in the United States in 1890. This method, they said, would truly reflect the national origins of the entire American population. The proposal delighted members of the House Committee on Immigration who had been in search of a method to admit "good blood" and keep out "bad blood." Besides adopting 1890 as the year on which to base quotas, the House committee voted to establish a procedure by which all immigrants would be issued certificates before departing from Europe. (This would eliminate the racing of ships and the lengthy Ellis Island inspections.) The number of immigrants per year would be cut from 357,803 to 161,184, and each nation's quota would be reduced from 3 percent to 2 percent. Experts told them that if this method were used, according to their preliminary projections, Czechoslovakia's total would be cut from 14,557 to 2,031, Hungary's from 5,638 to 474, Italy's from 42,057 to 3,912, Poland's from 21,076 to 5,156, Russia's from 21,613 to 1,992, Yugoslavia's from 6,426 to 851, and Turkey's from 7,388 to 129. On the other hand, Germany's would only be cut from 67,607 to 51,299, and the United Kingdom's would be reduced from 77,342 to 62,458. Highly pleased by these calculations, the committee, dominated by representatives from southern and western states, voted to send the bill to the House.

The measure that the committee approved also included a provision that excluded all immigrants who were ineligible to become citizens. Restrictionists aimed this clause at the Japanese, who, along with the Koreans, were the only group who fell into this particular category. The Japanese fit this description because an 1870 law had specified that only whites and those of African descent were eligible for naturalization, and a 1922 Supreme Court decision had declared that the Japanese were not "white" within the meaning of the naturalization statute. Those who favored this proviso ignored State Department warnings that the stipulation would inflame Japanese-American relations, which the Washington Conference had done so much to improve. If the Japanese had been treated as other nationalities were, they would have received a quota of 240, a number still too large for the rabid West Coast racists responsible for pushing this clause.

The House committee inserted the provision even though the Japanese had often tried to accommodate the United States on the immigration issue. In 1907 and 1908, following the initial eruption of anti-Japanese sentiment, the Japanese government exchanged a series of notes with the United States (known as the Gentlemen's Agreement). The Japanese agreed not to issue passports to common laborers desiring to emigrate to the United States. In 1921, Japanese officials had even agreed to deny passports to "picture brides," who had previously been allowed to leave. The Japanese government did not want to see its citizens emigrate to the United States, but it demanded that Japanese nationals be treated with respect. To bar all Japanese from entering the United States smacked of the treatment the Chinese had received, and Japan resented being treated as an inferior nation.

Once the bill reached the House, its passage was a foregone conclusion. The lengthy debate fully revealed the fears, hatreds, and resentments that motivated the legislation's supporters. Much of the discussion boiled down to one basic issue: what groups should constitute the population of the United States in the future. Many of those who spoke in favor of using the 1890 census as the basis by which to determine the quotas left no doubt that they favored that year to exclude immigrants from southern and eastern Europe. Over and over again, representatives argued that the United States suffered from "acute indigestion" as a result of receiving "unassimilable" groups. Speeches that raised warnings about the danger of the United States becoming a "mongrelized" nation could have been delivered at Klan rallies. Other congressmen spoke so openly about their fears that America had become "the garbage can and the dumping ground of the world" that the comments left one wondering what language the representatives used when speaking in private.

Assertions of American sovereignty, along with racial notions, figured prominently in speeches delivered by House members. Stridently nationalistic statements such as "the nation's immigration laws should be made for Americans and not to please foreigners" and "No foreign government has the right to tell the United States who we shall or shall not admit" sounded markedly similar to those made when the Senate rejected the Treaty of Versailles. And when learning that Italy, Japan, and other nations had criticized the pending legislation, congressmen fell over one another to be the first to denounce the "impudence of foreign nations."

Almost all of those who spoke in favor of the legislation came from areas of the country where few of the recent arrivals had settled. It is likely that no congressman who called for excluding the "foreign invader" had ever shook the callused and blistered hand of a Lithuanian packing-house worker, Italian textile worker, Jewish sewing-machine operator, Slovak coal miner, or any of the other countless immigrants who had contributed to America's economic development. In general, speeches on the House floor revealed how little the congressmen understood about the immigrant experience. They exaggerated the role of steamship companies in encouraging the entire process; they failed to realize that the very poorest peasants were not those most likely to depart for the United States; they did not understand that the foreign-language press, which they so harshly criticized, often encouraged Americanization; they ignored almost completely the extent to which the children of immigrants (the second generation) had adopted American customs, which often led to conflicts with their parents. Nevertheless, despite the welter of misconceptions, the few thoughtful speeches raised legitimate concerns about the need for a "breathing space" so America could absorb the large numbers of immigrants who had arrived during the previous thirty years.

Those who spoke out in opposition to the bill came from urban districts, leading to accusations that the immigrants' congressional defenders had been unduly influenced by the "foreign" vote. In actuality, because of gerrymandering and the failure of Congress to carry out reapportionment following the 1920 census, urban residents were underrepresented in the House. Many of the Irish representatives who opposed the legislation were angered by a report prepared by Harry Laughlin, the immigration committee's eugenics consultant, which concluded that the Irish made up a disproportionate share of the inmates in mental hospitals and in other institutions. Some of the most emotional speeches were made by Adolph Sabath, Samuel Dickstein, and other Jewish representatives, who took to the floor of the House to protest a bill that held one was "better" if "born in one part of Europe . . . than if [one] had been born in another part of Europe."

The maverick Republican Fiorello La Guardia served as one of the immigrants' most outspoken defenders on the House floor. Elected to Congress during the 1922 progressive revival, La Guardia represented New York City's heavily Italian East Harlem district. A melting pot all by himself, La Guardia had a Jewish mother and an Italian father, and was a practicing Episcopalian. Notably cosmopolitan, he spoke a number of languages and had served as an interpreter on Ellis Island. He was fond of exposing his opponents' hypocrisy, and he mocked southerners for their open violations of Prohibition and asked why Kentucky had so many more illiterates and law violators than New York City, a comment that a representative from the Bluegrass State considered "insolent, infamous, contemptible slander."

Almost the entire House debate centered on the merits of using the 1890 census as the base year from which to determine quotas. But by the time the measure reached the Senate, the bill's floor manager, David A. Reed of Pennsylvania, had begun to express concern that the use of the 1890 census appeared to be too blatantly discriminatory. Reed wanted to accomplish the same goal as Johnson, but he wanted the law to seem fairer. With the assistance of John B. Trevor, a colleague of Madison Grant, Reed came up with the idea of basing the quotas on a systematic survey of the national origins of the population of the United States in 1920. Reed and Trevor had no doubt that immigrants from northwestern Europe would receive the vast majority of slots using such a technique. The Senate version of the bill thus established that 1890 (and the 161,184 figure) would be used only until 1927, when a survey of the national origins of the American population would be completed. After 1927 (it actually went into effect in 1929), a total of 150,000 immigrants would be admitted yearly, and the quotas would be based on the national origins of the white population in 1920.

The House and Senate bills had easily passed by margins of 322 to 71 and 62 to 6 respectively, and both bodies had made it resoundingly clear that they wanted a measure in place when the 1921 emergency law expired on 31 May 1924. So when the two bills went to a joint House-Senate committee, the Senate version, without much difficulty, won approval and the Johnson-Reed Act went to the president for his signature.

Calvin Coolidge had not said much about the issue, but people knew he sympathized with the critics of the immigrants. The very embodiment of Puritan stock, he had never had any appreciable contact with the new immigrant groups. In his 1924 annual message to Congress, the president had spoken of the need to limit "new arrivals" and said "America must be kept American," a phrase restrictionists took to repeating. But opponents of the legislation held out the hope that inclusion of the anti-Japanese provision might lead to a veto. The Japanese ambassador to the United States had warned that the clause could have "grave consequences" for United States–Japanese relations, and Secretary of State Charles Evans Hughes had cautioned about the danger of undoing American efforts "to create a better feeling in the East." But Coolidge signed the bill, although he expressed regrets over the needless irritation to Japan.

Passage of the Johnson-Reed Act closed an epoch in American history. No longer would the United States provide asylum for Europe's oppressed. Those most desirous of emigrating belonged to precisely the groups that Congress had practically excluded from coming to the United States. Some wishful thinkers held out the hope that the law would be repealed when the United States recovered from its "post-war hatred," but the National Origins Act established the basic framework for United States immigration policy until the 1960s. Despite the immense significance of the law, its enactment received surprisingly little coverage in the mainstream press. The failure to analyze the bill's implications manifested the general insensitivity that nativists had shown for recent arrivals. The lack of attention also reflected the consensus among old-stock Americans that the time for a drastic change in policy had arrived, and they took the act's passage for granted.

News of the enactment of the legislation brought a universal cry of outrage from groups that had been branded as inferior. Insulted by the tiny totals granted their compatriots, Italian, Polish, Jewish, Armenian, and many other ethnic newspapers denounced a law that designated nationalities as desirable or undesirable.

The Japanese and Italian governments also reacted with indignation when they learned that the Johnson-Reed law had been enacted. Even Rumania, hardly in a position to do anything about it, rebuked the United States for assigning its citizens a quota of 831. Despite the protests, the Johnson-Reed Act did not seriously affect American foreign policy. But the law had serious consequences for the United States and for those who hoped to make the voyage to America. Some of the effects had been anticipated, but others surprised both supporters and opponents of the law.

The legislation, for example, had disastrous consequences for Jews. If the United States had at least continued the quota policy established in 1921, it is likely that approximately three hundred thousand eastern European Jews would have emigrated to America between 1924 and 1929. Instead, except for the few who emigrated to the Latin American countries and to Palestine, most of these would-be emigrants perished in the Holocaust. Advocates of restriction could not have anticipated these tragic results, although they had never shown any sympathy for Jewish victims of European anti-Semitic movements. In late 1924, American officials turned a deaf ear to thousands of Jewish refugees stranded in various European ports after they had been caught unaware by the passage of the Johnson-Reed Act—an eerie preview of events in the late 1930s.

Other groups felt the sting of the legislation. "Japanese immigrants," in the words of historian Yuji Ichioka, "interpreted the enactment of the 1924 Immigration Act as the culminating act of rejection by the United States." Those of the first generation, known as Issei, never shook off the "stigma of inferiority" and even the Nisei, the American-born second generation, feared their citizenship might be taken away. As it turned out, the federal government interned both groups during World War II. Armenians caught between the depredations of the Turks and the Kurds even sought refuge in the Soviet Union once they realized they could not come to America. Regardless of their nationality, many immigrants discovered that family members could not join them. And from Portugal to Greece to the Cape Verde Islands, home countries suffered because when fewer immigrants were able to go to the United States, there was less money flowing back in the form of remittances.

The most disillusioned groups turned out to be the Scandinavians. They were the only true Nordics according to the dictionary definition of the term, and their representatives had supported the idea of using 1890 as the basis for quotas. But at the last moment, they realized that Senator Reed's national-origins plan would favor British immigrants over all others. Nordic unity dissolved as

Representative Knud Wefald of Minnesota protested the "breach of faith" that gave preference to "peoples from the British slums" over "farmer lads and skilled laborers from Scandinavian countries." The protests came too late, and when the national-origins provision finally went into effect in 1929, only 2,377 Norwegians were allowed to enter the United States, whereas in 1923, 16,000 had arrived.

Because countries in the Western Hemisphere had been exempted from both the 1921 and the 1924 laws, Canadians and Mexicans remained free to emigrate to the United States. Canadians had generally been welcomed, but some restrictionists had urged that a quota be assigned to Mexico. Intense lobbying by agricultural interests, however, had overcome efforts to close America's back door. In any case, Mexicans had found it relatively easy to avoid paying the required ten-dollar head tax because the newly established United States Border Patrol lacked the means to prevent illegal crossings.

During the 1920s, approximately five hundred thousand Mexican immigrants arrived in the United States, and employers eagerly tapped this new source of cheap labor. Mexican immigrants filled a wide variety of jobs. In California, they replaced the Japanese as the principal source of labor in agriculture; in Arizona, they worked in copper mines, receiving wages far below those paid to "Anglos"; they did much of the repair work on railroads; they became the chief source of labor in Michigan sugar-beet fields; they filled steel jobs in Chicago, Gary, Lorain, and Youngstown; they joined the rush to Detroit's automobile factories. By the late 1920s, Los Angeles, home to more Mexican immigrants than any other city, supported a thriving Mexican-American cultural life. But once the Great Depression hit, in a new surge of anti-immigrant sentiment, many Mexicans faced forced repatriation.

From a long-term perspective, the quota laws made it more difficult for immigrant communities to sustain the institutional infrastructures they had developed. The individual groups had built a rich array of newspapers, fraternal organizations, mutual-aid and singing societies, gymnastic clubs, and many other institutions. During the 1920s, these organizations flourished as the first generation, which for the most part still lived in densely packed urban districts, generously supported them. But by the 1930s and the 1940s, the lack of replenishment by new arrivals led to the erosion of these institutions. The more Americanized second generation sought other outlets for its leisure and cultural life.

In a development that must have surprised restrictionists, the quota laws aided the Congress of Industrial Organizations (CIO) when it undertook its great organizing drives in the 1930s. When the first generation made up the bulk of the industrial work force, it was hard to build support for permanent unions among immigrants who distrusted one another, intended to return to Europe, or simply did not understand English well. But the second generation proved far more likely than their parents to identify with the American working class, and its members enthusiastically embraced a union movement that treated them as equals rather than as inferiors.

By 1928, these second-generation immigrants increasingly cast their ballots for the Democratic Party, which had become much more open to them than the Republicans. The Republicans by the middle and late 1920s had become even more ardent champions of the quota laws. In 1926, Secretary of Labor Davis boasted that immigration restriction had preserved the wages and purchasing power of American workers. Angered by the demonstrations to save Sacco and Vanzetti, in 1927 Albert Johnson, seemingly not happy unless he could exclude every Slav, Italian, and Jew, pushed for an alien registration law and for legislation to make it easier to deport aliens who participated in protests. And in 1928, Republicans, confident of victory, nominated Herbert Hoover, like Coolidge an embodiment of old-stock America, to face Al Smith, the representative of urban, immigrant America, in an election that highlighted many of the social forces that had divided Americans during the decade.

8

THE NEW ERA AND THE PRESIDENTIAL ELECTION OF 1928

THE 1928 PRESIDENTIAL ELECTION highlighted many of the most significant developments in the 1920s. Basking in the New Era prosperity, the Republicans nominated Secretary of Commerce Herbert Hoover, the epitome of the business system's success, and the underdog Democrats nominated Al Smith, the personification of Gotham, a city Americans loved to hate. Both candidates agreed on the essential soundness of the American economy, so the campaign focused on many of the social issues that had divided Americans. Controversy over Smith's religion and his criticism of Prohibition contributed to a revival of interest in politics and reversed the downward trend in voter participation that had been evident throughout the decade. To the surprise of no one, Herbert Hoover won an easy victory in an election held one year before the stock market crash ushered in a decade markedly different from the 1920s.

Business and the New Era

In 1928, the United States economy entered its fifth year of almost steady growth, and an economist writing in the liberal weekly *The Nation* noted: "Unquestionably this post-war period has been marked by America's economic coming of age." Brief recessions in 1924 and 1927 had little overall impact, and many academic experts expressed confidence that the business cycle (the wild swings between growth and depression) that had characterized American capitalism had been conquered. Prices had been stabilized and the ready availability of consumer credit allowed workers to purchase products turned out by American industry. The United States had become the world's leading creditor nation. The booming bull market indicated that investors had confidence in the future.

Business executives replaced politicians as the exemplars of progressivism. Instead of extolling the accomplishments of Theodore Roosevelt or Woodrow Wilson, journalists heaped praise on Henry Ford and General Electric's Gerard Swope. Despite the oligopolistic American economy, antitrust sentiment had seemingly died with La Follette. No longer portrayed as robber barons, businessmen basked in their rehabilitated public image and funded charities, symphony orchestras, and art museums filled with the de rigueur impressionist paintings.

Business and industry set the tone for many aspects of American life. A 1925 bestseller, *The Man Nobody Knows* by Bruce Barton, portrayed Jesus Christ as an advertising man. Handsome bank lobbies and magnificent art deco office buildings suggested a faith in the future. The machine-age precisionist artists Charles Demuth and Charles Sheeler found their inspiration in skyscrapers and smokestacks. Ministers and rabbis warned of the dangers of materialism, but shoppers packed department stores offering a vast array of goods, and filmgoers flocked to the ornate movie palaces that had replaced the nickelodeons. Business, having mastered the techniques of mass production and mass distribution, received full credit for having created a standard of living that surpassed all others in the world, and that provided far more than the basic necessities of food, clothing, and shelter.

By the mid-1920s, as the postwar tensions began to fade, Americans celebrated the accomplishments of Babe Ruth in baseball, Red Grange in football, Jack Dempsey in boxing, Bobby Jones in golf, and Helen Wills in tennis. Charles Lindbergh, whose solo 1927 New York–to–Paris flight stirred the nation, stood out as the hero in an era of heroes. Modest and unassuming, Lindbergh personified the marriage of technology and individualism that seemingly accounted for America's economic success.

Widespread distribution of the automobile served as the best indication that the United States had entered a new era. By 1929, between 50 and 60 percent of all American families owned a car. This was a phenomenal figure given the newness of the industry, and it was not matched again until 1949. Making full use of techniques suggested by Frederick Taylor, the father of scientific management, Ford and other automobile manufacturers reorganized their factories to ensure a smooth flow of production. The workers remained stationary while cranes and hoists brought the parts to them; thousands of single-purpose machine tools bored out the required parts; and the final product took shape on a series of assembly lines. By the early 1920s, one Model T rolled off the assembly line every ten seconds, and the term *Fordism* became synonymous with mass production.

Ford continued to enjoy an excellent reputation because he produced an affordable car for the masses and because it was mistakenly believed that he paid higher wages than other automobile manufacturers. But by mid-decade, General Motors had emerged as the dominant firm in America's most important industry. During the postwar depression, the du Pont family had gained ownership of controlling stock in General Motors. The du Ponts, in turn, had chosen Alfred P. Sloan, an MIT-trained engineer, to head the corporation. The very model of a 1920s corporate executive, Sloan played a major role in General Motors's emergence as the nation's largest corporation. With his encouragement, General Motors gave division executives considerable autonomy. Sloan also pioneered the General Motors Acceptance Corporation, which allowed new-car buyers to finance their purchases through the company. Above all, Sloan understood that the automobile had become a sign of status and that people chose a car, in part, to make a statement about themselves. Unlike Ford, who until 1927 stuck stubbornly to the Model T, General Motors manufactured different automobiles for different income groups and made annual style changes a newsworthy event.

By mid-decade, the automobile had become the linchpin of the American economy. Not only did the industry employ hundreds of thousands of workers directly, but it also had an important multiplier effect. Along with the machine-tool industry, the rubber, glass, steel, and petroleum industries all benefited from the growth of automobile manufacturing. Countless more people worked in constructing roads, selling automobiles and servicing them, and in creating the print advertisements that stimulated sales.

The automobile also drastically altered the way people lived. When Robert Lynd and Helen Lynd conducted their famous 1920s sociological study in Muncie, Indiana (published in 1929 as *Middletown*), one resident asked them: "Why on earth do you need to study what's changing the country? I can tell you in just four letters: A-U-T-O!" Indeed, the Lynds discovered that the automobile appeared to be changing peoples' lives in a number of ways. Some Muncie residents had become so determined to purchase a car that they owned an automobile before they had indoor plumbing. Driving the car itself had become a form of leisure, identified with freedom and mobility, and instead of attending community holiday celebrations, union meetings, or church services, many residents preferred to take a drive in the country. For some, it appeared to provide a relief from boring and tedious jobs. Parents blamed the automobile for the increase in premarital sexual activity evident in the 1920s.

The automobile may have had the greatest impact on small towns and rural districts where it gave people new options for shopping and for leisure. In the 1920s, the car had less of an impact on large cities, where people still lived in congested areas and relied on public transportation. But even in urban areas, the automobile had begun to encourage the growth of suburbs and had led to a decline in the interurban, a system of rail transportation that had connected large cities with communities thirty to sixty miles away. By the end of the decade, the passenger railroads and the streetcars had begun their long-term decline, in part because there was no prestige involved in boarding a trolley, even when it was headed for a leafy suburb.

The willingness to assume considerable consumer debt in order to purchase an automobile and new household appliances indicated that a fundamental shift in values had taken place. In earlier times, Americans had emphasized the importance of thrift and frugality, but the 1920s previewed the American society that fully emerged in the 1950s, one that placed far more emphasis on consumption and leisure. Even the ads had changed. In the 1890s, an individual was likely to pick a product out of a Sears Roebuck catalogue that described the actual mechanical workings of the item. By the 1920s, most Americans had been exposed to the full-color, splashy display ads that filled mass-circulation magazines and sought to convince consumers that ownership of a particular item would make them appear up-to-date. Appropriately, advertising, which emerged as an industry in itself, became concentrated in New York City, a metropolis identified with modernity.

By the eve of the 1928 presidential election, business had become the dominant if not the hegemonic force in American society. Through the introduction of new products, business had changed the way people lived their lives. To meet the needs of business, universities had begun to place more emphasis on science, engineering, and research. Because of the success of the open-shop campaign and welfare capitalism, business dominated the workplace, and it set the political agenda for the Coolidge administration, which emphasized economy in government, low taxes, and limited regulation of business. Therefore, once Calvin Coolidge decided not to seek reelection, Herbert Hoover—a man who more than any other figure had become identified with the American ideal of efficiency—became the logical Republican candidate at the end of a decade that had seen business emerge as the most dynamic force in American life.

Herbert Hoover and the American Business System

Most political observers had expected that Calvin Coolidge would again seek the Republican presidential nomination in 1928. Coolidge appeared to be a sure winner given that his administration had been free of scandal and that he had presided over the booming American economy. It thus came as a surprise when the taciturn president called reporters into a room on 2 August 1927 and, without explanation, handed each one of them a slip of paper reading "I do not choose to run for president in nineteen twenty eight." For a few months, speculation centered on whom the new Republican nominee might be, but when Herbert Hoover announced his candidacy in early 1928, it became a foregone conclusion that the secretary of commerce would be chosen by the Republicans to head the ticket.

Hoover emerged as the front runner for good reason, because his entire career represented an astonishing American success story. Born in Iowa and from a Quaker background, Hoover was orphaned at an early age. After moving to Oregon to live with relatives, he worked his way through Stanford University, where he studied geology. Upon graduation, he became a highly successful mining engineer and carried out extensive explorations in Australia and China. Having earned a fortune by the age of forty, Hoover made an unusual decision for a young man: he decided to devote the rest of his career to public service. During 1914 and 1915, he had earned international stature by his efforts to relieve hunger in Belgium following the German invasion of that neutral nation. Once the United States entered the war, he headed the newly established Food Administration, a federal agency that sought to stimulate production of essential grains and to limit domestic consumption. At the end of the war, Hoover had further enhanced his reputation when he headed the American Relief Association, which fed millions of civilians in wartorn areas of East Central Europe. For good reason, in the wake of the Versailles negotiations, John Maynard Keynes in *The Economic Consequences of the Peace* observed that Hoover had been "the only man who emerged from the ordeal of Paris with an enhanced reputation."

The war and Hoover's involvement in Europe played an important role in shaping his ideas. A foe of bureaucracies, he believed European governments to be overcentralized and too wedded to notions of state socialism. When he came home in 1919, he told reporters that he hoped he would never again have to return to the Continent, and despite his success as head of the Food Administration, he believed that the United States should avoid the type of coercive government policies followed by the Wilson administration during the war.

Hoover had become secretary of commerce on condition that he be given a free hand to shape all aspects of American economic policy. Between 1921 and 1928, the man whom historian Joan Hoff Wilson has described as the "postwar superman" did much to elevate this previously obscure cabinet post. Indeed, at times Americans may have wondered who was president: Harding, Coolidge, or Hoover. Besides taking the initiative in convening the 1921 conference on unemployment, he organized more than two hundred other conferences aimed at encouraging American corporations to cooperate and to move away from older forms of destructive competition. Along with helping to convince the steel industry to end the twelve-hour day, he played an important role in shaping the 1926 Railway Labor Act that granted unions collective bargaining rights and established mediation procedures whenever a railroad strike threatened. He actively campaigned to eliminate waste in industry and encouraged the growth of trade associations, which allowed firms engaged in like-minded endeavors to share information without facing the threat of antitrust suits. He reorganized the Department of Commerce into commodity divisions so as to encourage the growth of exports. He helped convince Coolidge to veto the McNary-Haugen Bill because he did not believe that the federal government should assume the responsibility of providing guaranteed prices for farmers. He served as chairman of the Special Mississippi Flood Committee following the disastrous Mississippi River flood of 1927, a position that cemented his reputation as the Great Humanitarian, although critics charged he used the tragedy for political purposes.

Hoover by the 1920s had also developed a well-thought-out philosophy that he articulated in his book *American Individualism*, published in 1922. In this work and in many of his other writings, Hoover sought to balance individual striving with the need for community, a source of tension for Americans ever since the Puritans had settled the Massachusetts Bay Colony. Hoover believed that a solution for this conflict could be found in a system that he variously described as "cooperative capitalism" or "cooperative individualism," a philosophy that revisionist historians have labeled associationalism. Hoover considered himself a progressive but given the faith that he placed in the private enterprise system and his distrust of government, his thinking most closely matches that of twentieth-century conservatives. Impressed by the emergence of welfare capitalism and the new era of labor-capital peace, Hoover believed that a more responsible and enlightened capitalist system had made the robber barons of an earlier era obsolete. Based on his wartime experiences, he feared the excesses of concentrated state power far more than any potential abuses of power by business. To American business, he gave full credit for the rise in the standard of living that had outpaced Europe and the rest of the world. For those who had not shared in the prosperity, he hoped that charities and local government could take care of their needs, an element of his philosophy often referred to as voluntarism.

Hoover could be quite cold and aloof. He viewed most issues as technical problems that could be solved by engineers, whom he considered to be a neutral force between employers and employees. He paid little attention to highly charged emotional issues that could not be resolved by technocrats. He did not speak out against the excesses of the Red Scare, and he rarely commented on the intolerance and nativism of the 1920s. During his career in business and government, he had only minimal contact with Catholics, Jews, or African Americans, and he appeared uncomfortable with people from a background different than his own.

As the decade wore on, Hoover had become more complacent, and many of his earlier criticisms of business had lost their edge by the late 1920s. Hoover also had never run for office before and had never been fully accepted by the Republican political leadership. But his reputation for being above politics served him well with an American public distrustful of politicians, and provided a striking contrast to Al Smith, a man who lived and breathed politics.

Al Smith and the Democratic Party

As the 1928 presidential election approached, the Democrats knew they had little chance of victory. Not only had Cox and Davis been trounced in 1920 and 1924, but the Republicans had controlled both the House and the Senate since 1918. Grover Cleveland in 1892 had been the last Democrat to win a typical presidential election, because both of Woodrow Wilson's victories could be considered flukes: in 1912 because of a split in the Republican Party and in 1916 because of the unusual circumstances brought on by the war in Europe.

By 1928, no one could be quite sure what the Democrats stood for. Unlike the Republicans, who had become known as the party of business, the Democrats lacked a cohesive element that could bind them together. The party's two principal constituencies, urban Irish Catholics and white southerners, shared little other than a commitment to localism and opposition to a strong central government. Since the deaths of Woodrow Wilson and William Jennings Bryan, the Democrats had lacked a nationally prominent leader who could speak for them. Franklin Delano Roosevelt, while recovering from poliomyelitis, had been working since the 1924 presidential election to build party unity and to restore morale, but the Democrats continued to be torn by factionalism.

Few Democrats even appeared interested in receiving the 1928 nomination. William Gibbs McAdoo, never fully able to shake the taint of scandal, withdrew from the race in 1927. Tom Walsh, a dry, progressive Roman Catholic Democrat from Montana with a reputation for rectitude, appeared to be an attractive candidate, but he fared poorly in the primaries. This left the field for Al Smith, then serving his fourth term as governor of New York, who received the nomination on the first ballot when the Democrats convened in Houston in June 1928.

Smith became the first Roman Catholic ever nominated for president by a major political party. It is not surprising that the Democrats established this precedent; they had been far more receptive to Catholic voters than had the Republicans. Nevertheless, given the intensity of the opposition to Smith and given that the Democratic nominee needed to receive two-thirds of the delegates' votes, it seems surprising that he faced so little opposition. A number of factors explain the ease with which he swept the convention. Following the 1924 New York City debacle, the Democrats had become determined to avoid bitter infighting. Smith had acceded to the choice of Houston as the convention site and as a further sign of harmony, he chose the dry Democratic senator Joseph Robinson of Arkansas as his running mate. Many party members who disliked or even detested Smith believed he had no chance of winning the presidential contest. By selecting him, they could appease Irish Catholics and other northern Democrats while clearing the decks for a different candidate in 1932. Finally, Smith's nomination indicated that the southern Democrats were losing influence in a party that could not hope to win a presidential election without carrying some of the big industrial states.

Smith's nomination set up a battle between two dissimilar candidates who had achieved the American dream in radically different ways. Although he identified himself as Irish, Smith came from a New York City family of mixed Irish and German descent. His father died when he was young and he received little formal schooling. While Hoover remained proud of his Stanford education, Smith liked to say that he had graduated from the Fulton Fish Market, a slap at those who boasted about their college educations. After working at various jobs, Smith had received his start in politics with the aid of Tammany Hall, New York City's Irish-dominated political machine. For the Irish, Tammany had been a source of jobs and an avenue of social mobility for men who lacked a formal education. Many other Americans, however, identified Tammany with political bosses, corruption, and bloc voting—associations that had a considerable basis in reality.

Smith had risen quickly in New York City and New York State politics. Representing a Lower East Side Manhattan constituency, he had first been elected to the state assembly in 1903 and had served on a commission that conducted a thorough investigation of industrial conditions following the 1911 New York City Triangle Shirtwaist Company fire, a disaster that cost the lives of 146 young women. The commission's exhaustive research had led to the passage of a number of factory-inspection and fire-prevention laws, making New York State a leader in this area. Personable and convivial, Smith had first been elected governor of New York in 1918, had narrowly lost in the 1920 Republican landslide, and then had won successive terms in 1922, 1924, and 1926 to a position that had often served as a stepping-stone to the White House.

Smith compiled an admirable record as governor of the nation's most populous state. A master of government administration, he reorganized state bureaus and departments in order to make them more efficient. Despite Tammany's unsavory reputation, New York government remained free of scandal during his four terms. Governor at the time of progressive retreat, he earned a reputation as a moderate reformer through his advocacy of conservation, state parks, laws protecting women and child wage earners, and workers' compensation. In contrast to Hoover, he had a number of women advisors, including Belle Moskowitz, a master political strategist and his most trusted confidant, and Frances Perkins, the Smith administration's top expert on labor matters.

Smith earned a national reputation because of his outspokenness on social issues. Largely self-taught, he had opposed the literacy test and had become known as a friend of the immigrants. He had gladly signed New York's anti-Klan law and had spoken out against the growing intolerance of the early 1920s. By 1923, when he signed a statute repealing New York's Prohibition enforcement law, he had become known, in the words of historian Douglas B. Craig, as the "most famous wet politician in the country."

Smith's views on Prohibition aroused strong emotions. To Smith, the Eighteenth Amendment represented an attack on immigrant customs and traditions by intolerant nativists and bigots. Most people assumed that Smith had continued to imbibe after the passage of Prohibition, and in 1922, Smith had supposedly commented to reporters: "Wouldn't you like to have your foot on the rail and blow the foam off some suds?" His comments and behavior had led prohibitionists to refer to him as Alcohol Al. For political reasons, Smith had said he only favored modification of the Volstead Act to permit light beers and wine, but almost no one doubted that he would have been delighted to see Prohibition repealed.

When he defended immigrants, opposed the Klan, and employed Jewish as well as women advisors, Smith appeared broadminded, but he lacked an overall vision of the nation's future. Besides having little knowledge of foreign policy, he also had little understanding of problems facing Americans who lived outside the urban Northeast. Very much a "New York provincial," Smith had not served in Congress and thus had not been forced to deal with national issues.

Even before the formal start of the race, Smith's selection of John K. Raskob to head the Democratic National Committee indicated that he would not challenge Hoover's business orientation. Raskob, like Smith, had risen from humble circumstances to a position of national stature. Having begun his career as a personal secretary to Pierre S. du Pont, Raskob had quickly moved up the ranks of the du Ponts' giant chemical firm, which had earned enormous profits during the war. Partly at Raskob's urging, the du Ponts had used these surplus funds to gain ownership of controlling shares in General Motors. At General Motors, Raskob, along with Alfred P. Sloan, had been the driving force behind the establishment of the General Motors Acceptance Corporation and had earned a national reputation as a business genius.

Raskob's appointment brought forth a firestorm of criticism from progressives and from western Democrats who had long harbored a strong dislike of Wall Street. Until 1926, Raskob had considered himself a Republican. Why then did Smith choose him to head the Democratic National Committee for the next four years? In part, Smith was comfortable with a man who shared his devout Catholicism and plebian origins. Lacking self-confidence himself, Smith also enjoyed being associated with a prominent businessman. More importantly, Raskob shared Smith's fervent opposition to Prohibition. Both Raskob and the du Ponts had become vehement critics of the Eighteenth Amendment, a measure they viewed as encouraging government interference with personal liberty and as establishing a dangerous precedent for government expropriation of business without compensation. The du Ponts and Raskob had become financial backers of the Association against the Prohibition Amendment, and Smith anticipated that they would be willing to help bankroll the Democrats, a party that in the past had often been forced to conduct underfinanced campaigns.

Raskob's appointment guaranteed that Smith would not challenge Republican economic policies (Raskob even moved the Democratic national headquarters to General Motors's New York City building) and that Prohibition would figure prominently in the Hoover-Smith race. Despite his hostility to a strong central government, Hoover, in a letter to William Borah, had described Prohibition as "a great social and economic experiment, noble in motive and far-reaching in purpose," and the Republicans had drafted a dry platform. The Democratic platform had also endorsed Prohibition but Smith had repudiated this stand in his "wet telegram" to the convention. Such a focus distressed Democrats who wished to call attention to the plight of farmers or more substantive issues than the right to drink. Nevertheless, controversy over Prohibition and Smith's religion created far more interest in the 1928 election than would otherwise have been the case.

Prosperity, Prohibition, and Prejudice: The 1928 Campaign

Herbert Hoover entered the 1928 campaign an overwhelming favorite to win the presidency. Given the usual Republican majority in a presidential election, the overall prosperity, and Hoover's string of personal successes, it seemed almost inconceivable that he could lose the election. Ever since 1896, when Mark Hanna stage-managed William McKinley's triumph over William Jennings Bryan, the Republicans had sought to identify their party with business and prosperity, an emphasis that implied that a Democratic victory could lead to financial panic and depression.

With the advent of radio, Hoover, uncomfortable with crowds, had a good excuse not to campaign, because he could reach an audience of forty million with a single address. One of his rare campaign stops came in Elizabethton, Tennessee, one of the Piedmont textile towns where workers in 1929 would conduct militant strikes. Hoover traveled to Tennessee because Republicans believed that Smith's religion gave them an opportunity to crack the Democratic stranglehold on the Solid South. Aside from this and a few other appearances, Hoover seemed content to run a safe and noncontroversial campaign.

Only at the end of the campaign, in a Madison Square Garden address heard by millions over the radio, did Hoover deliver a speech that captured his ideas, philosophy, and vision as they had evolved by 1928. The address stressed the progress the United States had made since the war, particularly in contrast with Europe, a continent that Hoover almost always referred to in a negative way. Using unusually strong language, Hoover warned of the dangers of a return to the "centralized despotism" of the wartime period and contrasted the "American system of rugged individualism" with European "paternalism," words that carried additional weight because of his previous role as head of the Food Administration. In a veiled reference to vague Democratic proposals to use the dam at Muscle Shoals to provide public power for the Tennessee Valley region, Hoover warned about the dangers of "bureaucracy" and of "state socialism." Echoing themes struck by Republican orators ever since Harding's 1920 "triumphant nationality" campaign, Hoover praised both the tariff and restrictive immigration laws for providing protection for the American worker.

The second part of the speech praised America's material progress. In words that sounded convincing in 1928 but haunted him for the rest of his life, Hoover repeatedly cited the rise in the standard of living as evidence of America's progress since the postwar recovery:

> It [the United States] has come nearer to the abolition of poverty, to the abolition of the fear of want, than humanity has ever reached before.

> The slogan of progress is changing from the full dinner pail to the full garage.

> We are nearer today to the ideal of the abolition of poverty and fear from the lives of men than ever before in all history.

While noting the difficulties of those who labored in the "textile, coal and agricultural industries," Hoover left little doubt that the last seven and one-half years of Republican administrations had led to an unprecedented rise in the standard of living.

Smith made little effort to challenge Hoover's business ideology. Whether because of his own conservatism, Raskob's influence, or the apparent success of American capitalism, Smith chose to ignore the glaring inequalities between the rich and the poor and warning signs such as a decline in new housing starts and a slowdown in the purchase of consumer durables, which indicated that the period of prosperity was about to end. To the consternation of free traders, Smith abandoned the Democratic commitment to a tariff for revenue only and instead embraced the Republican policy of protectionism. This "me-too" strategy had its perils, because voters were unlikely to believe that the Democrats could be more probusiness than the Republicans, just as in the 1950s, the Democrats sounded unconvincing when they tried to be more anti-Communist than the Republicans.

Smith did make some effort to call attention to the plight of farmers, whose discontent had continued to grow throughout a decade when world prices failed to reach their prewar high. Hoover appeared vulnerable on this issue because he had approved of Coolidge's veto of the McNary-Haugen Bill. In order to take advantage of Hoover's weakness in rural areas, Smith made a campaign swing through the Farm Belt. But he hedged and endorsed the principle of McNary-Haugen without fully embracing it. Besides, Smith had slight knowledge of agricultural issues, and a candidate who wore a brown derby, smoked cigars, used "The Sidewalks of New York" as a theme song, and spoke with a city accent faced insurmountable barriers in trying to convince farmers that he understood their problems. Progressive Republicans (with the exception of Nebraska's George

Norris), seeing little difference between the candidates, endorsed Hoover, although they expressed unease with the commerce secretary's total embrace of business.

Smith failed to stake out independent ground on other issues as well. Although he considered the use of quotas discriminatory, he did not challenge Hoover's embrace of the National Origins Act. He was critical of Republican plans to turn Muscle Shoals over to private industry, but he said little about the need for public power, even though much of the South lacked electrification. Despite the evident unrest of textile workers, he offered no concrete programs for those who labored in the sick industries. Fearful of alienating southern white voters, he made no effort to court the northern black population.

Foreign-policy issues hardly figured in the campaign at all. In 1928, American dollars flowed into Germany, enabling the Germans to make their scaled-down reparations payments to England and France, which in turn began to pay off some of their debts to the United States. The political situation on the Continent had apparently stabilized, and Hitler's Nazi movement, which had gained ground during the 1923 German crisis, appeared to many observers to have faded by 1927. In 1928, the United States had cosponsored the Kellogg-Briand Pact, a meaningless document that outlawed war as "an instrument of national policy." While American investment flowed overseas, the United States showed little interest in participating in meaningful international organizations. During the campaign, Smith abandoned the lingering rhetorical commitment to joining the League of Nations, an act that outraged diehard Wilsonians still active in the Democratic Party.

Given the consensus on domestic and foreign policy, Prohibition emerged as the single most important issue distinguishing the two candidates. Smith had called for "fundamental changes" in Prohibition but remained vague about exactly what he would propose if he became president. While steering away from advocating outright repeal of the Eighteenth Amendment, he had implied that he favored either altering the Volstead Act to permit light beers and wine or allowing each state to determine for itself the standard for categorizing a drink as intoxicating. Although he had signed the statute repealing New York's enforcement law, Smith insisted that he did not wish to see a return of the saloon.

Many Protestants continued to view Prohibition as an intensely moral issue that could not be compromised or even debated. Other supporters of the Eighteenth Amendment argued that it had aided the economy by making workers more productive and that it had led to an overall improvement in the nation's health. Hoover did not care much about the issue and may have been amused that some commentators misquoted him as having described Prohibition as the "noble experiment." Hoover knew that his endorsement of Prohibition would win him votes in the South, and regardless of his own viewpoint, the Quaker image of propriety that he projected appealed to many Americans who were upset by the pace of change in the 1920s as well as by the open violations of the law.

The campaign of 1928 is best remembered for the outburst of anti-Catholicism on the part of many Protestants, who could not stomach the idea of a Roman Catholic becoming president of the United States, especially one who had been an altar boy and who had kissed the ring of the papal legate at the 1926 Eucharistic Congress held in Chicago. Even those Protestants who fought bitterly with one another shared a belief that a Roman Catholic should not become president. Fundamentalism had emerged in the postwar period as a cause stressing the inerrancy of the Scriptures and hostile to modernist tendencies within Protestantism. Fundamentalists had directed most of their ire at liberal Protestants, but they also scorned Catholic ceremonies and rituals. Although their growth had been stemmed due to negative publicity they received for supporting the Tennessee law forbidding the teaching of evolution in public schools (the law that schoolteacher John Scopes had tested in the famous "monkey trial"), they remained a formidable force in the Bible Belt. Protestants from more-liberal denominations wondered whether a Catholic president could remain independent of Vatican control. Regardless of denomination, Protestants questioned whether the doctrine of papal infallibility (which they often distorted) meant that a Catholic president would be duty-bound to follow the dictates of the pope.

As the presidential contest entered its final weeks, some of Smith's opponents mounted a whispering campaign against him, spreading rumors, for example, that the New York governor had been arrested for drunken driving, even though he did not drive. Anti-Catholic fanatics circulated a number of anonymously authored pamphlets, similar to those used by the Klan, warning of the consequences of electing a man who had "kissed the papal ring." Others who objected to Smith on religious grounds made little effort to hide their personal belief that a Catholic should not become president. James Cannon, a Virginia Methodist bishop who in 1927 had become head of the Anti-Saloon League upon Wayne Wheeler's death, openly expressed hostility to a religion he described as "the Mother of ignorance, superstition, intolerance and sin," and warned people not to vote for a candidate representative of "the kind of dirty people that you find today on the sidewalks of New York." Popular revivalists Aimee Semple McPherson and Billy Sunday appealed to their flock to keep America Protestant, and

Alabama senator Thomas Heflin warned that the Pope would control America if Smith triumphed. Mabel Walker Willebrandt, an assistant attorney general with special responsibility for Prohibition enforcement, made one of the campaign's most controversial statements when she told the Ohio Conference of the Methodist Episcopal church: "There are two thousand pastors here. You have in your churches more than 600,000 members of the Methodist Churches in Ohio alone. That is enough to swing the election. The 600,000 have friends in other states. Write to them. Everyday and every ounce of your energy are needed to rouse the friends of Prohibition to register and vote." Although Hoover spoke out against religious prejudice, he did not do so in a vigorous way, and Smith supporters remained dissatisfied that the Republican candidate refused to condemn a Coolidge administration official whom they believed had blatantly appealed to people to vote on religious grounds.

Smith made some effort to respond to reasonable critics. In 1927, he carried out a dignified discussion on the pages of the *Atlantic Monthly* with Charles C. Marshall, a New York lawyer, who in an open letter to the New York governor had raised questions about potential conflicts between Catholic dogma and the Constitution. During the campaign, Smith deliberately traveled to the fundamentalist stronghold of Oklahoma City to make a major address, defending the right of a Roman Catholic to seek the presidency and pledging to uphold the separation of church and state if elected to the nation's highest office. Some historians, citing John F. Kennedy's more effective response to the Catholic issue in 1960, have questioned whether Smith went far enough in answering questions concerning possible conflicts between his duty to obey the Constitution and the pope. But many things had changed by 1960: liberal tendencies had emerged within Catholicism; the ecumenical movement had established a dialogue between Protestants and Catholics; American society itself had become more secular. In the context of 1928, there is probably not much more that Smith could have done in a nation that remained sharply divided along religious lines.

Ultimately, it is impossible to distinguish opposition to Smith based on his religion from other issues. A wet, Tammany, Catholic Democrat from New York City was an ideal type of what most horrified many Protestants. Many Catholics became determined to vote for Smith because of his religion and many liberals, lacking a viable third party to support, argued that at least a vote for Smith would be a vote for tolerance. Given the lack of disagreement on economic issues, these emerged as some of the key determinants of voting in the last election before the stock market crash.

The Republican Triumph and the Coming of the Great Depression

As expected, the Republicans scored a decisive triumph in the election. Hoover won more than twenty-one million votes to Smith's fifteen million, and won by a 444 to 87 margin in the electoral college. Most notably, the Republicans made gains in the South, carrying the states of Virginia, North Carolina, Florida, Tennessee, and Texas, where hostility to Smith's religion and Prohibition stance proved decisive. In Dixie, Smith only carried the Deep South states, where the Democratic Party had become identified with white supremacy and voters' hostility to African Americans proved more powerful than their prejudice against Catholics. The Republicans also did well with female voters, many of whom still thought of Prohibition as a women's issue, although only seven women were elected to Congress. In addition, the Republicans picked up thirty seats in the House and seven in the Senate, giving them large majorities in both bodies. Besides South Carolina, Georgia, Alabama, Mississippi, Louisiana, and Arkansas, the Democrats carried only Massachusetts and Rhode Island, states with large Catholic populations where the slump in the textile and shoe industries made a mockery of the notion that the United States had entered a new era.

In retrospect, the 1928 election marked the beginning of a shift toward the Democrats. Despite their defeat, the Democrats scored major gains in some of the nation's largest cities, winning Boston and New York City by decisive margins, narrowly carrying Milwaukee, Cleveland, and St. Louis, and almost winning in San Francisco, Chicago, Pittsburgh, and Baltimore. A dual dynamic explained these results. The Republicans, because of their hardline stance on Prohibition and immigration restriction, had little appeal for the recent arrivals, while the Democrats, simply by nominating a Catholic who had been known as a friend of the immigrants, had begun to win the loyalty of those designated inferior by the National Origins Act. Smith won the support of many immigrants from Catholic backgrounds, although Catholic women did not vote in large numbers. He also won the support of many Jews, who viewed him as a symbol of tolerance and who began to view the Democrats as far more open to them than the Republicans.

The truly major changes in American politics occurred in the 1930s as a result of the Great Depression and the New Deal. By 1936, the Democrats won large majorities from Catholics, Jews, industrial workers, and African Americans. Fortunately for the Democrats, they found in Franklin Roosevelt, who had first been elected governor of New York in 1928, a brilliant leader far more capable than Al Smith of overcoming the fierce divisions within the Democratic Party.

The 1920s ended a bit prematurely as the stock market crash of October 1929 brought a close to the Roaring Twenties. Certainly, if Al Smith by some miracle had been elected in 1928, the Democrats would have been blamed for causing the crash and would have been forced to deal with the unparalleled economic decline. Instead, Hoover, who never lost his faith in American business, tried to work with business in coping with the economic crisis of the early 1930s. After his defeat by Roosevelt in 1932, Hoover bitterly opposed the New Deal. But Al Smith also opposed the vast increase in federal power that resulted from Roosevelt's reforms, as the two candidates who had so celebrated the success of American capitalism in the 1920s could not adjust to its failures in the 1930s.

The Great Depression exposed weaknesses in the business system that Democrats and Republicans had ignored during the 1920s. Both farmers and workers lacked adequate purchasing power to buy the goods produced by American industry. Industrialists' success in preventing unionization meant that wages remained stable despite the huge gains in productivity. The failure of Europe to fully recover from the war—a failure partly caused by the United States' narrow-minded economic policies—limited the foreign markets that could be tapped. The federal government's taxation policies distributed income upward and the failure to regulate Wall Street encouraged the bull market of the late 1920s.

The 1930s were quite different from the 1920s. As a sign of the shift in emphasis from social to economic issues, those opposed to Prohibition gained its repeal in 1933 by arguing that opening up distilleries and breweries would create jobs. By 1936, many Americans celebrated Roosevelt, the New Deal, and the CIO rather than Henry Ford, Herbert Hoover, and the business system. Murals painted by Works Progress Administration artists embodied a different definition of Americanism than that which had prevailed in the 1920s, and writers, no longer a Lost Generation, embraced the working class. Liberalism replaced progressivism as the dominant reform ideology, and previously scorned groups gained recognition within the Democratic Party. Overseas, the three nations most dissatisfied with the results of World War I—Japan, Italy, and Germany—turned to variants of Fascism and embarked on an aggressive course that led to a world war with unimaginable horrors, a war that in many ways represented a continuation of the Great War. In foreign affairs as well as in domestic affairs, the 1920s provided only a respite for a nation and a world that never fully recovered from the 1914–18 conflagration.

BIBLIOGRAPHICAL ESSAY

THE PRIMARY AND SECONDARY SOURCES that have proved most helpful to me in preparing this book are given here. In addition to the primary sources listed below, I have made use of the *New York Times*, the *New Republic*, the *Nation*, the *Literary Digest*, the *World's Work*, the *Survey*, the *Christian Century*, the *American Mercury*, the Federated Press, and the Frank Walsh Papers at the New York Public Library.

Those interested in general histories of the 1920s should consult Preston William Slosson, *The Great Crusade and After, 1914–1928* (New York, 1930), Frederick Louis Allen, *Only Yesterday* (New York, 1931), William Leuchtenburg, *The Perils of Prosperity, 1914–1932* (Chicago, 1958, 1993), John D. Hicks, *Republican Ascendancy* (New York, 1960), Ellis Hawley, *The Great War and the Search for a Modern Order* (New York, 1979, 1992), Stanley Coben, *Rebellion against Victorianism* (New York, 1991), and Lynn Dumenil, *The Modern Temper* (New York, 1995). George Soule, *Prosperity Decade* (New York, 1947), is an extremely useful economic survey, and Stanley Coben, ed., *Reform, War, and Reaction, 1912–1932* (New York, 1972), contains a number of valuable primary sources. André Siegfried, *America Comes of Age* (New York, 1927), is a valuable account that captures the ethnic and racial tensions of the 1920s.

Chapter 1. Progressivism and the War

Richard Hofstadter, *The Age of Reform* (New York, 1955), remains the single most valuable analysis of the progressives. For progressivism, see also Robert Wiebe, *The Search for Order, 1877–1920* (New York, 1967), Robert M. Crunden, *Ministers of Reform* (Urbana, Ill., 1982, 1984), and John Milton Cooper, *The Warrior and the Priest: Woodrow Wilson and Theodore Roosevelt* (Cambridge, Mass., 1983). The merger movement that led to the formation of the trusts is well described in Naomi Lamoreaux, *The Great Merger Movement in American Business, 1895–1904* (New York, 1985).

The settlement house movement has produced a rich history, including Allen F. Davis, *Spearheads for Reform* (New York, 1967) and *American Heroine: The Life and Legend of Jane Addams* (New York, 1973), Rivka Shpak Lissak, *Pluralism and Progressivism: Hull House and the New Immigrants, 1890–1919* (Chicago, 1989), and Mira Carson, *Settlement Folk, Social Thought, and the American Settlement Movement, 1885–1930* (Chicago, 1990). Jane Addams, *Twenty Years at Hull House*, and Lillian D. Wald, *The House on Henry Street*, originally published in 1910 and 1915 respectively, remain classic accounts.

For urban reform in the progressive era, Tom L. Johnson, *My Story* (Kent, Ohio, 1911, 1953), Brand Whitlock, *Forty Years of It* (Cleveland, Ohio, 1914, 1970), and Frederic C. Howe, *The Confessions of a Reformer* (Kent, Ohio, 1925, 1988), provide fascinating accounts. For Johnson's battle with the streetcar companies, see also Barbara Clemenson, "The Political War against Tom L. Johnson, 1901–1909" (master's thesis, Cleveland State University, 1989). David P. Thelan, *Robert M. La Follette and the Insurgent Spirit* (Boston, 1976), is a fine biography that captures the progressive mentality.

For a superb account of World War I, see Marc Ferro, *The Great War, 1914–1918* (Boston, 1969, 1973). The war has spawned an enormous literature exploring its intellectual, social, and cultural effects. Some of the most influential works include Paul Fussell, *The Great War and Modern Memory* (New York, 1975), Robert Wohl, *The Generation of 1914* (Cambridge, Mass., 1979), and Morris Eksteins, *The Great War and the Birth of the Modern Age* (New York, 1989). Robert Graves, *Good-Bye to All That* (New York, 1929, 1985), is a moving and brilliant memoir, and Charles Fengvesi, *When the World Was Whole* (New York, 1970), captures the *Mitteleuropa* that would never be the same after 1914.

The prewar intellectual mood in the United States is brilliantly described in Henry F. May, *The End of American Innocence* (Chicago, 1959, 1964). See also Martin Green, *New York, 1913: The Armory Show and the Paterson Strike Pageant* (New York, 1988), and Adele Heller and Lois Rudnick, eds., *1915: The Cultural Moment* (New Brunswick, N.J., 1991).

The complex series of events that eventually led the United States to declare war on Germany is ably described in Ross Gregory, *The Origins of American Intervention in the First World War* (New York, 1971). The two principal accounts that address the domestic impact of the Great War are David M. Kennedy, *The First World War and American Society* (New York, 1980), and Ronald Schaffer, *America in the Great War* (New York, 1991). For the antagonism toward German Americans, see Frederick C. Luebke, *Bonds of Loyalty: German Americans and World War I* (De Kalb, Ill., 1974). Stephen L. Vaughn, *Holding Fast the Inner Lines: Democ-*

racy, Nationalism, and the Committee on Public Information (Chapel Hill, N.C., 1980), provides a complete account of the committee. For repression of the war's opponents, see Horace C. Peterson and Gilbert Fite, *Opponents of War, 1917–1918* (Madison, Wisc., 1957), and Paul L. Murphy, *World War I and the Origin of Civil Liberties in the United States* (New York, 1979). For the response of progressives to the wartime events, see John A. Thompson, *Reformers and War: American Progressive Publicists and the First World War* (New York, 1987).

Chapter 2. The United States Faces the Postwar World

For the conclusion of the war and the treaty negotiations, I have relied most heavily on John Maynard Keynes, *The Economic Consequences of the Peace* (New York, 1920), Martin Kitchen, *Europe between the Wars: A Political History* (New York, 1988), and Detlev J. Peukert, *The Weimar Republic: The Crisis of Classical Modernity* (New York, 1987, 1989). Jan William Schulte Nordholt, *Woodrow Wilson: A Life for World Peace* (Berkeley and Los Angeles, 1991), is an eloquent biography that expertly describes Wilson's flaws. See also August Heckscher, *Woodrow Wilson* (New York, 1991).

For insight into the role of nationalism and Americanism in shaping foreign policy, Selig Adler, *The Isolationist Impulse: Its Twentieth-Century Reaction* (New York, 1957), remains extremely valuable. Lloyd E. Ambrosius, *Woodrow Wilson and the American Diplomatic Tradition: The Treaty Fight in Perspective* (New York, 1987), has much fascinating detail. William C. Widenor, *Henry Cabot Lodge and the Search for an American Foreign Policy* (Berkeley and Los Angeles, 1980), is a first-rate intellectual biography. See also Ralph Stone, *The Irreconcilables: The Fight against the League of Nations* (New York, 1970), Ronald Steel, *Walter Lippmann and the American Century* (New York, 1980), and Robert James Madox, *William E. Borah and American Foreign Policy* (Baton Rouge, La., 1969). For events in Russia, I have made great use of Bruce Lincoln, *Red Victory: A History of the Russian Civil War* (New York, 1989). George F. Kennan, *Russia and the West under Lenin and Stalin* (New York, 1960), is a hard-hitting and eloquent analysis. See also Peter G. Filene, *America and the Soviet Experiment, 1917–1933* (Cambridge, Mass., 1967), John Lewis Gaddis, *Russia, The Soviet Union, and the United States: An Interpretive History* (New York, 1978, 1990), and Benjamin M. Weissman, *Herbert Hoover and Famine Relief to Soviet Russia, 1921–1923* (Palo Alto, Calif., 1974).

For an expert account that considers the perspective of all the major powers in East Asia, see Akira Iriye, *After Imperialism: The Search for a New Order in the Far East, 1921–1932* (Cambridge, Mass., 1965, 1968). For United States–Japanese relations, Charles E. Neu, *The Troubled Encounter: The United States and Japan* (Malabar, Fla., 1975, 1981), is extremely valuable. Walter B. Pitkin, *Must We Fight Japan?* (New York, 1921), provides a useful contemporary perspective. For events in China, Jonathan D. Spence, *The Search for Modern China* (New York, 1990), is a classic. Warren I. Cohen, *America's Response to China: A History of Sino-American Relations* (New York, 1990), provides a world of detail, and Thomas H. Buckley, *The United States and the Washington Conference, 1921–1922* (Knoxville, Tenn., 1970), is a readable, straightforward account.

For events in the Western Hemisphere, Joseph Tulchin, *The Aftermath of War: World War I and U.S. Policy toward Latin America* (New York, 1971), and Lester Langley, *The United States and the Caribbean in the Twentieth Century* (Athens, Ga., 1982), provide essential background information. Arthur C. Millspaugh, *Haiti under American Control, 1915–1930* (Westport, Conn., 1931, 1970), provides the perspective of a former United States official, and Hans Schmidt, *The United States Occupation of Haiti, 1915–1934* (New Brunswick, N.J., 1971), provides a detailed account of events in Haiti. For Cuban and Dominican developments, see Bruce J. Calder, *The Impact of Intervention: The Dominican Republic during the U.S. Occupation of 1916–1924* (Austin, Tex., 1984), and Louis A. Pérez Jr., *Cuba: Between Reform and Revolution* (New York, 1988). John Mason Hart, *Revolutionary Mexico: The Coming and Process of the Mexican Revolution* (Berkeley and Los Angeles, 1987), has a rich description of the extremely complicated events in Mexico. For aspects of American policy, see Robert Freeman Smith, *The United States and Revolutionary Nationalism in Mexico, 1916–1932* (Chicago, 1972). The critical role of oil in postwar policy is well described in John A. DeNovo, "The Movement for an Aggressive Oil Policy Abroad, 1918–1920," *American Historical Review* 61 (July 1956): 854–76.

For an article that thoroughly analyzes the Versailles revisions, see Jon Jacobson, "Is There a New International History of the 1920s?" *American Historical Review* 88 (June 1983): 617–45. See also John Braeman, "Power and Diplomacy: The 1920s Reappraised," *Review of Politics* 44 (July 1982): 342–69. American reaction to Mussolini is well described in John P. Diggins, *Mussolini and Fascism: The View from America* (Princeton, 1972).

Discussions of various aspects of United States foreign policy can also be found in Scott Nearing and Joseph Freeman, *Dollar Diplomacy: A Study in American Imperialism* (New York, 1925, 1969), Emily S. Rosenberg, *Spreading the American Dream: American Economic and Cultural Expansion, 1890–1945* (New York, 1982), and Warren I. Cohen, *Empire without Tears: American Foreign Relations, 1921–1933* (Philadelphia, 1987).

Chapter 3. Anything But "Normal": Postwar American Politics and the Demise of Progressivism

The immediate postwar political situation is covered in Burl Noggle, *Into the Twenties: The United States from Armistice to Normalcy* (Urbana, Ill., 1974), and Stuart I. Rochester, *American Liberal Disillusionment in the Wake of World War I* (University Park, Pa., 1977).

Aspects of the Red Scare and the Palmer Raids are covered in Norman Hapgood, ed., *Professional Patriots* (New York, 1927), Louis Post, *The Deportations Delirium of Nineteen-Twenty* (Chicago, 1923), Richard Gid Powers, *Secrecy and Power: The Life of J. Edgar Hoover* (New York, 1987), M. J. Heale, *American Anti-Communism: Combating the Enemy Within, 1830–1970* (Baltimore, 1990), and Stanley Coben, *A. Mitchell Palmer, Politician* (New York, 1963). For the American Legion and the ACLU, see William Pencak, *For God and Country: The American Legion, 1919–1941* (Boston, 1989), and Samuel Walker, *In Defense of American Liberties: A History of the ACLU* (New York, 1990).

Wesley M. Bagby, *The Road to Normalcy: The Presidential Campaign and Election of 1920* (Baltimore, 1962), is the standard account of the 1920 election. Douglas B. Craig, *After Wilson: The Struggle for the Democratic Party, 1920–1934* (Chapel Hill, N.C., 1992), David Burner, *The Politics of Provincialism: The Democratic Party in Transition, 1918–1932* (Cambridge, Mass., 1967, 1986), and J. Joseph Huthmacher, *Massachusetts People and Politics* (Cambridge, Mass., 1959), all expertly describe the divisions within the Democratic Party during the 1920s. James Oliver Robertson, *No Third Choice: Progressives in Republican Politics* (New York, 1983), is the only work that fully describes the continuing rift between the progressives and the Old Guard factions.

Stanley Shapiro has described the reasons for the 1920 third-party failure in four articles: "The Twilight of Reform: Advanced Progressives after the Armistice," *Historian* 38 (May 1971): 349–64, "The Great War and Reform: Liberals and Labor, 1917–1919," *Labor History* 12 (summer 1971): 323–44, "The Passage of Power: Labor and the New Social Order," *Proceedings of the American Philosophical Society* 120 (December 1976): 464–74, and "Hand and Brain: The Farmer Labor Party of 1920," *Labor History* 26 (summer 1985): 405–22.

John D. Hicks, *Rehearsal for Disaster: The Boom and Collapse of 1919–1920* (Gainesville, Fla., 1961), is the most complete account of the onset of the 1920–22 depression. Ellis Hawley, ed., *Herbert Hoover as Secretary of Commerce: Studies in New Era Thought and Practice* (Iowa City, 1981), provides a series of superb essays by scholars dealing with many aspects of domestic and foreign policy.

Robert K. Murray, *The Politics of Normalcy* (New York, 1973), is a thorough account of the Harding administration.

Aileen S. Kraditor, *The Ideas of the Woman Suffrage Movement* (New York, 1965), analyzes the different approaches of the suffragists. Nancy Cott, *The Grounding of Modern Feminism* (New Haven, 1982), is sweeping in its coverage and the starting point for an understanding of women in the 1920s. J. Stanley Lemons, *The Women Citizen: Social Feminism in the 1920s* (Urbana, Ill., 1973), is valuable for its coverage of legislation. Felice D. Gordon, *After Winning: The Legacy of the New Jersey Suffragists, 1920–1947* (New Brunswick, N.J., 1986), suggests that women did make some political gains during the 1920s. Estelle B. Freedman, "The New Woman: Changing Views of Women in the 1920s," *Journal of American History* 61 (September 1974): 372–93, is an important article, and Paula Fass, *The Damned and the Beautiful: American Youth in the 1920s* (New York, 1977), suggests that college women had things other than politics on their minds during the 1920s.

Norman H. Clark, *Deliver Us from Evil: An Interpretation of American Prohibition* (New York, 1976), is a splendid synthesis, notably sympathetic to the foes of alcohol. Ruth Bordin, *Woman and Temperance* (New Brunswick, N.J., 1981, 1990), is a pathbreaking study of the WCTU, and K. Austin Kerr, *Organized for Prohibition: A New History of the Anti-Saloon League* (New Haven, 1985), is the standard history of the ASL. J. C. Burnham, "New Perspectives on the Prohibition Experiment of the 1920s," *Journal of Social History* 2 (fall 1968): 50–68, raises a number of important questions. Joseph H. Timberlake, *Prohibition and the Progressive Movement, 1900–1920* (Cambridge, Mass., 1963), and Joseph R. Gusfield, *Symbolic Crusade: Status Politics and the American Temperance Movement* (Urbana, Ill., 1963), offer differing approaches to Prohibition during the Progressive Era. Charles Merz, *The Dry Decade* (Garden City, N.Y., 1931), provides a wealth of information from all points of view. The social history of Prohibition has yet to be written, but see Larry Engelmann, *Intemperance: The Lost War against Liquor* (New York, 1979), and Mary Murphy, "Bootlegging Mothers and Drinking Daughters: Gender and Prohibition in Butte, Montana," *American Quarterly* 46 (June 1994): 174–94. The best book on the saloon is Perry Duis, *Public Drinking in Chicago and Boston* (Chicago, 1983).

For rural discontent and the revival of progressivism, see Robert Morlan, *Political Prairie Fire: The Nonpartisan League, 1915–1922* (Minneapolis, 1955), Russell B. Nye, *Midwestern Progressive Politics: A Historical Study of Its Origins and Development, 1870–1959* (East Lansing, Mich., 1959), Don S. Kirschner, *City and Country: Rural Responses to Urbanization in the 1920s* (Westport, Conn., 1970), Le Roy Ashby, *The Spearless Leader: Senator Borah and the Progressive Movement in the 1920s* (Urbana, Ill., 1972), and Lawrence W. Levine, *Defender of the Faith: William Jennings Bryan: The Last Decade, 1915–1925* (New York, 1965).

The 1924 Democratic Party split is expertly covered in the books by Burner, *Politics of Provincialism*, and Craig, *After Wilson*. For a complete account, see Robert K. Murray, *The 103rd Ballot: Democrats and the Disaster in Madison Square Garden* (New York, 1976). The third-party movement is described in Kenneth Campbell Mackay, *The Progressive Movement of 1924* (New York, 1947, 1966), Alan R. Havig, "A Disputed Legacy: Roosevelt Progressives and the La Follette Campaign of 1924," *Mid-America* 53 (January 1971): 44–64, and Eugene M. Tobin, *Organize or Perish: America's Independent Progressives, 1913–1933* (New York, 1986).

The appearance of Frederic Howe's memoir provoked a fascinating discussion: "Where Are the Pre-War Radicals?" *Survey*, 1 February 1926, 556–66. See also Paul W. Glad, "Progressives and the Business Culture of the 1920s," *Journal of American History* 53 (June 1966): 75–89.

For women and reform in the 1920s, see Clarke Chambers, *Seedtime of Reform: American Social Service and Social Action, 1918–1933* (Minneapolis, 1963), and Robyn Muncy, *Creating a Female Dominion in American Reform, 1890–1935* (New York, 1991).

I have also made use of a number of memoirs and biographies, including William Allen White, *A Puritan in Babylon: The Story of Calvin Coolidge* (New York, 1938), Oswald Garrison Villard, *Fighting Years: Memoirs of a Liberal Editor* (New York, 1939), James Cox, *Journey through My Years* (New York, 1946), Harold Ickes, *The Autobiography of a Curmudgeon* (New York, 1943), George Creel, *Rebel at Large: Recollections of Fifty Crowded Years* (New York, 1947), and C. H. Cramer, *Newton D. Baker: A Biography* (New York, 1961, 1979).

Chapter 4. Capital Triumphant: The Postwar Decline of the American Labor Movement

I have relied on a number of general works in developing points made throughout this chapter. The starting point for an understanding of labor in this era is David Montgomery, *The Fall of the House of Labor: The Workplace, the State, and American Labor Activism, 1865–1925* (New York, 1987). I also highly recommend David Montgomery, "Thinking about American Workers in the 1920s," *International Labor and Working Class History* 32 (fall 1987): 4–38. Lizabeth Cohen, *Making a New Deal: Industrial Workers in Chicago, 1919–1939* (New York, 1990), represents a major breakthrough in the conceptualization of working-class history. Irving Bernstein, *The Lean Years: A History of the American Worker* (Boston, 1960, 1966), is an older history that remains extremely valuable. Robert Zieger, *Republicans and Labor, 1919–1929* (Lexington, Ky., 1969), is rich in detail and extremely informative about the 1922 events. John A. Fitch, *The Causes of Industrial Unrest* (New York, 1924), is an informed contemporary account by a writer with a deep sympathy for labor. Louis Adamic, *Dynamite: The Story of Class Violence in America* (New York, 1931, 1934), recounts many of the labor-capital struggles in this era. Sylvia Kopald, *Rebellion in Labor Unions* (New York, 1924), captures the hopes of left-wing insurgents in the postwar era. J. B. S. Hardman, ed., *American Labor Dynamics in the Light of Post-War Developments* (New York, 1928), is a rich collection of essays, most of which reflect the perspective of those close to the Amalgamated Clothing Workers of America. Anyone interested in labor events in this period can also learn a great deal by a thorough reading of the Federated Press, a labor news service, available on microfilm.

For the Seattle General Strike, see Robert L. Friedhiem, *The Seattle General Strike* (Seattle, 1964). For the Boston Police Strike, see Francis Russell, *City in Terror: The Boston Police Strike* (New York, 1975). For the 1919 textile strikes, see David J. Goldberg, *A Tale of Three Cities: Labor Organization and Protest in Paterson, Passaic, and Lawrence, 1916–1921* (New Brunswick, N.J., 1989). My discussion of events in steel relies heavily on David Brody, *Steelworkers in America: The Nonunion Era* (New York, 1960, 1969), and *Labor in Crisis: The Steel Strike of 1919* (Urbana, Ill., 1965, 1987). For specifics, see Commission of Inquiry, Interchurch World Movement, *Report on the Steel Strike of 1919* (New York, 1920, 1971). For the 1919 industrial conferences, see Haggai Hurvitz, "Ideology and Industrial Conflict: President Wilson's First Industrial Conference," *Labor History* 18 (fall 1977): 509–24, and Larry S. Gerber, "The United States and Canadian National Industrial Conferences of 1919: A Comparative Analysis," *Labor History* 32 (winter 1991): 42–65. Anyone who wishes to understand the lives, the hopes, the dreams, and often the despair of steelworkers in this era would benefit from reading Thomas Bell, *Out of This Furnace* (Pittsburgh, 1941, 1981). Many thanks to David Demarest for rediscovering this novel.

For the overall situation in coal, Melvyn Dubofsky and Warren Van Tine, *John L. Lewis: A Biography* (New York, 1977), is indispensable. For the background to the West Virginia mining wars and for many other aspects of coal miners' lives, see David Alan Corbin, *Life, Work, and Rebellion in the Coal Fields: The Southern West Virginia Miners, 1889–1922* (Urbana, Ill., 1981).

A number of historians have described aspects of welfare capitalism. I have relied on Stuart D. Brandes, *American Welfare Capitalism, 1880–1940* (Chicago, 1970, 1976), David Brody, "The Rise and Decline of Welfare Capitalism," in *Workers in Industrial America* (New York, 1980), 48–81, David J. Goldberg, "Richard A. Feiss, Mary Barnett Gilson, and Scientific Management," in *A Mental Revolution*, ed. Daniel Nelson (Columbus, Ohio, 1992): 40–57, Sanford M. Jacoby, *Employing Bureaucracy: Managers, Unions, and the Transformation of Work in American Industry, 1900–1945* (New York, 1985), and Howard M. Gitelman, "Welfare Capitalism Reconsidered," *Labor History* 33 (winter 1992): 1–31.

For the open-shop offensive, see Allen M. Wakstein, "Origins of the Open-Shop Movement, 1919–1920," *Journal of American History* 51 (December 1964): 460–75. For the impact of the postwar depression on organizing efforts, see Goldberg, *Tale of Three Cities*, and James R. Barrett, *Work and Community in the Jungle: Chicago's Packinghouse Workers, 1894–1922* (Urbana, Ill., 1987). See also Daniel Nelson, *American Rubber Workers and Organized Labor, 1900–1941* (Princeton, 1988).

More needs to be written about workers' reaction to the 1920–22 economic slump. Two valuable works are Eric Arneson, *Waterfront Workers of New Orleans: Race, Class, and Politics* (New York, 1991), and Marc Jeffrey Stern, *The Pottery Industry of Trenton: A Skilled Trade in Transition, 1850–1929* (New Brunswick, N.J., 1994). One can learn a great deal about the background to the 1922 textile strikes in Tamara K. Hareven, *Family Time and Industrial Time: The Relationship between the Family and Work in an Industrial Community* (New York, 1982).

For the coal situation, I have made great use of Dubofsky and Van Tine, *John L. Lewis*. For the Herrin events, see Paul M. Angle, *Bloody Williamson: A Chapter in American Lawlessness* (New York, 1952, 1988). John Brophy, *A Miner's Life* (Madison, Wisc., 1964), is a wonderful autobiography by one of the most respected of all labor leaders. See also Alan Kent Powell, *The Next Time We Strike: Labor in Utah's Coal Fields, 1900–1933* (Logan, Utah, 1985). The *United Mine Workers' Journal* is available on microfilm. For the 1922 shopmen's strike, I have drawn most heavily from Zieger, *Republicans and Labor*, and Colin Davis, "Bitter Conflict: The 1922 Railroad Shopmen's Strike," *Labor History* 33 (fall 1992): 433–55.

For the runaway shop and the southern textile industry, see Bernstein, *Lean Years*, and Jacquelyn Dowd Hall et al., *Like a Family: The Making of a Southern Cotton Mill World* (Chapel Hill, N.C., 1987), a book that integrates family, work, and community history. For a vivid description of a depressed northern textile community, see Louis Adamic, *My America* (New York, 1938).

For the building trades, see Michael Kazin, *Barons of Labor: The San Francisco Building Trades and Union Power in the Progressive Era* (Urbana, Ill., 1987), Mark Erlich, *With Our Hands: The Story of Carpenters in Massachusetts* (Philadelphia, 1986), Richard Scheirov and Thomas J. Suhrbur, *Union Brotherhood and Union Town: A History of the Chicago Carpenters' Union, 1863–1987* (Carbondale, Ill., 1988), and Philip J. Zausner, *Unvarnished: The Autobiography of a Union Leader* (New York, 1941), a quietly eloquent story of a union leader who battled graft.

The indispensable work on Sidney Hillman and the ACWA is Steven Fraser, *Labor Will Rule: Sidney Hillman and the Rise of American Labor* (New York, 1991). For the labor education movement, see Richard J. Altenbaugh, *Education for Struggle: The American Labor Colleges of the 1920s and 1930s* (Philadelphia, 1990), and Nat Hentoff, ed., *The Essays of A. J. Muste* (New York, 1970). For A. Philip Randolph, see Jervis Anderson, *A. Philip Randolph: A Biographical Portrait* (Berkeley and Los Angeles, 1972, 1986). For the Garland Fund, see Morton J. Siegal, "The Passaic Textile Strike of 1926" (Ph.D. diss., Columbia University, 1952). All of the initiatives can be followed in the pages of *Labor Age*. See also Thomas R. Brooks, *Clint: A Biography of a Labor Intellectual* (New York, 1987).

The standard history of the IWW is Melvyn Dubofsky, *We Shall Be All: A History of the Industrial Workers of the World* (Chicago, 1969). See also Patrick Renshaw, *The Wobblies* (Garden City, N.Y., 1967, 1968), Joyce Kornbluh, ed., *Rebel Voices* (Ann Arbor, Mich., 1964, 1968), Larry Peterson, "The One Big Union in International Perspective: Revolutionary Industrial Unionism," in *Work, Community, and Power: The Experience of Labor in Europe and America, 1900–1925*, ed. James E. Cronin and Carmen Sirianni (Philadelphia, 1983), 49–87, John S. Gambs, *The Decline of the IWW* (New York, 1932, 1966), and Joseph R. Conlin, ed., *At the Point of Production: The Local History of the IWW* (Westport, Conn., 1981). The standard history of the Communist Party in the early 1920s is Theodore Draper, *Roots of American Communism* (New York, 1957). For the division on the left, see James Weinstein, *The Decline of Socialism in America, 1912–1925* (New York, 1967).

A number of excellent works dealing with women workers have appeared in recent years. For the WTUL, a good starting point is Nancy Schrom Dye, *As Equals and as Sisters: Feminism, the Labor Movement, and the Women's Trade Union League of New York* (Columbia, Mo., 1980). For women telephone workers and the 1919 strike, see Stephen H. Norwood, *Labor's Flaming Youth: Telephone Operators and Worker Militancy, 1878–1923* (Urbana, Ill., 1990). The battle of women to retain their jobs as trolley conductors is well covered in Maurine Weiner Greenwald, *Women, War, and Work: The Impact of World War I on Women Workers in the United States* (Ithaca, N.Y., 1980, 1990). For an influential book dealing with women workers, see Leslie Woodcock Tentler, *Wage-Earning Women, Industrial Work, and Family Life in the United States, 1900–1930* (New York, 1979). Ileen A. DeVault, *Sons and Daughters of Labor: Class and Clerical Work in Turn-of-the-Century Pittsburgh* (Ithaca, N.Y., 1990), is a highly original work exploring the backgrounds and goals of clerical workers. Clerical workers are also the subject of Lisa Fine, *The Souls of the Skyscraper: Female Clerical Workers in Chicago, 1870–1930* (Philadelphia, 1990), and Sharon Hartman Strom, *Beyond the Typewriter: Gender, Class, and the Origins of Modern American Office Work, 1900–1930* (Urbana, Ill., 1992). For schoolteachers and department store employees, see Marjorie Murphy, *Blackboard Unions: The AFT and the NEA, 1900–1980* (Ithaca, N.Y., 1990), and Susan Porter Benson, *Counter Cultures: Saleswomen, Managers, and Customers in American Department Stores, 1890–1940* (Urbana, Ill., 1986). For many issues relevant to women workers, see Cott, *Grounding of Modern Feminism*, and Alice

Kessler Harris, "Problems of Coalition-Building: Women and Trade Unions in the 1920s," in *Women, Work, and Protest*, ed. Ruth Milkman (New York, 1985), 110–38.

For an understanding of automobile workers in the 1920s, I recommend Ronald Edsforth, *Class Conflict and Cultural Consensus: The Making of a Mass Consumer Society in Flint, Michigan* (New Brunswick, N.J., 1987), Joyce Shaw Peterson, *American Automobile Workers, 1900–1933* (Albany, N.Y., 1987), Stephen Meyer III, *The Five-Dollar Day: Labor Management and Social Control in the Ford Motor Company, 1908–1921* (Albany, N.Y., 1981), and Zaragosa Vargas, *A History of Mexican Industrial Workers in Detroit and the Middle West, 1917–1933* (Berkeley and Los Angeles, 1993). Kathy Peiss, *Cheap Amusements: Working Women and Leisure in Turn-of-the-Century New York* (Philadelphia, 1986), has stimulated much of the recent work on urban life. Selig Perlman, *A Theory of the Labor Movement* (New York, 1928), is still valuable for an understanding of American labor.

This chapter has also made use of Whiting Williams, *What's on the Worker's Mind* (New York, 1920), John R. Commons, "The Passing of Samuel Gompers," *Current History* 21 (February 1925): 670–76, Louis Levine, *The Women Garment Workers: A History of the International Ladies' Garment Workers' Union* (New York, 1924), Oscar Ameringer, *If You Don't Weaken* (New York, 1940), Len De Cax, *Labor Radical: From the Wobblies to the CIO* (Boston, 1970), Ronald W. Schatz, *The Electrical Workers: A History of Labor at General Electric and Westinghouse, 1923–1960* (Urbana, Ill., 1983), Frank Stricker, "Affluence for Whom? Another Look at Prosperity and the Working Classes in the 1920s," *Labor History* 24 (winter 1983): 5–33, Alexander Keyssar, *Out of Work: The First Century of Unemployment in Massachusetts* (New York, 1986), Daniel Ernst, "The Yellow-Dog Contract and Liberal Reform," *Labor History* 30 (spring 1989): 251–74, and Melvyn Dubofsky, *The State and Labor in Modern America* (Chapel Hill, N.C., 1994).

Chapter 5. African Americans in the Postwar Period

At various points in this chapter, I have made use of the *Chicago Defender* and the *Pittsburgh Courier*. For the 1919–22 period, I have relied heavily on the *Crisis*, the NAACP's journal, edited by W. E. B. Du Bois. Essential background material is also contained in David Levering Lewis, *W. E. B. Du Bois: Biography of a Race, 1868–1919* (New York, 1993), a splendidly written, magisterial biography. For the controversy surrounding *Birth of a Nation*, see Fred Silva, ed., *Focus on The Birth of a Nation* (Englewood Cliffs, N.J., 1971). The Great Migration is covered quite well in Florette Henri, *Black Migration: Movement North, 1900–1920* (Garden City, N.Y., 1975, 1976). Malaika Adero, ed., *Up South: Stories, Studies, and Letters of*

African-American Migrations (New York, 1993), is a fascinating collection of documents. For the perspective of historians who emphasize the purposeful nature of the migration, see Joe William Trotter Jr., ed., *The Great Migration in Historical Perspective: New Dimensions of Race, Class, and Gender* (Bloomington, Ind., 1991). For a work that traces migration to Pittsburgh through 1930, see Peter Gottlieb, *Making Their Own Way: Southern Blacks' Migration to Pittsburgh, 1916–1930* (Pittsburgh, 1987).

For the 1917 East St. Louis riot, see Elliot M. Rudwick, *Race Riot at East St. Louis, July 2, 1917* (Cleveland, Ohio, 1964, 1970). For a comprehensive account of the violent incidents in 1919, see Herbert Shapiro, *White Violence and Black Response: From Reconstruction to Montgomery* (Amherst, Mass., 1988). Events in Chicago have been extensively covered by a number of historians. See Allan H. Spear, *Black Chicago: The Making of a Negro Ghetto, 1890–1920* (Chicago, 1967), and William F. Tuttle Jr., *Race Riot: Chicago in the Red Summer of 1919* (New York, 1922, 1968). The events in Tulsa are covered in Scott Ellsworth, *Death in a Promised Land: The Tulsa Race Riot of 1921* (Baton Rouge, La., 1982). Wayne F. Cooper, *Claude Mckay: Rebel Sojourner in the Harlem Renaissance* (New York, 1987), is a fine biography.

For Marcus Garvey, I have relied heavily on Tony Martin, *Race First: The Ideological and Organizational Struggles of Marcus Garvey and the Universal Negro Improvement Association* (Dover, Mass., 1976, 1986), and Judith Stein, *The World of Marcus Garvey: Race and Class in Modern Society* (Baton Rouge, La., 1986). See also Mary Gambrell Rolinson, "The Universal Negro Improvement Association in Georgia," in *Georgia in Black and White: Explorations in the Race Relations of a Southern State, 1865–1990*, ed. John C. Inscoe (Athens, Ga., 1994), 202–24. John Henrik Clark, ed., *Marcus Garvey and the Vision of Africa* (New York, 1974), is a rich collection of documents and articles that contain diverse opinions about Garvey. See also the multivolume collection edited by Robert A. Hill, *Marcus Garvey: Life and Lessons* (Berkeley and Los Angeles, 1987).

W. Fitzhugh Brundage, *Lynching in the New South, 1880–1930* (Urbana, Ill., 1993), is a model historical study that astutely analyzes patterns of lynching in the South. The standard monograph dealing with the NAACP's campaign against lynching is Robert L. Zangrando, *The NAACP Crusade against Lynching, 1909–1950* (Philadelphia, 1980). See also Ida B. Wells Barnett, *The Autobiography of Ida B. Wells* (Chicago, 1970).

For the CIC and the role of southern women in the campaign against lynching, see Jacquelyn Dowd Hall, *Revolt against Chivalry: Jessie Daniel Ames and the Women's Campaign against Lynching* (New York, 1979). Vanessa Northington Gamble, *Making a Place for Ourselves: The Black Hospital Movement, 1920–1945* (New York, 1995), is a pioneering study that contains an extremely valuable account of the controversy surrounding the Tuskegee hospital. Lester C. Lamon,

Black Tennesseans, 1900–1930 (Knoxville, Tenn., 1977), is useful for the Fisk events and for many other developments as well. Raymond Walters, *The New Negro on Campus: Black College Rebellions of the 1920s* (Princeton, 1975), has a complete account of the campus unrest.

There is a rich literature that addresses the economic, social, and political situation in the South during the early twentieth century. Some of the most valuable books are Pete Daniel, *Breaking the Land: The Transformation of Cotton, Tobacco, and Rice Cultures since 1880* (Urbana, Ill., 1985), John Dittmer, *Black Georgia in the Progressive Era, 1900–1920* (Urbana, Ill., 1977), Neil R. McMillan, *Dark Journey: Black Mississippians in the Age of Jim Crow* (Urbana, Ill., 1989), Jack Temple Kirby, *Rural Worlds Lost: The American South, 1920–1960* (Baton Rouge, La., 1987), Wayne Flynt, *Poor But Proud: Alabama's Poor Whites* (Tuscaloosa, Ala., 1989), William A. Link, *The Paradox of Southern Progressivism, 1880–1930* (Chapel Hill, N.C., 1992), James D. Anderson, *The Education of Blacks in the South, 1860–1935* (Chapel Hill, N.C., 1988), Albert D. Kirwan, *Revolt of the Rednecks: Mississippi Politics, 1876–1925* (New York, 1951, 1965), John W. Cell, *The Highest Stage of White Supremacy: The Origins of Segregation in South Africa and the American South* (New York, 1982, 1985), Pete Daniel, *Standing at the Crossroads: Southern Life since 1900* (New York, 1986), Robert Higgs, "The Boll Weevil, the Cotton Economy, and Black Migration, 1910–1930," *Agricultural History* 50 (April 1976): 335–50, and Jack Temple Kirby, "The Transformation of Southern Plantations, ca. 1920–1960," *Agricultural History* 57 (July 1983): 257–76. For African-American life in a southern city, see Earl Lewis, *In Their Own Interests: Race, Class, and Power in Twentieth-Century Norfolk, Virginia* (Berkeley and Los Angeles, 1991). Richard Wright, *Black Boy* (New York, 1944, 1993), is a brilliant autobiographical novel. The *Southern Workman*, published by the Hampton Institute, contains a number of articles relevant to the renewed migration in 1923 and 1924.

For black male workers in the North, see Sterling D. Spero and Abram L. Harris, *The Black Worker* (New York, 1931, 1972), Dennis C. Dickerson, *Out of the Crucible: Black Steelworkers in Western Pennsylvania, 1875–1980* (Albany, N.Y., 1980), August Meier and Elliot Rudwick, *Black Detroit and the Rise of the UAW* (New York, 1979, 1981), Joe William Trotter Jr., *Black Milwaukee: The Making of an Industrial Proletariat, 1915–1945* (Urbana, Ill., 1988), and Gottlieb, *Making Their Own Way*. For African-American women workers, see Jacqueline Jones, *Labor of Love, Labor of Sorrow: Black Women, Work, and the Family from Slavery to the Present* (New York, 1985), and David M. Katzman, *Seven Days a Week: Women and Domestic Service in Industrializing America* (New York, 1978). For the Urban League, see Nancy J. Weiss, *The National Urban League, 1910–1940* (New York, 1974), and Arvarh E. Strickland, *History of the Chicago Urban League, 1910–1940* (Urbana, Ill., 1966). Randolph's efforts can be followed in Anderson, *A. Philip Randolph*.

The starting point for the black church is C. Eric Lincoln and Lawrence H. Mamiya, *The Black Church in the African-American Experience* (Durham, N.C., 1990). Ghetto formation is traced in Gilbert Osofsky, *Harlem: The Making of a Ghetto* (New York, 1963, 1966), and Kenneth L. Kusmer, *A Ghetto Takes Shape: Black Cleveland, 1870–1930* (Urbana, Ill., 1976).

For the black hospital movement, see Gamble, *Making a Place for Ourselves.* The Negro Leagues have been the subject of some excellent books, including Robert Peterson, *Only the Ball Was White* (New York, 1970, 1984), Donn Rogosin, *Invisible Men: Life in Baseball's Negro Leagues* (New York, 1983), and Phil Dixon and Patrick J. Hannigan, *The Negro Baseball Leagues: A Photographic History* (Mattituck, N.Y., 1992). Albert Murray, *Stomping the Blues* (New York, 1976, 1982), pulsates with the music itself.

Nathan Irvin Huggins, *Harlem Renaissance* (New York, 1971), is the starting point for the Harlem Renaissance, and David Levering Lewis, *When Harlem Was in Vogue* (New York, 1979, 1981), provides a great deal of fresh analysis. Steve Watson, *The Harlem Renaissance: Hub of African-American Culture* (New York, 1995), is a useful survey. The articles in Alain Locke, ed., *The New Negro* (New York, 1925, 1992), still sound fresh. Irma Watkins-Owens, *Blood Relations: Caribbean Immigrants and the Harlem Community* (Bloomington, Ind., 1992), is an outstanding contribution. See also Theodore Kornweibel Jr., *No Crystal Stair: Black Life and the Messenger, 1917–1928* (Westport, Conn., 1975), and Theodore G. Vincent, ed., *Voices of a Black Nation: Political Journalism in the Harlem Renaissance* (Trenton, N.J., 1973).

For an interesting analysis of African-American politics, see Raymond A. Mohl and Neil Betten, *Steel City: Urban and Ethnic Patterns in Gary, Indiana, 1906–1950* (New York, 1986). For the racial tensions in Detroit, see David Allan Levine, *Internal Combustion: The Races in Detroit, 1915–1925* (Westport, Conn., 1976). The disastrous effects of the Great Depression on the African-American community are movingly described in Richard Wright, *Twelve Million Black Voices: A Folk History of the Negro in the United States* (New York, 1941).

I have also made use of Martin Bauml Duberman, *Paul Robeson* (New York, 1988), Joseph Boskin, *Sambo: The Rise and Demise of an American Jester* (New York, 1986), Jacqueline Goggin, *Carter G. Woodson: A Life in Black History* (Baton Rouge, La., 1993), Jane Lang Schreiber and Harry N. Schreiber, "The Wilson Administration and the Wartime Mobilization of Black Americans, 1917–1918," *Labor History* 10 (summer 1969): 433–58, and Richard B. Sherman, "The Harding Administration and the Negro: An Opportunity Lost," *Journal of Negro History* 49 (July 1964): 151–68.

Chapter 6. The Rapid Rise and the Swift Decline of the Ku Klux Klan

In developing many of the points in this chapter, I have relied heavily on the *Fiery Cross* for 1923 and 1924, which filled its pages with news about Klan activity and which provides a good guide to the appeals used by the hooded order.

David M. Chalmers, *Hooded Americanism: The History of the Ku Klux Klan* (Durham, N.C., 1965, 1987), is the best overall history of the Klan. Kenneth T. Jackson, *The Ku Klux Klan in the City, 1915–1930* (New York, 1967), provides a pathbreaking focus on the urban Klan and contains a mass of detail. See also Richard K. Tucker, *The Dragon and the Cross: The Rise and Fall of the Ku Klux Klan in Middle America* (Hamden, Conn., 1991).

For valuable studies of the Klan written during its rise to influence, see Henry F. Fry, *The Modern Ku Klux Klan* (New York, 1922, 1969), John Moffatt Mecklin, *The Ku Klux Klan: A Study of the American Mind* (New York, 1924, 1963), and Stanley Frost, *The Challenge of the Klan* (New York, 1924, 1969).

Kathleen M. Blee, *Women of the Klan: Racism and Gender in the 1920s* (Berkeley and Los Angeles, 1991), is highly innovative and has sparked much of my thinking about the Klan. This chapter also relies on a number of local and state studies of the Klan, including Emerson Hungberger Loucks, *The Ku Klux Klan in Pennsylvania: A Study in Nativism* (New York, 1936), Charles C. Alexander, *The Ku Klux Klan in the Southwest* (Lexington, Ky., 1965), Robert Alan Goldberg, *Hooded Empire: The Ku Klux Klan in Colorado* (Urbana, Ill., 1981), Larry R. Gerlach, *Blazing Crosses in Zion: The Ku Klux Klan in Utah* (Logan, Utah, 1982), Shawn Lay, *War, Revolution, and the Ku Klux Klan: A Study of Intolerance in a Border City* (El Paso, Tex., 1985), William D. Jenkins, *The Ku Klux Klan in Ohio's Mahoning Valley* (Kent, Ohio, 1990), Leonard J. Moore, *Citizen Klansmen: The Ku Klux Klan in Indiana, 1921–1928* (Chapel Hill, N.C., 1991), Shawn Lay, ed., *The Invisible Empire in the West: Toward a New Historical Appraisal of the Ku Klux Klan in the 1920s* (Urbana, Ill., 1992), Nancy Maclean, *Behind the Mask of Chivalry: The Making of the Second Ku Klux Klan* (New York, 1994), Shawn Lay, *Hooded Knights on the Niagara: The Ku Klux Klan in Buffalo, New York* (New York, 1995), and Ronald E. Marec, "The Fiery Cross: A History of the Ku Klux Klan in Ohio" (master's thesis, Kent State University, 1967). For an excellent review article of the literature, see Leonard J. Moore, "Historical Interpretations of the 1920s Klan: The Traditional View and the Populist Revision," *Journal of Social History* 24 (winter 1990): 341–57.

For Catholic attitudes, I highly recommend Lynn Dumenil, "'The Insatiable Maw of Bureaucracy': Antistatism and Education Reform in the 1920s," *Journal of American History* 77 (September 1990): 449–524, and "The Tribal Twenties: 'Assimilated' Catholics' Response to Anti-Catholicism in the 1920s," *Journal of American Ethnic History* 10 (fall 1991): 21–49. M. Paul Holsinger, "The Oregon School Bill Controversy, 1922–1925," *Pacific Historical Review* 37 (August 1968): 327–41, and Edward Cuddy, "The Irish Question and the Revival of Anti-Catholicism in the 1920s," *Catholic Historical Review* 67 (April 1981): 236–55, are both valuable. For the Knights of Columbus, see Christopher J. Kauffman, *Faith and Fraternalism: The History of the Knights of Columbus, 1882–1992* (New York, 1982, 1992).

For opposition to the Klan, see David J. Goldberg, "Unmasking the Ku Klux Klan: The Northern Movement against the KKK, 1920–1925," *Journal of American Ethnic History* 15 (summer 1996): 31–48. For the fate of D. C. Stephenson, see M. William Lutholz, *Grand Dragon: D. C. Stephenson and the Ku Klux Klan in Indiana* (West Lafayette, Ind., 1991).

Chapter 7. Nordics to the Front: The 1924 National Origins Act

Three of the most useful histories of immigration are Thomas Archdeacon, *Becoming American: An Ethnic History* (New York, 1983), John Bodnar, *The Transplanted* (Bloomington, Ind., 1985), and Roger Daniels, *Coming to America* (New York, 1990).

Recent work on immigration has deeply enriched historians' understanding of the process of immigration and the various ways in which immigrants adjusted to life in the United States. The most outstanding contributions include Kerby A. Miller, *Emigrants and Exiles: Ireland and the Irish Exodus to North America* (New York, 1985), Robert Anthony Orsi, *The Madonna of 115th Street: Faith and Community in Italian Harlem, 1880–1950* (New Haven, 1985), Ewa Morawska, *For Bread with Butter: The Life World of East Central Europeans in Johnstown, Pennsylvania* (New York, 1985), Jon Gjerde, *From Peasants to Farmers: The Migration from Balestrand, Norway, to the Upper Middle West* (New York, 1985), and Ronald Takaki, *Strangers from a Different Shore: A History of Asian Americans* (Boston, 1989).

I have also benefited from Caroline Golab, *Immigration Destinations* (Philadelphia, 1977), John Bodnar, *Steelton: Immigration and Industrialization* (Pittsburgh, 1977, 1990), Joseph John Parot, *Polish Catholics in Chicago, 1850–1920* (De Kalb, Ill., 1981), and Marilyn Halter, *Between Race and Ethnicity: Cape Verdean American Immigrants, 1860–1965* (Urbana, Ill., 1993).

Stanley Feldstein and Lawrence Costello, eds., *The Ordeal of Assimilation: A Documentary History of the White Working Class* (New York, 1974), and John Chalbert, *Immigration: Opposing Viewpoints* (San Diego, 1992), are both outstanding collections of documents.

John Higham, *Strangers in the Land: Patterns of American Nativism, 1860–1925* (New Brunswick, N.J., 1955, 1988), remains a classic to which all historians of anti-immigrant movements are indebted. Robert A. Divine, *American Immigration Policy, 1924–1952* (New Haven, 1957), is also an invaluable source of information. For a synthesis that traces the "birds of passage," see Mark Wyman, *Round-Trip to America: The Immigrants Return to Europe, 1880–1930* (Ithaca, N.Y., 1993). For the New Orleans and Lattimer events, see R. Gambino, *Blood of My Blood* (New York, 1975), and Michael Novak, *The Guns of Lattimer* (New York, 1978).

Barbara Miller Solomon, *Ancestors and Immigrants: A Changing New England Tradition* (Chicago, 1956, 1972), is a splendid work that traces the involvement of the Boston Brahmins in the anti-immigrant movement. For Theodore Roosevelt's thinking on these issues, see Thomas G. Dyer, *Theodore Roosevelt and the Idea of Race* (Baton Rouge, La., 1980). Daniel J. Kevles, *In the Name of Eugenics: Genetics and the Uses of Human Heredity* (New York, 1985), is an essential work.

For the emergence of anti-immigrant sentiment, I have made use of Frank Julian Warne, *The Immigrant Invasion* (New York, 1913, 1971), H. A. Millis, *The Japanese Problem in the United States* (New York, 1915), John R. Commons, *Races and Immigrants in America* (New York, 1908), and Julius Weinberg, *Edward Alsworth Ross and the Sociology of Progressivism* (Madison, Wisc., 1972). The perspective of the AFL is traced quite well in A. T. Lane, *Solidarity or Survival? American Labor and European Immigrants, 1830–1924* (Westport, Conn., 1987). Oscar Handlin, *Race and Nationality in American Life* (New York, 1950, 1957), devotes a chapter to the Dillingham Commission.

For the immigrants' defenders, I have made particular use of Henry Beardsell Leonard, *The Open Gates: The Protest against the Movement to Restrict European Immigration, 1896–1924* (New York, 1980), Hamilton Holt, ed., *The Life Stories of Undistinguished Americans as Told by Themselves* (New York, 1980), Mary Antin, *They Who Knock at Our Gates: A Complete Gospel of Immigration* (Boston, 1914), Emily Greene Balch, *Our Slavic Fellow Citizens* (New York, 1910), and Mercedes Randall, *Improper Bostonian* (New York, 1964).

I have relied on the files of the American Jewish Committee in New York City for much of the material about the committee. See also Charles Reznikoff, ed., *Louis Marshall: Champion of Liberty* (Philadelphia, 1957). For the role of Jewish intellectuals as defenders of immigrants, see Elazar Barkan, *The Retreat of Scientific Racism: Changing Concepts of Race in Britain and the United States between the Wars* (New York, 1992), and Milton M. Gordon, *Assimilation in American Life* (New York, 1964).

For the Americanization movement, see Edward George Hartmann, *The Movement to Americanize the Immigrant* (New York, 1948), and Gerd Korman, *Indus-*

trialization, Immigrants, and Americanizers: The View from Milwaukee (Madison, Wisc., 1967). For the wartime use of IQ tests, see Schaffer, *America in the Great War.*

Aspects of the anti-Japanese movement are traced in Raymond Leslie Buell, "The Development of Anti-Japanese Agitation in the U.S.," *Political Science Quarterly* 38 (March 1973): 47–81, Roger Daniels, *Asian America: Chinese and Japanese in the United States since 1850* (Seattle, 1988), and Yuji Ichioka, *The World of the First-Generation Japanese Immigrants, 1885–1924* (New York, 1988).

There is voluminous literature on the Sacco and Vanzetti case, but I have relied most heavily on Nunzio Pernicone, "Carlo Tresca and the Sacco-Vanzetti Case," *Journal of American History* 66 (December 1979): 535–47, and Paul Avrich, *Sacco and Vanzetti: The Anarchist Background* (Princeton, 1991).

Madison Grant's ideas can be traced in Madison Grant, *The Passing of the Great Race, or the Racial Basis of European History* (New York, 1916), and Stoddard's in Lothrop Stoddard, *The Rising Tide of Color against White World-Supremacy* (New York, 1920) and *The Revolt against Civilization: The Menace of the Under Man* (New York, 1923). The *Saturday Evening Post* articles can be found in Kenneth L. Roberts, *Why Europe Leaves Home* (New York, 1922, 1977).

For anti-Semitism, see Leonard Dinnerstein, *Anti-Semitism in America* (New York, 1994), Susanne Klingenstein, *Jews in the American Academy, 1900–1940: The Dynamics of Intellectual Assimilation* (New Haven, 1991), and Marcia Graham Synnott, "Anti-Semitism and American Universities: Did Quotas Follow the Jews?" in *Anti-Semitism in American History*, ed. David A. Gerber (Urbana, Ill., 1987), 233–71. For Henry Ford, see Leo Ribuffo, *Right Center Left: Essays in American History* (New Brunswick, N.J., 1992).

A good sampling of business opinion can be found in the National Industrial Conference Board's Special Report 26, "Proceedings of the National Immigration Conference Held in New York City, December 13 and 14, 1923" (New York, 1924), which also contains some interesting testimony by representatives of the Armenian community. For the opinions of the secretary of labor, see James J. Davis, *The Iron Puddler: My Life in the Rolling Mills and What Came of It* (Indianapolis, 1922). African-American opinion is traced in David J. Hellwig, "Black Leaders and United States Immigration Policy, 1917–1929," *Journal of Negro History* 66 (summer 1981): 110–27. Jewish opinion is discussed in Sheldon Morris Neuringer, "American Jewry and United States Immigration Policy" (Ph.D. diss., University of Wisconsin, 1969). For Irish opinion I have made use of the *Irish World* (New York); for the Catholic church, I have used *Catholic Universe Bulletin* (Cleveland), *New World* (Chicago), and *America.* The daily press gave extensive coverage to the race to the ports in 1922 and 1923.

For the congressional debate, I have relied heavily on the *Congressional Record*, 68th Cong., 1st sess., 1924, vol. 65, pt. 6. For La Guardia, see Arthur Mann, *La Guardia: A Fighter against His Times* (New York, 1959), and Howard Zinn, *La Guardia in Congress* (Ithaca, N.Y., 1959). For the final shaping of the bill, in addition to works already cited, see Margo J. Anderson, *The American Census: A Social History* (New Haven, 1989).

The reaction of various immigrant groups to the passage of the 1924 bill is best traced in *Literary Digest*, 17 May 1924. In following reaction to the various proposals, I have also made extensive use of the *Jewish Independent* (Cleveland). See also Adam Urbanski, "Immigration Restriction and the Polish-American Press: The Response of Widomosci Codzienne, 1921–1924," *Polish American Studies* 28 (autumn 1971): 5–21.

For Mexican immigration, see Vargas, *History of Mexican Industrial Workers*, and George J. Sanchez, *Becoming Mexican American: Ethnicity, Culture, and Identity in Chicano Los Angeles, 1900–1945* (New York, 1993).

In developing this chapter, I have also used Robert E. Park, *The Immigrant Press and Its Control* (New York, 1922, 1970), John Bodnar, *Remaking America: Public Memory, Commemoration, and Patriotism in the Twentieth Century* (Princeton, 1992), John V. Baimonte Jr., *Spirit of Vengeance: Nativism and Louisiana Justice, 1921–1924* (Baton Rouge, La., 1986), Barbara Benton, *Ellis Island: A Pictorial History* (New York, 1985), and Humbert S. Nelli, *The Business of Crime: Italians and Syndicate Crime in the United States* (Chicago, 1976).

Chapter 8. The New Era and the Presidential Election of 1928

My discussion of the American economy during the 1920s has been informed by Louis Galambos and Joseph Pratt, *The Rise of the Corporate Commonwealth: U.S. Business and Public Policy in the Twentieth Century* (New York, 1988), John M. Dobson, *A History of American Enterprise* (New York, 1988), Raymond M. Wik, *Henry Ford and Grass-Roots America* (Ann Arbor, Mich., 1972), Roland Marchand, *Advertising the American Dream: Making the Way for Modernity, 1920–1940* (Berkeley and Los Angeles, 1985), Robert S. Lynd and Helen Merrell Lynd, *Middletown* (New York, 1929, 1956), Soule, *Prosperity Decade*, and Hawley, *Great War*. For Herbert Hoover, I have made extensive use of Joan Hoff Wilson, *Herbert Hoover: A Public Life* (Boston, 1978, 1984), and Hawley, *Herbert Hoover as Secretary of Commerce*.

As in chapter 3, my discussion of Smith and the Democrats is heavily dependent on Craig, *After Wilson*, and Burner, *Politics of Provincialism*. See also Kenneth Davis, *FDR: The Beckoning of Destiny, 1882–1928* (New York, 1971, 1927), Elisabeth

Isabels Perry, *Belle Moskowitz: Feminine Politics and the Exercise of Power in the Age of Alfred E. Smith* (New York, 1987, 1992), John M. Allswang, *A House for All Peoples: Ethnic Politics in Chicago, 1890–1936* (Lexington, 1971), and Oscar Handlin, *Al Smith and His America* (Boston, 1958).

Hoover's Madison Square Garden address can be found in Coben, *Reform, War, and Reaction.* Allan J. Lichtman, *Prejudice and the Old Politics: The Presidential Election of 1928* (Chapel Hill, N.C., 1979), is an innovative book that deals with many aspects of the 1928 race. Edmond A. Moore, *A Catholic Runs for President: The Campaign of 1928* (New York, 1956), remains the standard work on the role played by religion in the campaign. David E. Kyvig, *Repealing National Prohibition* (Chicago, 1979), is extremely useful for the Prohibition issue. Agricultural issues are addressed quite well in Hicks, *Republican Ascendancy.* For the role of labor, see Vaughn Davis Bornet, *Labor Politics in a Democratic Republic: Moderation, Division, and Disruption in the Presidential Election of 1928* (Washington, D.C., 1964). For foreign policy, see L. Ethan Ellis, *Frank B. Kellog and American Foreign Relations* (New Brunswick, N.J., 1961). An excellent source for the emergence of fundamentalism in the 1920s is George M. Marsden, *Fundamentalism and American Culture: The Shaping of Twentieth-Century Evangelicalism, 1870–1925* (New York, 1980). For the overall significance of the election, see Samuel Lubell, *The Future of American Politics* (New York, 1951), and Gerald H. Gamm, *The Making of New Deal Democrats: Voting Behavior and Realignment in Boston, 1920–1940* (Chicago, 1986, 1989).

INDEX

Library of Congress Cataloging-in-Publication Data

Goldberg, David Joseph.
    Discontented America : the United States in the 1920s / David J. Goldberg.
    p.   cm. — (The American moment)
    Includes bibliographical references and index.
    ISBN 0-8018-6004-0 (acid-free paper). — ISBN 0-8018-6005-9 (pbk. : acid-free paper)
    1. United States—History—1919–1933. 2. World War, 1914–1918—United States—
Influence. 3. United States—Social conditions—1918–1932. 4. Nineteen twenties.
I. Title. II. Series.
E784.G65   1999
973.91—dc21   98-36310
                                               CIP